94457

D1109652

7

Sexual Health Information for Teens

TEEN HEALTH SERIES

First Edition

Sexual Health Information for Teens

Health Tips about Sexual Development, Human Reproduction, and Sexually Transmitted Diseases

Including Facts about Puberty, Reproductive Health, Chlamydia, Human Papillomavirus, Pelvic Inflammatory Disease, Herpes, AIDS, Contraception, Pregnancy, and More

◆

Edited by Deborah A. Stanley

615 Griswold Street • Detroit, MI 48226

Bibliographic Note
Because this page cannot legibly accommodate all the copyright notices, the Bibliographic Note portion of
the Preface constitutes an extension of the copyright notice.

Edited by Deborah A. Stanley

Teen Health Series

Karen Bellenir, *Managing Editor*
David A. Cooke, MD, *Medical Consultant*
Elizabeth Barbour, *Permissions Associate*
Dawn Matthews, *Verification Assistant*
Laura Pleva Nielsen, *Index Editor*
EdIndex, Services for Publishers, *Indexers*

* * *

Omnigraphics, Inc.
Matthew P. Barbour, *Senior Vice President*
Kay Gill, *Vice President—Directories*
Kevin Hayes, *Operations Manager*
Leif Gruenberg, *Development Manager*
David P. Bianco, *Marketing Consultant*

* * *

Peter E. Ruffner, *President and Publisher*
Frederick G. Ruffner, Jr., *Chairman*

Copyright © 2003 Omnigraphics, Inc.

ISBN 0-7808-0445-7

Library of Congress Cataloging-in-Publication Data

Sexual health information for teens : health tips about sexual development, human
  reproduction, and sexually transmitted diseases : including facts about puberty,
  reproductive health . . . / edited by Deborah A. Stanley.
    p. cm. — (Teen health series)
  ISBN 0-7808-0445-7
    1. Teenagers—Health and hygiene. 2. Hygiene, Sexual. 3. Reproductive health.
  4. Puberty. 5. Sexually transmitted diseases—Prevention. 6. Sex instruction for teenagers.
  I. Stanley, Deborah A. II. Series.

RA777.S47 2003
613.9′51—dc22   2003053636

Table of Contents

Part III: Reproductive Health For Boys

Part IV: Sexuality And Social Issues

Part V: Preventing Pregnancy

Part VI: Avoiding Sexually Transmitted Diseases

Part VII: If You Need More Information

Preface

About This Book

The teen years can be a minefield of confusing and embarrassing experiences, with transitions in every aspect of life: interacting with family, socializing with friends, coping with a school workload and perhaps a first job, and enduring the physical changes that come with puberty and young adulthood. Teens often feel uncomfortable discussing these changes with adults and may be especially hesitant to approach parents or teachers with questions about sex. Yet many teens—whether or not they are sexually active—do need guidance in understanding the reproductive-health issues they may face.

This volume of the *Teen Health Series* provides information about all aspects of sexual health, from what's normal and what's not during puberty to facts on how sexually transmitted diseases are spread. Also addressed are questions about hygiene, diseases of the reproductive system that are not sexually transmitted, pregnancy and contraception, and societal issues such as date rape. An end section includes directories of resources for additional help and information.

How to Use This Book

This book is divided into parts and chapters. Parts focus on broad areas of interest. Chapters are devoted to single topics within a part.

Part I: What Happens At Puberty? provides basic information on the changes that come with puberty for boys and girls, including when to expect it to happen and why puberty is sometimes early or late.

Part II: Reproductive Health For Girls presents facts on hygiene, menstruation, and gynecological health. Included are chapters on what to expect when visiting the gynecologist for the first time; what to do about cramps, yeast infections, and other common problems; and how to begin performing breast self-exams.

Part III: Reproductive Health For Boys covers questions about circumcision and testicular injuries, as well as the importance and how-to's of testicular self-exams.

Part IV: Sexuality And Social Issues addresses a variety of topics including how to talk about sex with parents, ways to be affectionate without having intercourse, what abstinence means and how to decide whether it's right for you, and the dangers of date rape.

Part V: Preventing Pregnancy gives information on various contraceptives, including how to use them, how reliable they are, and what to do if they fail.

Part VI: Avoiding Sexually Transmitted Diseases presents important information about STDs, including how they spread, their symptoms and treatments, and how to lower the risk of contracting them.

Part VII: If You Need More Information includes resources for further learning on all of the topics addressed in this volume of the *Teen Health Series*.

Bibliographic Note

This volume contains documents and excerpts from publications issued by the following government agencies: Agency for Healthcare Research and Quality (AHRQ); Centers for Disease Control and Prevention (CDC); Department of Health Abstinence Education Program, State of Florida; National Institute of Allergy and Infectious Diseases (NIAID); National Institute on Drug Abuse (NIDA); Office on Women's Health of the U.S. Department of Health and Human Services; Substance Abuse and Mental Health Services Administration (SAMHSA); and the U.S. Food and Drug Administration (FDA).

In addition, this volume contains copyrighted documents from the following organizations and individuals: ABC-TV; American Social Health Association; Campaign for Our Children, Inc.; Center for Young Women's

Health; Consumer Health Interactive; Florida Department of Health; National Breast Cancer Foundation; National Campaign to Prevent Teen Pregnancy; National Crime Prevention Council; Nemours Center for Children's Health Media, a division of The Nemours Foundation; New World Communications, Inc.; Planned Parenthood Federation of America, Inc.; *Portland Press Herald/ Maine Sunday Telegram*; Procter and Gamble Company; Rodale, Inc.; Roger Tonkin; Sexuality Information and Education Council of the United States (SIECUS); Testicular Cancer Resource Center; Time, Inc.; and *USA Today*.

Full citation information is provided on the first page of each chapter. Every effort has been made to secure all necessary rights to reprint the copyrighted material. If any omissions have been made, please contact Omnigraphics to make corrections for future editions.

Acknowledgements

Special thanks to the many organizations, agencies, and individuals who have contributed materials for this volume of the *Teen Health Series* and to the managing editor Karen Bellenir, medical consultant Dr. David Cooke, permissions specialist Liz Barbour, verification assistant Dawn Matthews, indexer Edward J. Prucha, and document engineer Bruce Bellenir.

Note from the Editor

This book is part of Omnigraphics' *Teen Health Series*. The series provides basic information about a broad range of medical concerns. It is not intended to serve as a tool for diagnosing illness, in prescribing treatments, or as a substitute for the physician/patient relationship. All persons concerned about medical symptoms or the possibility of disease are encouraged to seek professional care from an appropriate health care provider.

At the request of librarians serving today's young adults, the *Teen Health Series* was developed as a specially focused set of volumes within Omnigraphics' *Health Reference Series*. Each volume deals comprehensively with a topic selected according to the needs and interests of people in middle school and high school. If there is a topic you would like to see addressed in a future volume of the *Teen Health Series*, please write to:

Part 1

What Happens At Puberty?

Chapter 1

Our Sexual Bodies

Why Is Sexuality So Important?

All of us are sexual. Our sexuality includes:

- Our bodies and how our bodies work
- Our genders—male or female
- Our gender identity—our feelings about being male or female
- Our sexual orientations—straight, gay, or bisexual
- Our values about life, love, and the people in our lives

And sexuality influences how we feel about all of these things and how we experience the world.

When we think of sexuality, we might just think about our bodies. We might just think about our sex organs. But our sexuality has as much to do with how we think and feel as it does with how we behave. Sexuality is a basic part of our physical, mental, emotional, and spiritual lives.

Our sexuality should be enjoyed and celebrated. It is not something to be ashamed of or embarrassed about. Healthy sexuality allows us to be open,

About This Chapter: Text in this chapter is from "The Facts of Life: A Guide for Teens and Their Families," reprinted with permission from Planned Parenthood® Federation of America, Inc. © 2002 PPFA. All rights reserved. For additional information, visit www.plannedparenthood.org or www.teenwire.org.

flexible, creative, safe, and responsible as we explore our sexual thoughts and feelings. It lets us recognize that sex can be fun and can also fulfill many emotional needs. Sex also has risks.

Having a healthy attitude about sexuality means knowing our values, beliefs, attitudes, limits, and boundaries, and respecting that knowledge by being responsible. It allows us to feel attractive, regardless of our age, gender, sexual orientation, race, religion, height, weight, or physical or mental ability. It lets us be ourselves.

Knowing as much as possible about our sexual selves, in terms of our beliefs, values, and physical needs will help us create responsible, healthy, and satisfying sexual lives.

Our Sexual Bodies

Girls and boys have different sex organs.

Only girls and women have vulvas. Only boys and men have penises. Vulvas and penises are located in the front of the body between the legs.

The labia, urethra, clitoris, and opening to the vagina are all part of the vulva. Sometimes, girls use mirrors to see the parts of their vulvas.

The labia majora and labia minora are two folds of fleshy tissue on the outermost parts of the vulva. The labia majora—the outer lips—are closer to the legs. Pubic hair grows there on most adolescents and adult women. The labia minora protect the inner vulva. They do not have pubic hair.

The opening of the vagina is in the middle of the vulva. It is a passageway to a woman's reproductive organs. Above it, the opening of the urethra is not easy to see. It provides a passageway for urine to flow from the bladder to the outside of the body.

Only the tip of the clitoris is visible at the top of the vulva in the soft folds where the labia meet. The rest of the clitoris reaches inside the body.

The penis is easier to see than the vulva. Two testicles that look like balls hang beneath it in a sac called the scrotum. A foreskin covers the glans at the tip of the penis unless it was removed in an operation called circumcision. Circumcision is usually done for cultural reasons. In most cases, it has no health benefits.

Girls and boys touch their sex organs for pleasure from the time they are babies. Most adults, children, and infants enjoy touching their sex organs and other parts of their bodies. The clitoris is designed to give women and girls pleasure when touched. The penis gives men and boys pleasure when touched.

Touching our sex organs for pleasure—masturbation—is a normal, healthy part of life. Masturbation and other kinds of sex play can lead to orgasm—an intense feeling of pleasure that happens when the tension that builds up during sex play is suddenly released.

Puberty Happens To Everybody

But it doesn't happen to everybody at the same time. Generally, girls start puberty earlier than boys. The bodies of some girls begin changing at age eight. Others don't start changing until they are 14. Boys' bodies start changing from age 10 to 12. Most often these changes are complete before a person is 20.

Some of the changes are the same for girls and boys. We get taller. We begin to grow hair under our arms and around our vulvas or penises. We sweat more, too, mostly under the arms. That's when a lot of people start washing more often and start using deodorants. Also, our voices deepen. This usually happens more suddenly in boys than in girls.

Many of us get pimples during puberty on the face, back, chest, or buttocks. We get them as our skin starts growing thicker and the glands under it start making more oil. Our pores become clogged and infected. That's another good reason to wash and shampoo often.

Hormones Make Our Bodies Grow Up

Our bodies make chemicals called hormones that guide our growth into women and men—estrogen and progesterone in girls and testosterone in boys. Often we grow so fast that we feel clumsy. We even may have uncomfortable growing pains, usually in our arms and legs.

Estrogen causes lots of the changes. Girls' breasts begin to get fuller. Often one breast grows faster than the other. Their hips get rounder. Their waists get narrower. Their vulvas and clitorises grow slightly, too.

Girls may have a white, sticky discharge from their vaginas called leukorrhea. They shouldn't worry about it unless the vulva becomes itchy or irritated. If it does, a girl should visit her doctor or clinician.

Boys' testicles get bigger and hang lower. Usually one hangs lower than the other. Their penises grow larger and get hard more often—and unexpectedly. Boys gradually start growing beards after their voices change. Sometimes boys' breasts become tender and somewhat enlarged, too. This is called gynecomastia. It usually lasts only a year or two, and then the size of the breasts returns to normal.

We inherit our size, eye color, and skin color from our parents. We also inherit large breasts or small breasts, thin legs or thick legs, big penises or small penises, and thick beards or thin beards. Most of the time we inherit average breasts, legs, penises, or beards. But we are all very different, no matter what—and that's normal.

Clitorises, labia, penises, and breasts vary in shape and size.

The appearance of the outer folds of the labia—the labia majora—varies in size, shape, and color from woman to woman. The color of the labia minora is also different for every woman. In some women, the labia are smooth—in others, they are wrinkled.

The clitoris may be smaller than a pea or bigger than a fingertip. It reaches inside the body up to five inches.

Soft adult penises are usually between 3-1/4 and 4-1/4 inches long.

✎ **Weird Words**

Gynecomastia: Enlargement and tenderness of male breasts, which lasts only a year or two, then the size of the breasts returns to normal.

Leukorrhea: White, sticky discharge from the vagina.

Spermarche (sper-MAR-key): The time when sperm is first produced.

Some may be shorter, longer, thinner, or thicker. Five to seven inches is the average length of a hard penis.

Women's breasts are different in shape and size. The nipples may be flat or raised. They, and the area around them—the aureole—differ in color from woman to woman. A woman's breasts can give her sexual pleasure when touched. Small or large, her breasts can also produce milk after she has a baby.

Some people prefer big penises or big breasts. However, being attractive depends more on personality—how we think of ourselves, present ourselves, take care of ourselves, and respect ourselves and other people.

Body Image

The ways our bodies change in adolescence can affect how we see ourselves. Our feelings about appearance make up our body image. Our parents, the media, or other kids all influence the way we think about our bodies. But we can decide to respect and accept ourselves and the bodies we have, even if others don't.

We can look at our bodies for what they are—ours.

During Puberty, Things Happen Inside The Body, Too

Most girls start having periods. Most boys start having wet dreams. And girls and boys begin having a lot more thoughts and feelings about sex.

Important changes are happening inside the body. The reproductive system is maturing. Boys begin producing sperm—the male reproductive cells. Girls' ovaries begin to ripen eggs—the female reproductive cells.

Pregnancy can happen if only one sperm joins with an egg. The sperm can reach the egg if a boy or man puts his penis in or near the vagina. Often our reproductive systems grow up faster than we do. That's why girls can get pregnant and boys can cause pregnancy before they finish growing up.

As Boys Become Men

Boys and men have erections. Boys and men become sexually excited by sexual thoughts, wet dreams, or sex play with themselves or another person. Their penises fill with blood and get hard and erect. Boys and young men get erections for no reason at all. "Spontaneous erections" can be very embarrassing.

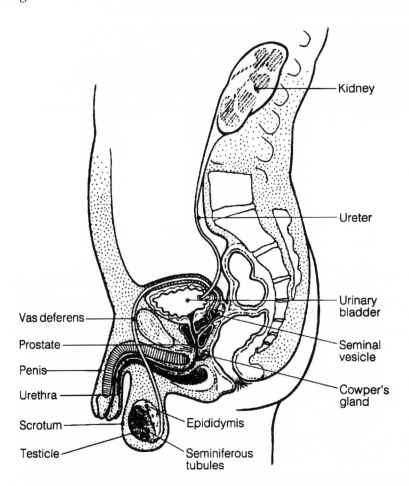

Figure 1.1. A Man's Reproductive System. Sperm are made in the testicles. There are millions in every drop of healthy semen. They move from the testicles to the seminal vesicles through tubes called the vas deferens. In the seminal vesicle, they mix with other fluids to form semen.

A sticky liquid spurts out of erect penises if men get very excited. This is called ejaculating or "coming." The spurting is called ejaculation. The liquid is semen or "cum," not urine. Ejaculation and urination cannot happen at the same time.

Semen contains sperm and is also called "ejaculate." Boys and men may have orgasms without ejaculation. They may ejaculate without orgasm. A hard penis becomes soft again after orgasm. And it will become soft again even without orgasm or ejaculation.

Sperm are made in the testicles. There are millions in every drop of healthy semen. They move from the testicles to the seminal vesicles through tubes called the vas deferens. In the seminal vesicle, they mix with other fluids to form semen. Usually, a teaspoonful to a tablespoonful of semen is released at a time.

The time when sperm is first produced is called spermarche (sper-MAR-key). Boys' bodies make sperm all their lives. New sperm develop every minute. Sperm are absorbed by the body if they are not ejaculated.

Wet dreams often come as a surprise. Most boys and men have wet dreams. This happens if they get erections and ejaculate during their sexual dreams. These dreams leave them wet or sticky around their bellies and penises. Some boys wake up thinking that they've wet the bed. Some boys never have wet dreams. Dreams or no dreams—both are normal.

As Girls Become Women

Girls and women have orgasms during sexual dreams. Women and girls become sexually excited by sexual thoughts and dreams or sex play with themselves or another person. Their vaginas become wet, their clitorises become erect, and if they become very sexually excited, they may have orgasms or a series of orgasms. In some women, a clear fluid spurts out of the urethra during sexual excitement or orgasm. This is also called ejaculation.

The vagina connects the sex organs of the vulva to the other reproductive organs inside the body. The soft folds of the walls of the vagina adjust to the size of the penis during vaginal intercourse and stretch during childbirth.

Girls and women also have two ovaries, a cervix, a uterus, and two fallopian tubes.

Each ovary holds hundreds of thousands of pinpoint-sized eggs. Girls are born with all the eggs they will ever have. One ovary releases a mature egg about once a month. This is called ovulation. Before ovulation, the uterus builds up a spongy, soft lining. It is made of tissue and blood. This lining is like a nest for the egg if pregnancy happens.

After ovulation, the egg moves through a fallopian tube toward the uterus. Most of the time, the egg breaks apart before it gets there. Then the tissue and blood aren't needed. They flow out of the uterus, through the cervix and

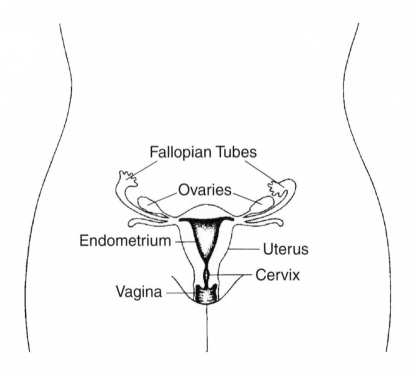

Figure 1.2. A Women's Internal Sex And Reproductive Organs. Girls and women have two ovaries, a cervix, a uterus, and two fallopian tubes.

vagina out of the body. This is called menstrual flow or a "period." Different women have different amounts of flow during their periods. About only three or four tablespoonfuls of it are blood—although it may seem like more.

But the egg doesn't always break apart. If the egg meets a sperm in the fallopian tube, they can join together. The joining of the egg and sperm is called fertilization. Pregnancy begins if a fertilized egg attaches itself to the lining of the uterus. The lining stays in place until the pregnancy ends. That's why pregnant women do not have periods.

The first time menstruation happens is called menarche (meh-NAR-key). Some families celebrate menarche as the time when a girl becomes a woman. Other families are more private about it. But whether or not menarche is celebrated, it is an exciting and important moment in a girl's life. It is also normal for girls to feel nervous or scared when they start getting their periods.

The time from the first day of one period to the first day of the next is called a menstrual cycle. On average, menstrual cycles begin between the ages of 12 and 13. They end when women are between 45 and 55 years old.

Periods last about five days. It may be seven to 21 days from the beginning of a woman's period to ovulation. Then there are usually 14 to 16 days from ovulation to the beginning of the next period.

During puberty, it's not unusual for three, four, five, or six months to go by between periods. Eventually, they happen every four or five weeks. Sometimes there is a spotting of blood between periods. Some women know when they are going to have their periods by the way their bodies feel. Others don't. Some women keep a record of their periods on a calendar to become more familiar with their cycle.

Some girls and women may have physical or emotional discomfort up to two weeks before menstruating. This is called premenstrual syndrome (PMS). Usually mild, PMS happens in fewer than half of all women.

Women use sanitary pads or tampons to absorb menstrual flow. Every package has instructions. Tampons and sanitary pads come in different sizes and varieties. Some are for lighter flows. Some are for heavier flows.

Pads stay in place by sticking inside the underwear. A tampon fits inside the vagina. The walls of the vagina hold it in place. Each tampon has a string that hangs out of the vagina. The tampon is removed easily by pulling the string slowly. Tampons or pads and regular bathing are all a woman or girl needs to stay clean during her period. Douches, vaginal deodorants, and perfumed pads and tampons are unnecessary and may irritate the vulva and vagina.

Some girls wonder if tampons will stretch the hymen and make them lose their virginity. The hymen is a thin skin that stretches across the opening of the vagina. There is usually an opening in it to let menstrual flow out of the body.

The hymen is very important to some people. They believe that a girl without a hymen is no longer a virgin—that a boy has put his penis in her vagina. Girls are born with various sizes and openings of the hymen. Some may even appear to have no hymen—others stretch theirs open during certain kinds of exercise like bicycling or horseback riding. Tampons don't usually stretch the hymen open all the way.

Girls and women who use tampons change them every three or four hours, or more often if bleeding is heavy. Too many bacteria can develop if a tampon is left in place too long. This can cause a rare illness called toxic shock syndrome (TSS). Although very rare, TSS is very serious. If you vomit and develop a high fever, diarrhea, muscle aches, sore throat, dizziness, faintness, or weakness, and a sunburn-type rash while using a tampon, take it out and see your clinician—fast. You can reduce your risk by using a pad or less absorbent tampon while sleeping.

Usually, women and girls do not have serious problems with their periods. Some feel depressed or moody. Some have cramps on the first day or two of their periods. Exercise and a healthy diet may reduce cramps. Putting a hot-water bottle or heating pad on the abdomen can help, too.

Usually cramps aren't severe enough to prevent normal activities. If they are, a girl should talk with her parent, the school nurse, a teacher, or a clinician. There are very good medicines that lessen the pain of menstrual cramps.

Chapter 2

What Happens At Puberty: For Girls

Puberty is the time when your body begins to change from a girl's body to a woman's body. It can take several years, and usually happens between the ages of nine and 17. Girls often start puberty before boys do.

Puberty happens when your brain and your sex organs send messages to the rest of your body. These messages are carried by chemicals called hormones. Hormones prepare your body and mind for sexual maturity (or adulthood).

Changes On The Outside

During puberty, girls' hips start to widen. You may not even notice this because it's a very subtle change. Next, hair starts to grow under your arms, around your genitals, and finer hair begins to show on your legs and arms. Your breasts will start to change in size and shape. This change may happen fast or slow, depending on who you are.

You will probably begin to sweat more under your arms, and your sweat may smell different. This is easy to deal with—shower or bathe more often and begin using deodorant or antiperspirant if you don't like the smell.

About This Chapter: Text in this chapter is from "Puberty: For Girls," Reprinted with permission from Planned Parenthood® Federation of America, Inc. © 2002 PPFA. All rights reserved. For additional information, visit www.plannedparenthood.org or www.teenwire.org.

During puberty, both girls and boys may develop acne (also called "pimples" or "zits"). Acne is very common and fairly easy to treat. Your health care provider can help you find a treatment that's right for you.

Sometimes the hormones of puberty can cause changes in your mood, making you feel more upset or excited about things than you used to. This is normal and it's a good idea to share your feelings with someone you trust, especially if you feel very sad or frustrated. Everyone goes through puberty, so you should be able to find an adult who understands to help you sort out your feelings.

Changes On The Inside

Hormones cause changes in your internal reproductive organs to get them ready to go through menstrual cycles and someday perhaps have a baby. At some point during puberty, you will start to have menstrual cycles and you will begin to get your monthly period. Most girls start having periods around the same age that their moms did, so you might want to ask your mom how old she was when she started. This is a good way to start talking to your mom about puberty.

Your first menstrual cycle starts inside where you can't see it, when an egg is released from your ovary. This is called ovulation. The ovaries usually release only one egg a month. The egg travels down the fallopian tube on its

✎ **Weird Words**

Acne: A condition that causes pimples on the face or body. Acne is affected by hormonal changes, so it is a common part of puberty.

Breasts: Soft, protruding organs on the upper front of a woman's body that secrete milk after pregnancy. During puberty, a young woman's breasts usually increase in size.

Genitals: The external reproductive organs.

Hormones: Substances produced by the body to stimulate specific cells or tissues into action. Hormones are responsible for the changes of puberty.

Sperm: The male sex cell. When a sperm fertilizes a female egg, pregnancy results.

way to the uterus. It's hard to tell when this all happens, but it's usually about two weeks before you get your period.

In the meantime, the uterus has prepared itself by growing a thick inner lining of blood. This lining will be very important if you have a baby. If you have sex with a man and your egg is fertilized by his sperm, the fertilized egg may implant itself into this lining, and pregnancy will begin. Otherwise, the lining starts to come off after a few days and leaves your body as menstrual flow through the vagina. This is the bleeding that lasts about five to seven days and is called your period.

Your Period

Periods are part of a monthly cycle that most healthy women's bodies go through during their reproductive years. You don't usually see or feel the rest of the cycle, so your period is an indicator that the cycle happened.

The menstrual flow is usually heaviest during the first few days. Some women get cramps before or during their periods. This is normal and usually goes away with Tylenol or ibuprofen. If you have a lot of cramping, you can get help from your health care provider. Some women feel irritable, bloated, or have any number of other symptoms before their period starts. These symptoms are temporary and are called PMS, which stands for premenstrual syndrome.

At first, most women have irregular periods, meaning they don't have them every month, or at the same time from month to month. Most women become more regular after a year, although some women never do. Most women's cycles are between 28 and 32 days long. There are a few things that will make your period late:

- Stress—worrying about family problems or exams or other things

- Exercise—many female athletes have irregular periods

- Big changes in your life—taking a trip somewhere, moving

- Pregnancy—this is important to think about if you are sexually active, even if you use birth control

- Birth control—hormonal methods of birth control (the Pill, implants and injections) can cause your periods to change or stop. This is something you should talk about with the person who prescribed your birth control.

- Illness—sometimes being sick or not feeling well can cause your period to be late.

☞ Remember!!

Puberty can be an awkward, uncomfortable time, so it's important to find someone you can talk to a parent, relative, teacher, or health care provider who can answer your questions.

Puberty is something everyone goes through and it can be a very uncomfortable, awkward, and lonely time. It is a good time to learn about your body and how it works. It is also a good time to start talking to your mom or dad about their experiences when they were your age. You can also talk a health care provider if you have questions that you don't want to ask your parents.

Chapter 3

What Happens At Puberty: For Boys

Puberty is the process of growing from a boy into a man that every boy will go through sometime between the ages of about 9 to 14. Your body changes at its own pace, which is largely determined by your genes. Some boys begin puberty earlier or later than their friends. Boys grow at different ages and rates. You may begin at age 9 or age 14 or anywhere in between. Some boys seem to grow overnight and some see gradual changes over a period of years. Puberty usually starts earlier for girls than boys. For a few years, girls your age will probably be larger and taller than you.

Will I Look Different?

Physically your body will begin to look more like an adult man. Sometime between the ages of 9 to 14, special glands in your brain release hormones into your body that produce changes in your size, appearance and much more. During this time you'll notice changes in:

- Your size. You'll grow taller and your weight will increase.

- Your body shape. Your shoulders will become wider and your muscles start to develop.

About This Chapter: Reprinted with permission from "Male Puberty," part of the *Tips to Grow By*® series produced as a public service by the Children's Medical Center of Akron, Ohio. © 2001 Children's Medical Center of Akron. For additional information, visit www.akronchildrens.org/kids-teens.

- Your body hair. It will grow under your arms, in the pubic area (the area between your legs), on your face, on your arms and legs and possibly on your chest, back and lower stomach.

- Your skin. It becomes thicker and more oily as your oil glands become more active. Keep your hair and skin clean to help avoid pimples.

- Your sweat glands become more active which means you sweat more. Wear deodorant to eliminate body odor. Bathe daily and keep your clothes clean.

- Your voice. It usually gets deeper and may crack at times.

- Your sex organs. Your penis will grow in size and your testicles will grow and descend. You will begin to produce sperm, tiny, tadpole-shaped cells that make you capable of becoming a father.

- Your coordination. You may temporarily feel off balance or clumsy at times. This is due to the rapid growth your body is going through.

- Your chest. You may notice breast lumps or tenderness due to hormonal changes, this is usually normal.

You're at the age where it is totally normal to be curious about sex. You are feeling sensations in your body that maybe you haven't felt before. They may include:

- Erection or hardening of the penis. This happens when the blood vessels of the penis become engorged with blood. This is usually caused by either mental or physical sexual stimulation, but it can be caused by other reasons too.

- Ejaculation or release of semen from the erect penis. Semen is a whitish, sticky fluid that contains sperm cells and is released during sexual stimulation, masturbation or sexual intercourse. Your penis can't release urine at the same time it releases semen.

- Masturbation or handling your sex organs to arouse sexual feelings. This is common and will not harm you in any way. If it makes you feel worried or guilty, talk to an adult you like and trust or talk to your doctor.

- Wet dreams or nocturnal emissions are the release of semen while you're asleep. It is a natural body function and is very common during your teen years. It's not bad and won't harm you.

- Orgasm or climax is a series of intense feelings and physical responses around the time of ejaculation. An orgasm can accompany a wet dream, masturbation, sexual intercourse or stimulation.

How Will I Feel?

Puberty can be a very emotional time. You'll begin to have more intense feelings of love and joy and also of loneliness and sadness. As you get older you'll have more responsibilities at home and at school. You'll also begin to decide what's important to you, what kinds of friends you want to have and the kind of person you want to be.

You'll probably want some independence from your parents, yet still find comfort in the security they provide. Your parents are proud that you're maturing into a young adult, yet they may get their feelings hurt because you'd rather spend time with your friends than with them. You may also argue with them over the fairness of house rules, family obligations, chores, etc.

♣ **It's A Fact!!**
Think Before You Act

Your body is now physically able to have sexual intercourse and produce a baby. Actions you take now could affect your health and happiness in the future.

Sexually transmitted diseases (STDs) are spread by sex. Many are silent infections, which means there aren't any signs or symptoms to let you know anything is wrong. Some STDs increase your risk of cancer or your ability to have a baby in the future and some, like AIDS, can kill you.

Try sharing your feelings with your parents and coming up with solutions that all of you can live with. The teenage years can also make you feel insecure. Being popular and belonging to a group may be very important to you, having friends can help you feel secure.

If you aren't accepted by a particular group, try and seek out friends elsewhere. Remember that you are a valuable and important person and you shouldn't have to change or do things you don't want to do just to be accepted as someone's friend. If you feel pressure from your friends to do something you don't want to, ask yourself whether what they want you to do could hurt you or help you.

As you probably know, girls go through a monthly cycle called menstruation or their "period." During a girl's monthly cycle an egg is released from her ovaries. If the egg is fertilized by a sperm cell, it will implant in the girl's uterus and grow into a baby. If the egg isn't fertilized, the lining of the uterus (a mixture of blood and tissue) leaves the body over a one to 10 day "period" each month. Girls can become pregnant at any time of the month. Occasionally, sperm can enter the vagina through close sexual contact without the penis ever being inserted into the vagina.

Never let anyone pressure you into having sex and certainly don't force or pressure someone to have sex with you. Using pressure or trickery to get a girl to have sex with you is a sign of emotional

☞ Remember!!
There is no safe time of the month to have unprotected sex!

immaturity and can get you in big trouble with the law if the girl claims she was "date raped." Just because you get sexually excited about a girl doesn't necessarily mean you are in love with that girl. Love is a deep emotional attachment that involves more than just sexual excitement.

Having sex before you or your partner is ready may leave one or both of you with feelings of anger or regret. It's best to wait until you're sure of your feelings, you're able to accept any possible results and you're ready to make a lifelong commitment to one person. Being a parent of an unplanned child will limit your social life and change your future. Parents must work hard for many years to provide a home, food, clothing, health care, education and guidance to their children. This is a huge responsibility even for married adult couples who plan the timing of their families.

Be responsible and seek the advice of an adult. If you do decide to become sexually active, it's important to talk to a trusted adult who can counsel you on the use of birth control, or contraception, which refers to methods used to prevent pregnancy. The only method that is 100 percent effective at preventing pregnancy or sexually transmitted disease is abstinence (not having sex at all). There are several types of birth control available for women. For men, a condom (or "rubber"), is reliable when properly used. It's a sheath made of latex or other material that fits over the penis to catch sperm when you ejaculate. Only condoms made of latex can help prevent the spread of STDs.

Take Care Of Yourself

When you feel good, you look good. During puberty it's extra important to take care of your body by eating a healthy diet consisting of a variety of foods from the five basic food groups. Get enough rest and exercise. Both will help increase your energy and reduce your stress levels. Bathe and shower regularly to help prevent body odor and acne breakouts.

If you have questions about the changes your body is going through, find an adult you trust. Remember he or she went through puberty too. If you are 15 or 16 and find that your body hasn't begun to show any signs of puberty, you may have a low hormone level. See your doctor so that he can further investigate what may be causing the problem.

Chapter 4

When Puberty Comes Early

Marissa Carter, a Galveston, Texas, housewife, could not believe it when her daughter Sharon, at the tender age of 4, seemed to be developing breasts. The tiny buds that appeared on the little girl's chest were gone within a couple of weeks, but three years later, they reappeared, and this time they grew—along with pubic hair and hair in Sharon's armpits. "I felt this was too early for her to be developing," recalls Carter. "Gosh, I was flat as a board at her age."

So after a series of medical consultations, the Carters (all these names have been changed at the families' request) put Sharon on Lupron, a hormone that slams the brakes on puberty—only to see their happy little girl go into terrible mood swings. "I had a child acting like she was in menopause," says Carter. The parents decided to stop the treatment, and by age 9, Sharon had full-blown breasts and was getting her period.

Laura Stover took her daughter Karen to a specialist when the girl began growing pubic hair at age 5. The doctor put Karen through a battery of blood tests to rule out ovarian tumors (which can force glands to churn out puberty-triggering hormones). But there was no apparent medical problem, and by age 8, Karen had full pubic growth. "We didn't allow her to go to any slumber parties," says Stover. "Or to change bathing suits in front of other children."

Cecilia Morton, in Santa Maria, Calif., has not one but two daughters who developed early. Clara, now 13, started sprouting breasts and pubic hair when she was 8 and began menstruating a year later, at summer camp. Says her mother: "It was scary and embarrassing because the girls in her cabin didn't have their periods yet." Then Clara's little sister Susan, a kindergartner, began developing at the same time. Although Susan's tests were normal, Morton put her on hormone treatments. "We already see how men look at Clara," she says. "If my younger one didn't have the medication, I can't even imagine the problems we'd be having."

If these were isolated cases, they might be chalked up to statistical flukes. But it seems as if everywhere you turn these days—outside schools, on soccer fields, at the mall—there are more and more elementary schoolgirls whose bodies look like they belong in high school and more and more middle schoolers who look like college coeds. "Young girls [in the 5- to 10-year-old range] with breasts or pubic hair—we encounter this every day we're in clinic," says Dr. Michael Freemark, chief of pediatric endocrinology at Duke University Medical Center in Durham, North Carolina.

It's as if an entire generation of girls had been put on hormonal fast-forward: shooting up, filling out, growing like Alice munching on the wrong side of the mushroom—and towering Mutt and Jeff-like over a generation of boys who seem, next to the girls, to be getting smaller every year.

What's going on? Is it something in the water? That's a possibility. Scientists think it may be linked to obesity, though they've also proposed a witches' brew of other explanations, from chemicals in the environment to hormones in cow's milk and beef. But the truth is that all anyone knows for certain is that the signs of sexual development in girls are appearing at ever younger ages. Among Caucasian girls today, 1 in every 7 starts to develop breasts or pubic hair by age 8. Among African Americans, for reasons nobody quite understands, the figure is nearly 1 out of every 2.

✎ Weird Words

Endocrinology: The branch of medicine that is concerned with hormones.

Insulin: A hormone produced in the pancreas which regulates the amount of glucose, or sugar, in the blood. Overweight girls tend to have higher levels of insulin, which can stimulate the production of sex hormones.

Leptin: A protein produced by fat cells which is necessary for the progression of puberty. Some experts believe that overweight children produce too much leptin, leading to early puberty.

Lupron: A hormone that can be used to stop early puberty.

Ovarian Tumor: A growth on one of the ovaries (the part of the female reproductive system which produces eggs) that can cause overproduction of hormones leading to early puberty.

Pesticides: Chemicals used to kill insects, often used on farms. Exposure to pesticides is suspected to be a possible cause of early puberty.

Even more troubling than the physical changes is the potential psychological effect of premature sexual development on children who should be reading fairy tales, not fending off wolves. The fear, among parents and professionals alike, is that young girls who look like teenagers will be under intense pressure to act like teenagers. Childhood is short enough as it is, with kids bombarded from every direction by sexually explicit movies, rock lyrics, MTV videos and racy fashions. If young girls' bodies push them into adulthood before their hearts and minds are ready, what will be forever lost?

The danger, as authors Whitney Roban and Michael Conn pointed out in a report for the Girls Scouts of America called *Girls Speak Out*, is that the stages of childhood development—cognitive, physical and emotional—have got out of synch. Roban and Conn call this "developmental compression" and pepper their study with poignant quotes from girls struggling to cope with pressures they are ill equipped to handle. "Boys," complains a fourth-grader in their report, "are gaga over girls with breasts."

In retrospect, pediatricians and psychologists say, there have been hints for the past decade or so that something strange was going on. But it wasn't until 1997 that anyone put her finger on it. That's when Marcia Herman-Giddens, now an adjunct professor at the University of North Carolina School of Public Health, published her famous paper in the journal *Pediatrics*. Herman-Giddens noticed in her clinical work that more and more young girls were coming in with breasts and pubic hair. Intrigued, she launched a major study of 17,000 girls to get a statistical handle on the problem.

What she and her colleagues found was that the changes of puberty were coming in two stages, each with its own timetable. The average age of menarche, or first menstruation, had already fallen dramatically (from 17 to about 13) between the middle of the 19th century to the middle of the 20th— mostly owing to improvements in nutrition. (Menstruation is considered the technical start of puberty; the outward signs of sexual maturity usually come earlier.) But since the 1960s, average age of first menstruation has basically remained steady at 12.8 years. For African Americans, it's currently about six months earlier, possibly reflecting genetic or nutritional differences.

What was striking about Herman-Giddens' report was the onset of secondary sexual characteristics: breast buds and pubic hair. Significant numbers of white girls—some 15%—were showing outward signs of incipient sexual maturity by age 8, and about 5% as early as 7. For African Americans, the statistics were even more startling. Fifteen percent were developing breasts or pubic hair by age 7, and almost half by age 8.

The *Pediatrics* report answered many questions, but much about the subject remains a mystery. The study couldn't accurately gauge, for example, how much the average age of onset of breast development (as opposed to menstruation) has dropped or over what period. That's because a key piece of research that helped set the standard age at 11 was a small study in the 1960s of white girls raised in English orphanages. But Dr. John Dallas, a pediatric endocrinologist with the University of Texas Medical Branch in Galveston, points out that the British girls may have been poorly nourished— a factor known to delay puberty. African-American girls were studied even less rigorously. "For all we know," says Dallas, "African-American girls could have been earlier developers for a long time."

The *Pediatrics* study is also limited because it does not include enough Asian-American or Hispanic girls to draw conclusions about these groups. Herman-Giddens agrees: "We in the public health and medical community really need to get data on American girls of all racial and ethnic groups." They also need to get data on boys, who haven't been studied in any systematic way. Herman-Giddens is pursuing the question now but says it isn't easy. "With girls," she says, "you can see breasts budding. With boys, the equivalent sign is an increase in size of the testes. It's very subtle. Even a physician may not be aware of it if they are not looking carefully."

Finally, somebody needs to look at what's going on in other countries. Is this a peculiarly American phenomenon? Or are girls developing breasts and reaching puberty at younger and younger ages all over the world?

The uncertainties swirling around the phenomenon make it difficult for scientists to nail down a cause, but that hasn't stopped them from coming up with a long list of potential candidates. The theory that has the broadest support among scientists holds that early puberty is somehow tied up with a much more familiar phenomenon: weight gain. America is in the midst of an epidemic of overweight and obese kids; between the late '70s and the early '90s, the percentage of children ages 6 to 11 who were overweight nearly doubled, from 6.5% to 11.4%, according to the National Center for Health Statistics.

Dr. Paul Kaplowitz, a pediatric endocrinologist with the Virginia Commonwealth University School of Medicine in Richmond, VA, explains, "We've known for a long time that very overweight girls tend to mature earlier, and very thin girls, such as anorexics, tend to mature later than normal. We think mildly overweight girls may be maturing early as well." Kaplowitz emphasizes that the correlation is merely statistical; not every girl with a little extra baby fat will develop breasts early.

Exactly why obesity and early development should be linked is not well understood. But Kaplowitz suspects early breast development may be encouraged by a protein called leptin. "We know that fat cells produce leptin," he says. "And leptin is necessary for the progression of puberty." Another clue, according to Duke's Freemark, is that overweight girls have more insulin circulating in their blood. Says Freemark: "Those higher levels of insulin appear to stimulate the production of sex hormones from the ovary and the adrenal gland."

While the consensus favors a fat connection, other explanations haven't been ruled out. One is chemical pollution in the food chain—specifically, DDE, a breakdown product of the pesticide DDT, and PCBs, once used as flame retardants in electrical equipment. Both chemicals are plausible suspects because they mimic hormones that play a key role in the development of the reproductive system. Beyond that, says Dr. Walter Rogan, an epidemiologist at the National Institute of Environmental Health Sciences in Research Triangle Park, NC, both chemicals are ubiquitous in the environment, and they persist in the body for years after exposure.

For that reason, he chose PCBs and DDE for one of the very few large, long-term studies of chemical exposure and puberty in humans. Rogan and his colleagues began with some 600 pregnant women, measuring concentrations of the chemicals in their bodies. When their babies were born, the researchers then measured levels in the mothers' breast milk. Finally, the team monitored the children as they grew and entered puberty.

The most prominent effect, reported last spring in the *Journal of Pediatrics*, was that boys exposed to DDE and girls exposed to PCBs were heavier than their unexposed peers at age 14. The study also noted an intriguing fact: girls with high prenatal PCB exposure tended to hit the first stages of puberty a bit earlier than others. Rogan stresses that the numbers were too low to be statistically significant. "If there is an effect of environmental chemicals on puberty," he says, "it's pretty small, because we studied these kids in detail over a long period of time, and we didn't see it." But, Rogan adds, "I can't rule it out."

Could other substances besides PCBs and DDE influence sexual development? Perhaps, Rogan says. But few compounds are as persistent and pervasive. Hormones given to livestock, for instance—another frequently invoked possibility—break down very quickly in the body. "I have not studied the effects of hormones in beef or dairy cattle," Rogan says. "It's not something I'm running out to study either."

What merits another look, some researchers believe, is a suite of chemicals used to make plastics. One is Bisphenol A, or BPA. Like DDE and PCBs, it is a chemical cousin of estrogen's, and it has been shown to affect the reproductive systems of lab mice. Another category of plastics ingredients, phthalates, may have played a role in a rash of cases of very early puberty in Puerto Rico back in the 1980s, with girls as young as 2 growing breasts and pubic hair. And while no cause has yet been determined, a study published last month suggests that a possible culprit could be phthalates, which are used, among other things, to make plastics flexible. It's by no means an ironclad case, however, and the plastics industry doubts that there's any link. But, says Rogan, "what went on in Puerto Rico is a good question and one that needs more study."

> ☞ **Remember!!**
> Some young people's bodies develop early, but their emotional maturity is no greater than that of other kids their age. It can be difficult to relate to your peers when you look much older than they do.

Then there are those who believe the sexualized messages bombarding kids from all sides could be triggering changes in the brain that are jump-starting development. Drew Pinsky, a physician and co-host of MTV's recently canceled Loveline advice program, is a proponent of this notion. "MTV," he asserts, "is absolutely one of the factors in early puberty." But even though the idea sounds nutty, says Herman-Giddens, "it would not be scientific to dismiss it. If someone cuts a nice juicy grapefruit in front of you, you salivate. Seeing things can affect us physiologically."

Whatever the cause—and it may eventually turn out to be a mix of some of or all these factors—doctors say early development has become too widespread to be treated as a medical aberration. In the past, girls who developed breasts before age 8 were often given hormone therapy to slow things down. But in a report being prepared for the Pediatric Endocrine Society, Kaplowitz and co-author Dr. Sharon Oberfield of Columbia University argue that most girls between 6 and 8 who develop breasts or pubic hair should be reclassified as normal and left untreated. "Three-, four- and five-year-old girls should still be managed aggressively," he says, "but there are far fewer of these."

That doesn't mean that breasts on seven-year-olds can simply be ignored. Mentally and emotionally, these kids are no different from their undeveloped peers. "They're not dyeing their hair purple and talking on the phone all the time," says Dr. Francine Kaufman, head of pediatric endocrinology at Childrens Hospital Los Angeles. "They're still 7."

But they don't look it, which can lead to all sorts of problems. For one thing, it makes these girls very obviously different from their peers—a position that can be deeply embarrassing for early and late developers alike. More ominously, says Susan Millstein, a professor of pediatrics at the University of California, San Francisco, "people think they're older, and the kinds of pressures put on them are more than they can handle." Marissa Carter, Sharon's mother, puts it more bluntly. "Girls who look more mature for their age are like honey," she says. "They attract older boys."

For Chicago friends Angelica Andrews, 13, and Emily Jacobson Ranalli, 12, that kind of attention is such a source of pride that the girls are willing to use their real names. Says Angelica: "The boys tease me. They ask me, 'Have you had plastic surgery?' My friends get kind of jealous." Emily, giggling, says, "I've been mistaken for 17." But even they see a downside to looking a half-decade older than they really are. "Life gets harder and harder when you're developed," admits Angelica. "Boys walk up and hit your butt. They won't stay away. They're like dogs."

The physical dangers of sexual harassment and sexually transmitted diseases—and, for those who start menstruating early as well, pregnancy—are only the most obvious fallout of premature development. Academic pressure, drugs and alcohol in the schools, peer pressure and sexually explicit media are all conspiring to foreshorten childhood, with consequences that are still not well understood. "One of the big shocks during the whole Clinton debacle," says William Damon, director of Stanford's Center on Adolescence, "was that people were trying to filter out phrases like 'oral sex,' when in fact there were no eight-year-olds who didn't already know what that was." One result of these influences is that girls are wearing highly sexualized, adult clothing in middle school and below—even when they don't have adult bodies.

Yet this acceleration of growing up comes precisely at a time when life should be less about Eminem and more about M&M's. Between 8 and 12, explains psychologist Mary Pipher, author of *Reviving Ophelia*, a best-selling book on female adolescence, girls are in the so-called latency period, when they turn their backs on boys and bond with their peers—other girls. "Theoretically, it's a time when they're really gathering a lot of strength—they're doing well in sports, they're investigating the world, they're confident learners, and they're confident socially. They're marshaling their forces to be able to go into puberty."

♣ **It's A Fact!!**

What Causes Early Development?

Doctors suspect fat cells, but pesticides, chemicals and hormones in food could also be involved.

- PCBs—These long-lived chemicals, once used in the electric power industry, may jump-start reproductive development.

- Phthalates—A study speculates that they may have caused two-year-olds in Puerto Rico to grow breasts. But the link is far from proved.

- Hormones In Meat And Milk—They're given to help cattle grow bigger, produce more. But some think the hormones linger in food and wreak havoc.

- Fat Cells—Leptin, a protein secreted by these cells, is involved in the progression of puberty. The nation's obesity epidemic makes leptin a prime suspect.

- DDE—Though the U.S. banned the pesticide DDT in 1972, this breakdown product persists in the environment.

Cultural pressure alone tends to short-circuit the latency period, when a child usually develops a sense of who she is and where she fits in the world. When a girl's body develops early, she is more likely to hook up with a boy—and leave her group of girl friends—before the developmental work of the latency period is done. "That," says Pipher, "has all sorts of harmful social, academic and psychological consequences."

Moreover, says MTV's Pinsky, early development feeds into what's already one of the toughest aspects of being a young person in the U.S. today. "Kids don't feel good about themselves," he says. "There's a pandemic of that. Society says, 'Here's how you feel good: get lots of money, look like Britney Spears, have sex, do drugs, do extreme sports.' And it works—in the moment." Eventually, though, the high wears off, and, he says, kids' self-esteem is lower than ever.

So if worried parents shouldn't medicate their prematurely pubescent daughters, what can they do? "If I had a daughter who had a period at 9," says Pipher, "I'd say, 'This does not mean you're a woman; it means you're a nine-year-old having a period, and we are going to proceed accordingly.'" That means clothing, books and music appropriate to a girl's chronological age, not her physical age. It also means having her hang out with her family, where peer pressure to act sophisticated isn't a problem. "One of the best things for a nine-year-old," says Pipher, "is having her spend a lot of time with grandparents, cousins and so on—people who value her for something besides how sexy and popular she is."

Most important, agree virtually all the experts, is that parents keep communicating with their daughters. "It doesn't matter what you tell them," argues Pinsky. "Just get the dialogue going, because when they hit puberty, they'll have questions and they will ask you if they feel comfortable." Nothing is more important than that connection, he says. "It's the child that can't trust adults who is going to do whatever their biological impulses or their peers or the ambient culture suggests to them."

It was family support that got Sharon Carter safely though her bout with early puberty. "I am really very excitable," says her mom, "and I had to get all that under control and make her feel that what she was going through was normal." The result, says Sharon: "I don't remember much about all that. I couldn't go swimming when I had my period. And I still can't, and I love to swim. That's the only difference it made with me."

Angelica Andrews also has her parents watching out for her. Recently, the teenager experienced her first French kiss—but her family knew all about it, and the boy was immediately instructed not to call again until she was 16, or maybe 18. It's unfortunate that such vigilance has become necessary for the families of many 12- and 13-year-olds, whereas a generation ago, most parents could relax until a girl was 16 or 17. But as Angelica puts it, "Welcome to the 21st century."

Chapter 5

When Puberty Comes Late

Jeff hates gym class. It's not that he minds playing soccer or basketball or any of the other activities. But he does dread going into the locker room at the end of class and showering in front of his friends. While the other guys' bodies are growing and changing, his body seems to be stuck at a younger age. He's shorter than most of the other guys in his grade, and his voice hasn't deepened at all. It's embarrassing to still look like a little kid.

Abby knows what it's like to feel different, too. The bikini tops that her friends fill out lie flat on her. Most of them have their periods, too, and she hasn't had even a sign of one. Abby doesn't even really have to shave her legs or underarms, although she does it just to be like everyone else.

Both Jeff and Abby wonder and worry, "What is wrong with me?"

What Is Delayed Puberty?

Puberty is the time when your body grows from a child's to an adult's. You'll know that you are going through puberty by the way that your body changes. If you're a girl, you'll notice that your breasts develop and your

About This Chapter: "Delayed Puberty," provided by TeensHealth, one of the largest resources online for medically reviewed health information written for parents, kids, and teens. For more articles like this one, visit www.TeensHealth.org, or www.KidsHealth.org. © 2002 The Nemours Center for Children's Health Media, a division of The Nemours Foundation.

pubic hair grows, that you have a growth spurt, and that you get your period (menstruation). The overall shape of your body will probably change, too—your hips will widen and your body will become curvier. If you're a guy, you'll start growing pubic and facial hair, have a growth spurt, and your testicles and penis will get larger. Your body shape will also begin to change—your shoulders will widen and your body will become more muscular. These changes are caused by the sex hormones (testosterone in guys and estrogen in girls) that your body begins producing.

Puberty takes place over a number of years, and the age at which it starts and ends varies widely. It generally begins somewhere between the ages of 7 and 13 for girls, and somewhere between the ages of 9 and 15 for guys, although it can be earlier or later for some people. This wide range in age is normal, and it's why you may develop several years earlier (or later) than most of your friends.

Sometimes, however, teens pass this normal age range for puberty without showing any signs of body changes. This is called delayed puberty.

✎ Weird Words

Constitutional Delay: Another term for delayed puberty; this means the physical changes that come with puberty have not begun within the usual age range.

Klinefelter Syndrome: A condition that affects males and results in a tall, thin physique, enlarged breasts, and infertility. It is caused by the presence of an additional X chromosome in the person's genetic makeup.

Turner Syndrome: A condition affecting females that causes developmental abnormalities and infertility. It is the result of a missing X chromosome in the person's genetic makeup.

What Causes Delayed Puberty?

There are several reasons why puberty may be delayed. Most often, it's simply a pattern of growth and development in a family; a guy or girl may find that his or her parent, uncle, aunt, brothers, sisters, or cousins developed later than usual, too. This is called constitutional delay (or being a "late bloomer"), and it usually doesn't require any kind of treatment. These teens will eventually develop normally, just a little bit later than most of their peers.

Medical problems can also cause delays in puberty. Some people with chronic illnesses like diabetes, cystic fibrosis, kidney disease, or even asthma may go through puberty at an older age because their illnesses can make it harder for their bodies to grow and develop. Proper treatment and better control of many of these conditions can help make delayed puberty less likely to occur.

A person who's malnourished—without enough food to eat or without the proper nutrients—may also develop later than peers who eat a healthy, balanced diet. For example, teens suffering from anorexia nervosa, an eating disorder, often lose so much weight that their bodies can't develop properly. Girls who are extremely active in sports may also be late developers because their level of exercise keeps them so lean. (Girls' bodies require a certain amount of fat before puberty and menstruation can occur.)

Delayed puberty can also occur because of problems in the pituitary or thyroid glands, which produce hormones important for body growth and development. In other cases, there are abnormalities in the chromosomes (which contain the body's construction plans) that interfere with normal growth processes. Turner syndrome occurs when one of a female's two X chromosomes is abnormal or missing. This causes problems with growth and with the development of the ovaries and production of sex hormones. (Women who have untreated Turner syndrome are shorter in height than normal, are infertile, and may have other medical problems.)

Males with Klinefelter syndrome are born with an extra X chromosome (XXY instead of XY). This condition can slow sexual development.

What Do Doctors Do?

About one of every 100 teens has delayed puberty. The good news is that if there is a problem, doctors usually can help these teens develop more normally. So if you are worried that you're not developing as you should, you should ask your parents to make an appointment with your doctor.

Your doctor will perform a physical examination and ask about your medical history and the growth patterns of your family members. He or she will chart your growth to see if your growth pattern points to a problem. He or she may also order blood tests to check for thyroid, pituitary, chromosomal, or other problems. You may also have a "bone age" X-ray, which allows the doctor to see whether your bones are maturing normally.

> ♣ **It's A Fact!!**
>
> About one in 100 teens has delayed puberty, but doctors can usually help them to develop more normally.

In many cases, the doctor will be able to reassure you that there's no underlying physical problem; you're just a little bit later than average in developing. If the doctor does find a problem, however, he or she might also refer you to a pediatric endocrinologist (pronounced: en-doe-krih-NAH-luh-jist, a doctor who specializes in treating kids and teens who have growth problems) or other specialist for further tests or treatment.

Even after the doctor has reassured them that they are normal, some teens who are late developers may have a difficult time waiting for the changes of puberty to finally get going. In some cases, doctors may offer teens a short course (usually a few months) of treatment with hormone medications to get the changes of puberty started. Usually, when the treatment is stopped a few months later, the teen's own hormones will take over from there to complete the process of puberty.

Dealing With Delayed Puberty

It can be really hard to watch your friends grow and develop when the same thing's not happening to you. You may feel like you're never going to catch up. People at school may joke about your small size or your flat chest. Even when the doctor or your parents reassure you that things will be OK eventually—and even when you believe they're right—it's difficult to wait for something that can affect how you feel about yourself.

If you're feeling depressed or having school or emotional problems related to delays in your growth and development, ask your mom or dad, your doctor, or another trusted adult to find a counselor or therapist whom you can talk to. This person can help you sort out your feelings and suggest ways to cope with them.

Delayed puberty can be difficult to handle—but it's a problem that can generally be solved. Ask for help if you have any concerns about your development. And remember that in most cases you will eventually catch up with your peers.

 Remember!!

Delayed puberty can be caused by a number of medical problems, including:

- malnutrition

- problems with the thyroid gland

- problems with the pituitary glands

- abnormalities in the chromosomes

Or, it can just happen.

Part 2

Reproductive Health for Girls

Chapter 6

Your First Trip To The Gynecologist

You may be worried about your first pelvic exam. It's very normal to be anxious about something when you don't know what to expect. Hopefully after reading this chapter, you will be reassured that it is simple, isn't painful and takes only about 5 minutes. It is also normal to feel embarrassed or uneasy about your first exam. However, if you know what to expect, it may help you relax. Your health care provider understands how you feel and will be sensitive and gentle, and answer any questions you have.

What Is A Pelvic Or Gynecological Exam?

A pelvic exam is a way for your health care provider to examine your female organs and check for any gynecological problems.

When Should I Have My First Pelvic Exam?

There are no definite rules as to when you should have your first pelvic exam. Most health care providers agree that you should have your first exam

About This Chapter: Text in this chapter is from "Information About Your First Pelvic Exam," by Phaedra Thomas, R.N., B.S.N., Resource Center Nurse Coordinator, from the Center for Young Women's Health website (www.youngwomenshealth.org). This information is reprinted with permission from the Center for Young Women's Health, Children's Hospital of Boston, 333 Longwood Avenue, 5th floor, Boston, MA 02115, 617-355-2994 (phone), 617-232-3136 (fax), cywh@tch.harvard.edu (E-mail). For additional information, visit the Center's website at www.youngwomenshealth.org, © 2002 Center for Young Women's Health.

when you are 18 years old or when you begin to have sex. Whatever comes first. There are other important reasons to have a pelvic exam. These may include:

- Unexplained pain in your lower belly or around the pelvic area, where your vagina is;

- Vaginal discharge or wetness on your underwear that causes itching, burns or smells bad;

- No menstrual periods by age 15 or 16;

- Vaginal bleeding that lasts more than 10 days;

- Missed periods; especially if you are having sex;

- Menstrual cramps so bad that you miss school

Will I Need A Pelvic Exam If I'm A Virgin?

Even if you are a virgin (you've never had vaginal intercourse), you may need a pelvic exam if you are having any of these problems. Having a pelvic exam doesn't change anything, just as using tampons doesn't change your hymen (the skin that partly covers the opening to your vagina).

What Should I Do Before The Exam?

- When you make your appointment, be sure to let the secretary or nurse know that this is your first pelvic exam. The nurse can answer your questions and help explain what to expect so you won't be worried.

> ✔ **Quick Tip**
> Having your first pelvic exam can be stressful and embarrassing, but relaxation techniques such as deep breathing can make it less uncomfortable.

- Do not have sex, use vaginal creams, or douche for 24 hours before the exam.

What Kind Of Questions Will My Health Care Provider Ask Me?

Your health care provider will ask you questions about:

- Your general health, allergies and medications you are taking;

- Your menstrual period, such as how old you were when you first got it, how long it lasts, how often it comes, how much you bleed, the first day that your last period started, if you have cramps, and at what age your breasts started to develop.

- Whether you have ever had sex or have been sexually abused.

- If you have vaginal itchiness or an unusual discharge (drainage) or odor from your vagina.

Getting Ready

- If you find it comforting, your mom, friend or sister can stay with you. The nurse will too.

- After you have given your medical history, been weighed and had your blood pressure checked, you will be asked to put on a gown.

- You will need to remove your clothes including your underwear and bra.

What Happens During The Exam?

- Your health care provider will explain the steps to the exam and ask you to lie down on the exam table. You will be given a sheet to put over your stomach and legs.

- You will then be asked to move down to the end of the table and place your feet in stirrups (these are holders for your feet).

- With your knees bent, you will be asked to let your knees fall to each side allowing your legs to spread apart.

This is usually the part when most adolescent and adult women feel embarrassed. This feeling is normal too. Just remember that although this is your first exam, this is routine for health care providers and their only concern is for your health.

There are 3 parts to this exam. Sometimes not all parts of the pelvic exam are necessary. Ask your health care provider which part(s) will be done for your examination.

The External Exam

• Your health care provider will first look at the outside of your vagina.

The Speculum Exam

• The speculum is an instrument made of metal or plastic. Your health care provider will place the speculum into your vagina. After it is inserted, it will be gently opened so that your health care provider can see your vagina and your cervix (the opening to your uterus). If you like, you can ask your health care provider for a mirror so that you can see what your cervix looks like.

• After checking your vagina and cervix, your health care provider may take a thin wooden stick and a special tiny brush and gently wipe away some of the cells from your cervix. This is a Pap test, which detects

✎ **Weird Words**

Pelvic Exam: The method used by a health care provider to examine a woman's reproductive organs.

Speculum: The instrument a health care provider uses to examine the inside of the vagina and the cervix. A speculum can be made of metal or plastic.

Uterus: The part of a woman's reproductive system in which a baby is carried during pregnancy; also called the womb.

early changes of the cervix before they become cancer. Most girls have normal Pap tests.

• If you are having vaginal discharge, your health care provider will take another sample to check for yeast and other causes of discharge.

• If you are having sex, your health care provider will take another sample from the cervix to check for sexually transmitted diseases. When all of these samples have been taken, your health care provider will close the speculum and gently take it out.

The Bimanual Exam

> **♣ It's A Fact!!**
> A pelvic exam is done in three parts: the external exam, the speculum exam, and the bimanual exam. Sometimes not all three parts are necessary.

• The last part of the pelvic exam is done to check your female organs (your tubes, ovaries and uterus or womb). Your health care provider will insert one or two gloved fingers into your vagina. With the other hand, your doctor will gently apply pressure to the lower part of your belly. You may feel slight discomfort or pressure when he or she presses in certain places, but it shouldn't hurt. If you do feel pain, it is important to tell your health care provider.

• Sometimes your provider will do a rectal exam. This involves inserting one finger into your anus (the opening where bowel movements leave your body) This is usually done at the end of the bimanual exam. Like other parts of the exam, if you relax and take slow deep breaths, it should not be uncomfortable.

What Happens When The Exam Is All Over?

• When the exam is over, your health care provider will answer any questions you have and tell you when to make your next appointment. He or she will also talk to you about any medications you may need and tell you when and how you will get the results of the exam.

Chapter 7

Facts On Abnormal Pap Tests

If you are reading this chapter, you probably have already had a Pap smear test and may have been told by your health care provider that your Pap smear results were abnormal. Maybe you're scared and wondering what this means and how it will affect you. It is normal to feel worried when you get abnormal test results of any kind. However, knowing the possible reasons for abnormal results will help. Let's first review a little bit about what a Pap smear is. Then we'll give an explanation of abnormal Pap tests.

What Is A Pap Test?

A Pap test, also called a "Pap smear," is part of a pelvic exam. The word "Pap" is short for Papanicolaou, which is the last name of the doctor that studied early detection of changing cervical cells. A Pap test is usually done every year after you are sexually active or yearly after you turn 18, whichever comes first. It is the only way to check the cells on your cervix for changes that can lead to cancer. This test does not check for STD's (sexually transmitted

About This Chapter: Text in this chapter is from "Abnormal Pap Tests: A Guide for Teens," by Phaedra Thomas, R.N., B.S.N., Resource Center Nurse Coordinator, from the Center for Young Women's Health website (www.youngwomenshealth.org). This information is reprinted with permission from the Center for Young Women's Health, Children's Hospital of Boston, 333 Longwood Avenue, 5th floor, Boston, MA 02115, 617-355-2994 (phone), 617-232-3136 (fax), cywh@tch.harvard.edu (E-mail). For additional information, visit the Center's website at www.youngwomenshealth.org, © 2002 Center for Young Women's Health.

diseases, like chlamydia and gonorrhea). If you think you might have an STD, you will need to have other tests as part of your pelvic exam.

How Is A Pap Smear Done?

As part of your pelvic exam, your health care provider will take a thin wooden stick and a tiny brush and gently wipe away some of the cells from your cervix. Most girls don't feel anything at all. A few girls may feel a little cramping as their cervix is gently brushed. If you feel anything, it usually lasts less than 1 minute. These cells are placed on a glass slide and sent to a laboratory.

> ### ✎ Weird Words
>
> Biopsy: A procedure sometimes done during a colposcopy in which the doctor takes a very small sample of tissue from the cervix in order to check it for abnormalities.
>
> Colposcopy: A method used to look more closely at the cervix; this procedure is often used as a follow-up to an abnormal Pap test.
>
> Human Papilloma Virus (HPV): A virus that causes growths on the vulva, vagina, and cervix, and can lead to cancer if left untreated.
>
> Pap Test: Also called a Pap smear; a type of test done during a pelvic exam in which the doctor collects a sample of cells from your cervix to check them for changes that could lead to cancer.

A trained technician then examines the sample of cells under a microscope to see if the cells are normal or if there are any problems. The lab then gives the results to your health care provider, who will contact you if the results are not normal.

Does It Mean That I Have Cancer If I've Been Told I Have An Abnormal Pap?

No.

This is a common reaction but is usually not the reason why your Pap test is abnormal. The most common reason for an abnormal Pap smear is a vaginal or cervical infection that causes changes in the cells of your cervix. Most of these changes can be followed closely until they return to normal. Sometimes special treatments are needed. If you have already had a Pap smear, you have made a good decision to think ahead about your health. Regular Pap smears and treatment, if needed, can prevent most types of cervical cancer.

What Does My Pap Test Result Really Mean?

Although most Pap tests come back as normal, sometimes (about 1 time in 10) the result comes back as abnormal. The following is a description of the terms that are used to explain an abnormal Pap smear.

- Normal—This means that your cervix is healthy. If this is your first Pap smear, you won't need another Pap smear for 1 year.

- Unsatisfactory—For some reason the sample of cells was not a good sample and can't be read by the lab technician. The cause for this may include an infection, or if you had your period at the time of the test or if there were not enough cells to look at. Your doctor will decide if the Pap test needs to be repeated within 2-3 months or if it can wait until your next yearly exam.

- Benign changes—This means that your Pap smear was basically normal. However, you probably have an infection that is causing inflammation of the cervical cells. Your doctor will probably do a pelvic exam to check for the definite causes of the infection and prescribe treatment. Your doctor will tell you when you need to have a follow-up Pap smear.

- ASCUS (which is short for "Atypical Squamous Cells of Undetermined Significance")—This simply means there are some funny looking cells that we are not sure what they mean. You will be given advice about what follow up you may need. You may simply need a repeat Pap smear in 4 months, or you may need a more sensitive test called a colposcopy (a procedure done in your doctor's office using a high powered microscope so the doctor can look at your cervix).

- SIL (Squamous Intraepithelial Lesion) Low Grade Changes—These results often mean that you have been infected with the Human Papilloma Virus (HPV), which puts you at risk for developing cancer of the cervix. You will be given advice about what follow-up you may need. You will need a colposcopy.

- SIL, High Grade Changes—These results mean that the cells on your cervix have changed. The results are more serious than low grade changes. You do not have cancer now but without treatment, you are at a high risk for developing cervical cancer. Your doctor will arrange for you to have a colposcopy. It is very important for you to keep this appointment so you can have treatment as soon as possible.

- Cancer—Treatment is necessary right away. Treatment may include surgery. The earlier the treatment, the better your chances are of staying healthy.

What If I Need A Repeat Pap Smear?

Your health care provider may decide to repeat your Pap smear in 3-4 months if this is the first abnormal Pap smear result you have had. You should schedule your Pap smear:

- after any vaginal or cervical infection, yeast infection or STD has been treated (wait 2 weeks after your last dose of medicine).

- after your period has stopped completely.

It is very important to keep this appointment!

Also:

1. Always use a method of birth control you can depend on, if you are sexually active.

2. Contact your health care provider if you think you might be pregnant.

3. Nothing should be placed in your vagina for 48 hours before your Pap test. This includes tampons, douches, creams, and foams.

4. Do not have sexual intercourse for 48 hours before the test.

5. Tell your health care provider if you have any other health conditions or allergies.

What If I Have Cervical Changes Caused By The Human Papilloma Virus (HPV)?

HPV is the most common cause for cervical changes. This virus is spread through sexual contact. HPV causes lesions or growths on the vulva, vagina and cervix. If the lesions are not treated, they can result in a pre-cancerous condition. Since treatment is available, it is likely that your health care provider will advise you to have a colposcopy.

What If My Doctor Wants Me To Have A Colposcopy?

A colposcopy is a way for your doctor to look closely into your vagina and cervix. This is possible by using a colposcope.

What Will Happen During A Colposcopy?

After the nurse asks questions (for example, "When was your last period?"), and gives you information about what to expect, you will be given a gown to wear and be asked to remove your clothing from the waist down. You will then lie down on the exam table and place your feet in foot holders (the same position as a pelvic exam). Next, the doctor will gently insert a speculum into your vagina in order to separate the vaginal walls so your cervix can be seen easily. The colposcope is then placed at the opening of your vagina. Your doctor will be able to see your cervix through the magnifying lens.

☞ Remember!!

An abnormal result on your Pap test does not automatically mean you have cancer or another disease.

It might make you feel better to know that the colposcope is only placed at the outside of your vagina. Your doctor will first paint the cells or lesions on your cervix with a staining solution. The solution changes color when it touches unhealthy cells, so your doctor can get a better look. If there are unhealthy cells, it is likely that your doctor will do a biopsy. This is when your doctor gently removes a sample of tissue (smaller than 1/4 of the size of a pencil eraser) with an instrument similar to a pair of tweezers. The tissue sample is then placed in a jar with a preservative liquid and is sent to the lab to be checked out.

Will The Colposcopy Procedure Hurt?

The colposcopy itself usually isn't uncomfortable. It is really a long pelvic exam and a way for your doctor to look at your cervix. A biopsy, sometimes done at the time of a colposcopy, may be a bit uncomfortable, but this part takes less than one minute. When the tiny tissue sample is removed some young women feel nothing while others describe a "pinching" feeling or "mild cramps."

The entire colposcopy procedure takes between 15-20 minutes. Your doctor may suggest taking an over the counter pain reliever such as ibuprofen or naproxen sodium before the procedure to help decrease any discomfort you may have. You can also ask about taking the medicine you normally take for menstrual cramps.

What Happens After The Colposcopy Is Over?

After the colposcopy, your doctor will explain what he or she saw through the high powered lens and if a sample of tissue was taken. It usually takes about 2-3 weeks for the results of the biopsy to be ready. Your doctor will let you know how you will be contacted. Make sure to make a follow-up appointment.

- It is common to have slight bleeding or spotting that lasts a few days after the biopsy.

- Use pads (not tampons) for any bleeding you might have.

- You may see brownish material or clumps along with blood on your underwear or pad. This is not tissue. This is from a certain kind of solution your doctor used, called Monsel's. The brownish clumps will last about 1 to 5 days.

- It's even possible to have a blackish discharge if the doctor used a solution called silver nitrate to control the bleeding. Again, this will not last long.

- Do not have sexual intercourse, douche or use tampons for at least 2 weeks.

What Should I Be Concerned About After A Colposcopy?

There are certain things your doctor should be contacted about immediately:

- Call if you have any heavy bleeding (heavier than your normal menstrual period).
- Call if you have any bright red bleeding and you are not on your period.
- Call if you have a vaginal discharge that has an odor (other than blood).
- Call if you have severe abdominal (belly) pain.

Chapter 8

The Deal With Feminine Hygiene

As you've probably noticed, puberty comes with all kinds of changes—including the way your body looks and even the way it smells. These changes are a normal part of becoming a woman, but they can be a real source of anxiety for girls. You may wonder what you can do to feel as clean as possible during your period or whether you should use the feminine products you see advertised all the time.

Pads And Tampons

Super, slender, overnight, with or without wings, deodorant, maxi, mini... as if learning about menstruation weren't confusing enough, all these products can seem overwhelming, too! You've probably seen TV or magazine ads proclaiming their feminine products are the best. But what's the best one for you? And how on earth do you use it?

Once you begin menstruating, you'll need to use something to soak up the menstrual blood—either a pad or a tampon. Pads are made of layers of cotton, and they are sometimes also called sanitary pads or sanitary napkins.

About This Chapter: This information was provided by TeensHealth, one of the largest resources online for medically reviewed health information written for parents, kids, and teens. For more articles like this one, visit www.TeensHealth.org, or www.KidsHealth.org. © 2001 The Nemours Center for Children's Health Media, a division of The Nemours Foundation.

Some have extra cotton on the
sides (called "wings") that
fold over the edges of
your underwear to better
hold the pad in place and
prevent leakage. Some teen
girls normally have periods
with heavier bleeding that can
last for a week, and others routinely
have lighter periods with less bleeding that may only last for 4 to 5 days.
Pads come in several different thicknesses for heavier or lighter menstrual
periods or for day or nighttime use. Some pads come with a deodorant or
deodorizing substance in them. All pads have a sticky strip on the bottom
that helps them to adhere to your underwear.

> ✔ **Quick Tip**
>
> Never try to flush a sanitary pad down
> the toilet. It will probably block the
> toilet and make it overflow.

Pads are easy to use: you peel off the strip that covers the adhesive, press
the pad into the crotch of your underwear, and you're done. It's best to change
pads every 3 or 4 hours, even when you're not menstruating very much. Why?
Because regular changing prevents buildup of vaginal bacteria and elimi-
nates odor. Naturally, if your period is heavy, you should change pads more
often because they may get saturated more quickly. Once you've removed
your pad, wrap it in toilet paper and put it in the trash can (or if you're in
school, in a special disposal box that's found in most stalls). Never try to
flush a pad down the toilet—they're too big and will make a huge mess and
back up the toilet.

Another choice for feminine protection during your menstrual period is
to use tampons. A tampon is also made of cotton, but it's compressed into a
tiny tubular shape. Unlike a pad, which catches menstrual blood after it leaves
the body, tampons absorb blood from inside the vagina. Like pads, tampons
come in different sizes for heavier and lighter periods, and they can also
come in deodorizing scents. Tampons are also available with or without applicators—they can either be inserted into the vagina using a special card-
board or plastic tube-like applicator or with just your fingers.

Tampons are also easy to use, but you do need to learn how to put them
in. If tampons appeal to you, it's best to try them out before you get your first

period, so you know how to insert them. Follow the directions that come with the tampons carefully, and be sure to relax. Some girls find that using tampons with applicators is much easier because the applicator tube gives them something to hold onto and helps them guide it properly into the vagina.

Many girls who are using tampons for the first time worry about things, like whether the tampon will get lost inside them or whether a virgin can use a tampon. Luckily, tampons can't ever get lost inside you—the opening at the cervix (located at the top of the vagina) is just too tiny for a tampon to get through. Most tampons have a string attached to one end that stays outside your body and can be used to remove the tampon at any time. Virgins can certainly use tampons with no problem— many teen girls do—and a girl who uses a tampon won't lose her virginity that way.

Like a pad, a tampon needs to be changed every 3 or 4 hours or when it's saturated with blood. Because you can't see it as you would with a pad, you'll need to remember when it's time to change, or spotting and leakage will occur on your underwear. Pull gently on the string that is attached to the end of the tampon, pull it out, wrap it in toilet paper, and throw it in the trash. Don't flush it in the toilet unless it says on the box that it's flushable. If it's time to change your tampon and you can't find the string, don't worry! A tampon can't get lost inside you, remember? You'll need to reach in with your fingers to find it. It may take a minute to do because the string might be a bit hard to grab.

A final word about tampons: it's very important that you change them every few

✎ Weird Words

Cervix: The opening at the top of the vagina. It is too small for a tampon to fit through.

Douche: A product used to wash out the vagina. Medical experts say that douching can actually be harmful to your health.

Staphylococcus And Streptococcus: Two types of bacteria that can cause toxic shock syndrome (TSS).

Tampon: A tube-shaped piece of cotton with a string attached which is inserted into the vagina to absorb menstrual flow.

hours and that you wear the absorbency type that is right for you. Never put a tampon in and leave it in all day or all night, thinking that you won't need to change it because your period is so light. If you do, you put yourself at risk for a rare, but very dangerous disease called toxic shock syndrome (TSS). TSS results from a bacterial infection that may occur from certain super absorbent tampons, especially if they are left in longer than is recommended. Bacteria (certain strains of *Staphylococcus* and *Streptococcus*) can grow within the tampon, enter the body from inside of your vagina, then invade the blood-stream, releasing toxins that make you sick enough to die if you don't get medical treatment.

Symptoms of TSS include high fever, vomiting, feeling extremely ill, weak, and dizzy, and a rash that looks like a sunburn. If you ever have these symp-toms while wearing a tampon, remove it and tell an adult immediately. Have someone take you to the nearest emergency room as soon as possible. You can go into shock with TSS if you wait too long to seek medical treatment.

Remember though, that TSS is rare, and most women will never become ill from using tampons, especially if they follow the guidelines for changing them regularly.

When deciding whether to use pads or tampons, it's really up to you. Some girls like tampons because you can go swimming with no problem, and they are easy to store in a purse or pocket. Other girls like pads because they are easy to use, and you don't need to remind yourself to change them. Some women even go back and forth: sometimes they use tampons and some-times they use pads, depending on the situation, where they're going to be, and their menstrual flow. Some women use pads at night and tampons dur-ing the day.

Douches And Feminine Sprays

Douches (from the French word for "wash," douching refers to wash-ing out the vagina, usually with a prepackaged mix of fluids) and femi-nine sprays (or deodorants) supposedly keep a woman's vaginal area smell-ing fresh and clean. For a lot of girls who are just starting to deal with menstrual periods and other vaginal secretions, these products sound appealing—you might think, "Who wants to smell?! I don't want people to know I have my period!"

The truth is that unless a doctor says so, you never need to douche—and feminine sprays and deodorants aren't a good idea either. Feminine sprays and douches are often heavily scented and can create allergic reactions or even infections in the vagina. Your vagina has its own natural cleaning system that flushes out bacteria, so you don't need to add any chemicals to help it.

Under usual circumstances, no one ever smells any odors from your vagina. But some infections, such as bacterial vaginosis, can lead to an unpleasant fishy odor. The treatment for that odor is not a spray, but a prescription medication that treats the infection rather than covering it up. If you think you may have a problem, you should see a doctor or gynecologist right away. As far as your periods go, if you change your pads or tampons frequently and wear clean clothes, no one can ever smell that either.

It's easy to keep your vagina clean without making it smell like a floral shop. Washing every day with a mild soap and plenty of warm water will do the trick. Warm bathing rather than showering daily during your period may reduce menstrual cramps and give you reassurance about feeling clean. During your period, change your pads or tampons often (at least every 3 to 4 hours) and change your underwear if you happen to soak through your pad or tampon.

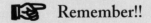 **Remember!!**

You should never use a douche unless your doctor tells you to.

Chapter 9

A Guide To Using Tampons

You may feel nervous about using a tampon for the first time. It is normal to feel nervous, especially if you have any unanswered questions about tampons. Hopefully, this chapter will answer your questions, address your worries, and make your first experience with tampons a positive one.

There are many myths about tampons. Test your knowledge, to see how much you really know about tampons.

Myth Or Fact? Take The Tampon Facts Quiz

1. Tampons are a healthy alternative to pads.

   True   False

2. If I use a tampon, I am at a very high risk for infections.

   True   False

About This Chapter: Text in this chapter is from "A Guide To Using Your First Tampon: Information Sheet," by Noel DiCarlo, Children's Hospital League's Resource Center Intern, from the Center for Young Women's Health website. This information is reprinted with permission from the Center for Young Women's Health, Children's Hospital of Boston, 333 Longwood Avenue, 5th Floor, Boston, MA 02115, 617-355-2994 (voice), 617-232-3136 (fax), cywh@tch.harvard.edu (E-mail). For additional information, visit the Center's website at www.youngwomenshealth.org, © 2002 Center for Young Women's Health.

3. A tampon can get lost inside of me.

    True   False

4. If I use tampons, I will no longer be a virgin.

    True   False

5. I can swim while wearing a tampon.

    True   False

6. Tampons fall out with physical activity.

    True   False

Read the following for the answers.

What Are Tampons And How Do They Work?

Tampons, like pads, are products used to absorb your menstrual flow. They are made of soft cotton pressed together to form a cylinder-like shape, so that they can be easily inserted into the opening of the vagina. A tampon absorbs your menstrual flow, or blood, before it has a chance to leave the body. Tampons come in all different sizes and absorbencies and can be purchased at most convenience stores or supermarkets.

How Do You Insert A Tampon?

You may be worried and nervous about using your first tampon. Talk to your mom or a friend who has used tampons. It is important to first learn how to use a tampon and then, just relax. The more you relax, the easier the insertion will be. When you are nervous, your muscles tense up, making insertion even harder. For your first time, you may want to try using a tampon when your menstrual flow is heavy; this should allow the tampon to glide in more easily. Choose the smallest size tampon for the first time. By following these simple guidelines, and those that come with your package of tampons, your first experience with tampons should be easy.

1. Sit or stand in a comfortable position. Some women prefer to place one leg on the toilet seat or tub, while others prefer to squat down. After you

find a position that is most comfortable for you, hold the tampon with the fingers that you write with. Hold the middle of the tampon, at the spot where the smaller, inner tube inserts into the larger, outer tube. Make sure the string is visible and pointing away from your body.

2. With your other hand, open the labia (the folds of skin around the vaginal opening) and position the tampon in the vaginal opening.

3. Gently push the tampon into the opening, aiming for the small of your back. Stop when your fingers touch your body and the applicator, or outer tube, is completely inside the vagina.

4. Once the applicator or outer tube is inside of you, use your index finger to push the inner tube (the tube where the removal string is connected) through the outer tube.

5. Once the inner tube is all the way in, use your thumb and middle finger to remove the applicator or outer tube. Make sure that the string hangs outside of the vaginal opening. Later, in order to remove a tampon, just pull downward on the removal string.

If the tampon is inserted correctly, you should not feel it. If you feel uncomfortable in any way, you may have inserted the tampon incorrectly or the tampon may not be placed far enough into the vagina. If this occurs, just remove the tampon and start again with a new tampon. Remember that practice makes perfect. If you don't get it on the first try, your second try will most likely be successful. Instead of getting frustrated and giving up, relax and try again.

What If I Still Don't Succeed?

If you don't succeed after several times, see your health care provider. It may be that you were born with a very small opening in your hymen and you can't insert tampons. This is true in only about 2% of teens, but it could be a problem.

A mirror is often helpful so that you can see where your vaginal opening is. Sometimes, even using a small amount of vaginal lubricant (K-Y Jelly) on the end of the tampon will help the first one glide in.

✎ **Weird Words**

Hymen: The membrane that partially closes the opening of the vagina.

Labia: The inner and outer folds of skin at either side of the vagina.

Lubricant: A slippery substance such as K-Y Jelly that can be used to make tampon insertion easier.

What Is TSS?

You've probably heard of this disease before, and how it may be connected to tampon use. TSS (Toxic Shock Syndrome) is an infection that is very rare, but potentially dangerous. TSS can affect anyone, male or female. However, it occurs most frequently in young women who wear tampons. You will probably never get TSS, but it's good to know what the symptoms are and how to avoid putting yourself at risk.

Tampons themselves do not cause TSS. TSS is caused by bacteria called *Staphylococcus aureus*. When a tampon is left inside your vagina for too long, it creates a perfect environment for different types of bacteria, including *Staphylococcus aureus*, to grow. To avoid developing TSS, follow these guidelines when using tampons:

- Change your tampons frequently (at least every 4-8 hours).

- Choose the correct tampon absorbency. Use smaller sized tampons when your flow is lighter. TSS occurs more often when super-absorbent tampons are used. Don't use these unless your menstrual flow is particularly heavy.

- Alternate between pad and tampon use. You might want to use pads at night, and tampons in the daytime.

- Wash your hands before inserting or taking out your tampon.

- Don't use tampons to absorb anything other than your menstrual flow. Only insert a tampon once menstrual blood is present.

If you experience the following symptoms while wearing a tampon, remove the tampon, and contact your health care provider immediately. These symptoms may seem similar to those of the flu. If they occur while you are menstruating and wearing a tampon, they may signal TSS. Otherwise, they may indicate another infection. It is recommended that you see your health care provider regardless. Symptoms of TSS include:

- Sudden high fever

- A sunburn-like rash

- Diarrhea

- Dizziness, fainting, or lightheadedness

- Vomiting

By following these simple guidelines, chances are you'll never have to worry about TSS. However, it is a good idea to recognize the symptoms, just in case.

So What Now?

Check the answers to the quiz that you took at the beginning. Good luck with your first tampon.

❧ It's A Fact!!
Tampons make it easier to participate in physical activities, especially swimming and other water sports.

1. Tampons are a healthy alternative to pads.

   TRUE. Whether you use pads or tampons, it's your choice. You should base your decision on what you feel most comfortable using. Whatever your decision, both methods are healthy and safe ways to absorb your menstrual flow.

2. If I use a tampon, I am at a very high risk for infections.

   FALSE. Tampons do not put you at a very high risk for infections. If used correctly, tampons are a safe way to absorb your menstrual flow. There is, however, a very slim chance that you can develop Toxic Shock Syndrome.

3. A tampon can get lost inside of me.

    FALSE. It is impossible for a tampon to get lost inside your body. Once a tampon is inserted into the vagina, the muscles in your vagina hold the tampon in place. Also, the opening of the cervix (the structure located above the vagina) is too small for any object like a tampon to enter. Normally the string hangs outside so that all you need to do is pull on it to remove the tampon. Occasionally, however, the string that allows a young woman to pull out the tampon can also get inserted with the tampon. If this should occur, don't panic. All you need to do is relax and manually remove the tampon with your fingers.

4. If I use tampons, I will no longer be a virgin.

    FALSE. Using a tampon will not affect your virginity. The only way to lose your virginity is through vaginal intercourse.

5. I can swim while wearing a tampon.

    TRUE. One of the benefits to using tampons is that you can participate in all water and physical activities, whether or not you have your period. Occasionally, the tampon may absorb some water. Don't worry, this will only cause the tampon to become a little wet with water and will have to be changed shortly after swimming.

6. Tampons fall out with physical activity.

    FALSE. When a tampon is properly inserted into your vagina, the muscles inside your vagina naturally hold the tampon in place so it can't fall out, even when playing active sports. When it's time to change or remove your tampon, these same muscles relax so the tampon can come out.

Chapter 10

Toxic Shock Syndrome And Tampon Safety

TSS (toxic shock syndrome) is a rare but serious disease that has been associated with tampon use. TSS is recognizable and treatable. But—most importantly, there are actions you can take to reduce the risk of developing it.

This chapter will help you learn the facts about TSS: symptoms, remedies, and prevention. It also includes a guide to choosing the right tampon absorbency—key to avoiding the risk of TSS.

Toxic Shock Syndrome

You've probably heard about this disease before, but how much do you really know about it? This chapter will help you find out who can get it, how to recognize the symptoms, and what you should do if you think you or someone else might have it.

TSS is a rare disease but because it is potentially serious, it's important to know about it and what action to take if you think you have the symptoms.

About This Chapter: Text in this chapter is from "TSS/Tampon Safety," from the Tampax website (www.tampax.com). Reprinted with permission from www.tampax.com. © 2002 Procter & Gamble Company.

Your Questions Answered

What is TSS?

Toxic Shock Syndrome (TSS) is a rare, but potentially serious disease that has been associated with tampon use. In rare cases, TSS can be fatal. TSS is believed to be caused by toxin-producing strains of the *staphylococcus aureus* bacterium.

What causes TSS?

The bacterium that causes TSS is found most commonly on the skin, in the nose, armpit, groin or vagina. In fact, about one third of the population carry it without any problem at all. However, in a very small number of people, certain strains of the bacterium produce toxins that can cause TSS. Most people have the antibodies in their bloodstream to protect them from the toxin if it is produced, but many do not.

Can anyone get TSS?

TSS can affect anyone—men, women or children. Some cases of TSS are caused by infections following insect bites, burns or surgery. About half of the reported cases are associated with women using tampons.

Can you catch TSS from other people?

No. TSS is not a contagious disease.

What is the link between TSS and tampon use?

The link is not clearly understood. However, tampon research shows that the risk of tampon-related TSS is associated with absorbency: the higher the

---

✎ Weird Words

Absorbency: The amount of liquid a tampon can hold. Higher-absorbency tampons are more likely to cause TSS.

Antibiotics: Medications used to treat bacterial infections, including TSS.

Antibodies: Substances in your blood that can prevent you from contracting toxic shock syndrome. Most people have antibodies against TSS, but some do not.

Alarmist: A person who overreacts to potential danger. If you have any of the symptoms of TSS, see your health care provider—don't worry about being an alarmist.

absorbency the higher the risk; the lower the absorbency the lower the risk. That is why a woman should always use the lowest absorbency tampon for her menstrual flow.

Can the risk of tampon-related TSS be reduced?

There are several things that can be done. Women should use the lowest absorbency tampon for their menstrual flow. The risk of tampon-related TSS may also be reduced by using pads as an alternative from time to time during a period.

The Symptoms

What are the symptoms of TSS? Some of the symptoms are much the same as the flu, but they can become serious very quickly. The warning signs of TSS are:

✔ **Quick Tip**

Dear Iris,

I recently started using tampons. At the beginning of my period I use a super tampon which lasts about 5-6 hours. I would like to wear a tampon to bed since it is more comfortable (I sleep for about 8 hours). Can I wear a super plus tampon to bed so it lasts 8 hours or should I just wear a pad?

Thanks,
Jo

Dear Jo,

I think you can try to wear a super plus at night as long as you are flowing heavily and you change the tampon not later than 8 hours after you inserted it.

Iris Prager, Ph.D., North American Education Manager for Tampax

- sudden high temperature (102 degrees F/38.9 degrees C or higher)

- vomiting

- diarrhea

- a sunburn-like rash

- muscle aches

- dizziness

- fainting or feeling faint when standing up

✔ Quick Tip

Dear Iris,

I accidentally left the same tampon in for a month. I don't know how I did this. Is anything going to happen from this? Do I need to see a doctor?

Thanks,
Stacey

Dear Stacey,

Tampons cannot get lost in the vagina. If you accidentally left one in from your last period you might experience localized inflammation, causing a discolored vaginal discharge and a foul odor. Squat down and insert your thumb and forefinger into your vagina. Sweep the fingers back and forth and try to feel the cord or tampon itself. Once you feel the tampon/cord, grasp it and pull it out. If you cannot find the tampon you will have to see a doctor. It is important that you get the tampon out as soon as you can. No tampon should be left in your vagina for more than 8 hours.

Iris Prager, Ph.D., North American Education Manager for Tampax

What should I do if I get these symptoms?

If you have any of these symptoms and are wearing a tampon you should remove the tampon immediately and contact your doctor for immediate treatment. Tell the doctor that you have been using tampons and suspect that you may have TSS. Don't worry about being an alarmist. What's important is to get speedy treatment.

Is it possible to get TSS more than once?

A person who has had TSS can develop it again. If a women has had TSS in the past, she should seek medical advice before using tampons again.

The Treatment

With early diagnosis, TSS can generally be effectively treated with antibiotics and other medicines to counteract the symptoms.

Chapter 11

Your Period: What's Normal And What's Not

Menstruation is a woman's monthly bleeding. It is also called menses, menstrual period, or period. When a woman has her period, she is menstruating. The menstrual blood is partly blood and partly tissue from the inside of the uterus (womb). It flows from the uterus through the small opening in the cervix, and passes out of the body through the vagina. Most menstrual periods last from three to five days.

What Is The Menstrual Cycle?

Menstruation is part of the menstrual cycle, which helps a woman's body prepare for the possibility of pregnancy each month. A cycle starts on the first day of a period. The average menstrual cycle is 28 days long. However, a cycle can range anywhere from 23 days to 35 days.

The parts of the body involved in the menstrual cycle include the brain, pituitary gland, uterus and cervix, ovaries, fallopian tubes, and vagina. Body chemicals called hormones rise and fall during the month and make the menstrual cycle happen. The ovaries make two important female hormones,

About This Chapter: Text in this chapter is from "Menstruation and the Menstrual Cycle," a fact sheet produced by the U.S. Department of Health and Human Services (DHHS), Office on Women's Health, 2002. Available online at http://www.4woman.gov/faq/menstru.htm.

estrogen and progesterone. Other hormones involved in the menstrual cycle include follicle-stimulating hormone (FSH) and luteinizing hormone (LH), made by the pituitary gland.

What Happens During The Menstrual Cycle?

In the first half of the menstrual cycle, levels of estrogen rise and make the lining of the uterus grow and thicken. In response to follicle-stimulating hormone, an egg (ovum) in one of the ovaries starts to mature. At about day 14 of a typical 28-day cycle, in response to a surge of luteinizing hormone, the egg leaves the ovary. This is called ovulation.

> **✤ It's A Fact!!**
>
> While most menstrual periods last from three to five days, anywhere from two to seven days is considered normal. For the first few years after menstruation begins, periods may be very irregular. They may also become irregular in women approaching menopause. Sometimes birth control pills are prescribed to help with irregular periods or other problems with the menstrual cycle.

In the second half of the menstrual cycle, the egg begins to travel through the fallopian tube to the uterus. Progesterone levels rise and help prepare the uterine lining for pregnancy. If the egg becomes fertilized by a sperm cell and attaches itself to the uterine wall, the woman becomes pregnant. If the egg is not fertilized, it either dissolves or is absorbed into the body. If pregnancy does not occur, estrogen and progesterone levels drop, and the thickened lining of the uterus is shed during the menstrual period.

What Is A Typical Menstrual Period Like?

During the menstrual period, the thickened uterine lining and extra blood are shed through the vaginal canal. A woman's period may not be the same every month, and it may not be the same as other women's periods. Periods can be light, moderate, or heavy, and the length of the period also varies. While most menstrual periods last from three to five days, anywhere from two to seven days is considered normal. For the first few years after menstruation begins, periods may be very irregular. They may also become irregular in women approaching menopause. Sometimes birth control pills are prescribed to help with irregular periods or other problems with the menstrual cycle.

Sanitary pads or tampons, which are made of cotton or another absorbent material, are worn to absorb the blood flow. Sanitary pads are placed inside the panties; tampons are inserted into the vagina.

What Kinds Of Problems Do Women Have With Their Periods?

Women can have various kinds of problems with their periods, including pain, heavy bleeding, and skipped periods.

- Amenorrhea—the lack of a menstrual period. This term is used to describe the absence of a period in young women who haven't started menstruating by age 16, or the absence of a period in women who used to have a regular period. Causes of amenorrhea include pregnancy, breastfeeding, and extreme weight loss caused by serious illness, eating disorders, excessive exercising, or stress. Hormonal problems (involving the pituitary, thyroid, ovary, or adrenal glands) or problems with the reproductive organs may be involved.

- Dysmenorrhea—painful periods, including severe menstrual cramps. In younger women, there is often no known disease or condition associated with the pain. A hormone called prostaglandin is responsible for the symptoms. Some pain medicines available over the counter, such as ibuprofen, can help with these symptoms. Sometimes a disease or condition, such as uterine fibroids or endometriosis, causes the pain. Treatment depends on what is causing the problem and how severe it is.

- Abnormal uterine bleeding—vaginal bleeding that is different from normal menstrual periods. It includes very heavy bleeding or unusually long periods (also called menorrhagia), periods too close together, and bleeding between periods. In adolescents and women approaching menopause, hormone imbalance problems often cause menorrhagia along with irregular cycles. Sometimes this is called dysfunctional uterine bleeding (DUB). Other causes of abnormal bleeding include uterine fibroids and polyps. Treatment for abnormal bleeding depends on the cause.

At What Age Does A Girl Get Her First Period?

Menarche is another name for the beginning of menstruation. In the United States, the average age a girl starts menstruating is 12. However, this does not mean that all girls start at the same age. A girl can begin menstruating anytime between the ages of 8 and 16. Menstruation will not occur until all parts of a girl's reproductive system have matured and are working together.

How Long Does A Woman Have Periods?

Women usually continue having periods until menopause. Menopause occurs around the age of 51, on average. Menopause means that a woman is no longer ovulating (producing eggs) and therefore can no longer become pregnant. Like menstruation, menopause can vary from woman to woman and may take several years to occur. Some women have early menopause because of surgery or other treatment, illness, or other reasons.

How Often Should I Change My Pad/Tampon?

Sanitary napkins (pads) should be changed as often as necessary, before the pad is soaked with menstrual flow. Each woman decides for herself what is comfortable. Tampons should be changed often (at least every 4-8 hours). Make sure that you use the lowest absorbency of tampon needed for your flow. For example, do not use super absorbency on the lightest day of your period. This can put you at risk for toxic shock syndrome (TSS). TSS is a rare but potentially deadly disease. Women under 30, especially teenagers, are at a higher risk for TSS. Using any kind of tampon—cotton or rayon of any absorbency—puts a woman at greater risk for TSS than using menstrual pads. The risk of TSS can be lessened or avoided by not using tampons, or by alternating between tampons and pads during your period.

The Food and Drug Administration (FDA) recommends the following tips to help avoid tampon problems:

- Follow package directions for insertion.

- Choose the lowest absorbency for your flow.

- Change your tampon at least every 4 to 8 hours.

- Consider alternating pads with tampons.

- Know the warning signs of toxic shock syndrome.

- Don't use tampons between periods.

If you experience any of the following symptoms while you are menstruating and using tampons, you should contact your health care provider immediately:

- High fever that appears suddenly

- Muscle aches

- Diarrhea

- Dizziness and/or fainting

- Sunburn-like rash

- Sore throat

- Bloodshot eyes

☞ Remember!!

When Should I See A Health Care Provider About My Period?

You should consult your health care provider for the following:

- If you have not started menstruating by the age of 16.

- If your period has suddenly stopped.

- If you are bleeding for more days than usual.

- If you are bleeding excessively.

- If you suddenly feel sick after using tampons.

- If you bleed between periods (more than just a few drops).

- If you have severe pain during your period.

Chapter 12

Menstrual Cramps

What Are Menstrual Cramps?

For decades, the medical establishment thought of menstrual cramps as an ailment that was minor at best. Doctors tended to deal with it by either dismissing the pain as a psychological problem or prescribing painkillers or tranquilizers. Today researchers have come a long way toward a fuller understanding of menstrual cramps and the pain they cause some 30 to 60 percent of women each month.

Are There Different Types Of Menstrual Cramps?

Most women who have cramps are experiencing what's known as dysmenorrhea. Most often this condition is classified as primary dysmenorrhea, meaning that it isn't caused by a physical abnormality of the reproductive organs. This type of dysmenorrhea usually takes the form of sharp, spasmodic pains in your lower abdomen at the beginning of your period, or a day or two earlier, and it lasts two to three days. The condition is most common among young women in their teens and twenties; it usually moderates with age and may disappear if you give birth. According to some estimates, as

About This Chapter: Text in this chapter is from "Menstrual Cramps (Dysmenorrhea)," by Paige Bierma, from the BluePrint for Health website (blueprint. bluecrossmn.com). Copyright © 1999 Consumer Health Interactive; last updated 2002.

many as 10 percent of young women have such severe cramps of this type that they're unable to maintain their normal schedules one or two days per month. In some women the cramping is so painful that they can't walk, and a few have compared it to the contractions of childbirth.

Another kind of menstrual pain that's common in primary dysmenorrhea feels more like a dull ache in the lower back and pelvis. It's more likely to affect older women and can sometimes get worse with age and multiple pregnancies.

Another type of menstrual cramps is a much less common disorder known as secondary dysmenorrhea, also marked by pelvic and lower-back pain. Unlike that of primary dysmenorrhea, however, the pain is a symptom of another disease or condition that may require treatment—perhaps endometriosis, pelvic inflammatory disease, uterine fibroids, and adenomyosis (in which uterine tissue grows into the wall of the uterus).

> ♣ **It's A Fact!!**
>
> Menstrual cramps are classified as either primary or secondary dysmenorrhea. Secondary dysmenorrhea is caused by an abnormality of the reproductive system, such as endometriosis, while primary dysmenorrhea is not.

What Are The Symptoms?

If you have primary dysmenorrhea, you'll feel either sharp cramps or dull pelvic pain. You may also have backaches, headaches, pain in the inner thighs, diarrhea or constipation, nausea and vomiting, dizziness, bloating, weight gain, and breast tenderness. Many of these symptoms are attributed to PMS (premenstrual syndrome), but stem from the same source as the dysmenorrhea.

The symptoms of secondary dysmenorrhea include pelvic and back pain, spotting between periods, pain during or after sex, a pus-like vaginal discharge, fever or chills, frequent urination, and changes in bowel movement.

What Causes Menstrual Cramps And Pain?

The cramps of primary dysmenorrhea are caused when your uterus contracts to push out the menstrual blood. Hormonal changes occurring naturally throughout your cycle can add to the pain; it's thought that imbalances between the hormones progesterone and estrogen worsen menstrual cramping. And when there's an over abundance of the hormone-like chemicals called prostaglandins, the uterus goes into spasms and racking cramps can result. (Some studies have shown that a woman with cramps has an unusually high level of the hormone prostaglandin F2 alpha in her menstrual blood.)

The use of an intrauterine device, or IUD, for birth control can markedly increase menstrual cramping.

What Are My Treatment Options?

Cramps associated with primary dysmenorrhea can often be eased with non-prescription pain-relievers and anti-inflammatory drugs like ibuprofen, aspirin, and naproxen. If your cycle is regular, you may be able to avoid cramps by taking these medicines one day before your period is due to arrive.

Having a warm bath or lying down with a heating pad or hot water bottle on your lower abdomen may also help. Exercise, believe it or not, can make you feel better; if you're up to it, a walk around the block or a few sit-ups will stimulate your muscles to release feel-good endorphins. On the other hand, if your symptoms make it hard for you to work or even sit up straight, your doctor may prescribe a stronger drug or put you on birth control or estrogen pills, which decrease your body's production of prostaglandin.

Depending on what disorder is causing it, secondary dysmenorrhea is treated with drugs and possibly surgery.

When Should I See A Doctor About Menstrual Pain?

Call your doctor for an appointment:

- If your pain is severe or lasts longer than two to three days.
- If your cramps don't seem like normal menstrual cramps or are occurring at the wrong time of the month.

• If you feel pain during or after sexual intercourse.

• If you have an abnormal vaginal discharge.

• If something just seems wrong.

Don't be shy about asking your doctor questions during your annual gynecological exam, either.

Are There Lifestyle Changes I Can Make To Lessen Cramps Caused By Primary Dysmenorrhea?

Regular aerobic exercise (like walking or swimming for 20 minutes three times a week) has been shown to decrease menstrual pain in some women. And, according to a recent study, daily calcium supplements appear to lessen symptoms of PMS, including cramping.

What Kinds Of Things Are Likely To Make My Cramps Worse?

Some gynecologists think that smoking, stress, lack of sleep, poor posture, caffeine (found in coffee and most soft drinks), and a diet high in fat and salt are all culprits.

Are There Any Alternative Treatments?

Yes. Although few scientific studies have been done in this area, many women have reported benefits from acupressure, acupuncture, and various

---

✎ Weird Words

Adenomyosis: An abnormal growth of the uterine tissue which can cause dysmenorrhea.

Fibroids: Benign (noncancerous) tumors that can grow on the walls of the uterus and can cause dysmenorrhea.

Prostaglandins: Hormone-like chemicals that can cause uterine cramps.

herbal remedies, which are believed to help lessen menstrual cramps as well as the symptoms of PMS. The ancient Chinese arts of acupuncture and acupressure are based on the belief that by stimulating specific points on the body with hair-thin needles or a practitioner's hand pressure can unblock the flow of energy within the body and relieve pain.

> ✔ **Quick Tip**
>
> Unfortunately, some people, even some health care providers, don't believe women when they say they have extreme menstrual pain. If you have really bad cramps, it's not all in your head, so if your health care provider doesn't believe you or help you, find another one who will.

In the herb department, cramp bark or black cohosh and evening primrose oil are all thought to safely relieve menstrual cramps.

Obstetrician/gynecologist Christian Northrup, author of *Women's Bodies, Women's Wisdom*, also reports that dietary changes have brought her patients relief from menstrual cramps. She recommends that women can decrease their intake of eggs, red meat, and dairy products or switch to organic dairy foods, on the theory that milk containing added hormones and antibiotics may stimulate female hormones in ways we don't yet understand. Among her other recommendations:

• Get plenty of essential fatty acids, which are found in canned sardines, salmon, flaxseed oil, and ground flaxseed, among other things (according to Northrup, this seems to moderate cramps even if you don't change your diets in other ways).

• Take extra magnesium and a multivitamin and mineral supplement.

• Take extra vitamin E during your menstrual cycles.

• As much as you can, eliminate trans-fatty acids from your diet (these are found in foods like commercially prepared pastries, which contain margarine, solid vegetable shortening, and other partially hydrogenated oils).

- Cut down on stress.
- Try yoga or massage.

Chapter 13

Severe Menstrual Pain And Heavy Bleeding

Severe Menstrual Pain

What is severe menstrual pain?

Some women have extreme cramping just before and during their period. The technical term for this is dysmenorrhea. If you have this kind of pain, you should seek treatment. Severe menstrual pain may be a symptom of endometriosis.

What can be done about severe menstrual pain?

Several types of medicine are used to treat painful cramps. These include:

• Over-the-counter pain relievers, such as aspirin, ibuprofen, naproxen (for example, Aleve), or acetaminophen may be helpful.

• If over-the-counter medicines don't work, your doctor can give you a prescription for a stronger pain reliever, such as codeine.

• Birth control pills or other medicines may be used to reduce cramping.

About This Chapter: Text in this chapter is excerpted from "Common Uterine Conditions: Options for Treatment," Agency for Healthcare Research and Quality (AHRQ), 1998. Available online at http://www.ahrq.gov/consumer/uterine1.htm. Reviewed in January 2003, by Dr. David A. Cooke, MD, Diplomate, American Board of Internal Medicine.

- Surgery usually is not necessary if severe menstrual pain is the only problem.

Very Heavy Menstrual Bleeding

What is very heavy menstrual bleeding?

As you get closer to menopause, it may be hard to tell when your period is going to start. The time between your periods may be longer or shorter than usual. When it does start, bleeding may be very heavy and last for several weeks.

✔ **Quick Tip**
Severe pain and heavy bleeding during your periods are both reasons to see your health care provider. Both conditions are treatable, so there is no reason to suffer through them without medical assistance.

You may have dysfunctional uterine bleeding or DUB. DUB most often affects women over 45. Usually it is caused by an imbalance in the chemicals in the body (hormones) that control the menstrual cycle.

Younger women also may have heavy bleeding. Usually it is because of an irregular menstrual cycle. A woman may go for several months without a period, but the lining of her uterus continues to build up. When finally her body sheds the uterine lining, she may have very heavy bleeding.

The symptoms can be very upsetting and may make you feel limited in the things you can do. Sometimes, the symptoms are a sign of a more serious problem.

Your doctor will probably do a blood test. Depending on the results, your medical history, and your age, the doctor may recommend that you have a biopsy to rule out endometrial hyperplasia.

What treatments are used for very heavy menstrual bleeding?

- Birth control pills or other medicines may be helpful.

- Another choice is watchful waiting.

- A surgical procedure called endometrial ablation may help to relieve very heavy menstrual bleeding. Endometrial ablation causes sterility (inability to become pregnant), but it does not trigger menopause. The long-term effects of endometrial ablation are unknown.

Do you have a bleeding disorder?

If you have very heavy periods (lasting more than 7 days or soaking more than one pad or tampon every 2 to 3 hours), frequent or long-lasting nosebleeds, easy bruising, or prolonged oozing of blood after dental work, you may have a bleeding disorder such as von Willebrand Disease. This is not the same as very heavy menstrual bleeding, but it can be an underlying cause.

✎ **Weird Words**

Dysfunctional Uterine Bleeding (DUB): A condition that can cause heavy menstrual bleeding. DUB usually occurs in women over 45 and is caused by a hormonal imbalance.

Dysmenorrhea: The medical term for painful menstruation.

Endometrial Ablation: A surgical treatment for very heavy menstrual bleeding which causes sterility (inability to become pregnant) but does not trigger menopause (the hormonal changes that normally occur between ages 45 and 50).

Endometriosis: A medical condition in which tissue travels outside of the uterus to other parts of the body, causing painful periods.

Hemophilia: A condition which prevents the blood from clotting when it should. It can be an underlying cause of heavy menstrual bleeding.

Chapter 14

Endometriosis: Painful, But Treatable

"The pain was so sharp I thought I'd ruptured my appendix, but the doctor said, no, it wasn't that. It was between my periods, so I didn't connect it with menstruation. I was 16.

"Over the next 10 years, I had more and more of these 'pain attacks,' and my periods gradually became heavier and more painful.

"When I was pregnant with my first child, I was virtually pain-free. But shortly after he was born, each month around ovulation, I went to bed in tears from horrible pain. And I bled so much during menstruation I didn't dare leave the house. I went back to the doctor. It was endometriosis."

—A woman from Des Moines, Iowa

Endometriosis is a mysterious, often painful, and disabling condition in which fragments of the lining of the uterus (womb) become embedded, or implanted, elsewhere in the body.

About This Chapter: Text in this chapter is from "On the Teen Scene: Endometriosis: Painful, but Treatable," by Dixie Farley, *FDA Consumer*, January-February 1993, revised January 1995 and September 1997. FDA Publication No. 93-1205. Reviewed and updated in January 2003, by Dr. David A. Cooke, MD, Diplomate, American Board of Internal Medicine.

Of the more than 3,000 patients registered with the research program of the International Endometriosis Association in Milwaukee, 41 percent report having symptoms as teenagers. About 5 million American women and girls, some as young as 11, have endometriosis, according to the association.

"These girls have terrible pain," says Lyle Breitkopf, M.D., a gynecologist in New York City. "Typically, they come to the school nurse month after month—maybe six to eight of their 12 menstrual cycles—needing something for pain or being sent home vomiting, writhing on the floor."

For the woman from Des Moines, 25 years with endometriosis led to removal of her uterus, fallopian tubes, and ovaries a number of years ago. For many women today, new medicine and less drastic surgery reduce endometriosis symptoms and preserve reproductive organs. The Food and Drug Administration has approved several drugs to treat endometriosis and regulates medical devices, such as lasers, used in surgical treatment.

✎ Weird Words

Adhesions: Scar tissue that forms from endometriosis and binds organs together.

Ectopic Pregnancy: A potentially life-threatening condition in which an egg becomes fertilized and begins to develop outside of the uterus, for example, in one of the fallopian tubes. Endometriosis is linked to a higher rate of ectopic pregnancy.

Gynecologist: A doctor who specializes in women's reproductive health.

Implants: Bits of uterine tissue that break away and become embedded elsewhere in the body, for example, on the intestines. Endometrial implants bleed each time the sufferer has her period, but because they are not inside the uterus, the blood has no way to leave the body and must be absorbed by the tissues around it, causing severe pain.

Infertility: The inability to become pregnant. Endometriosis can cause infertility.

Laparoscopy: A surgical procedure used to examine the internal organs without the need for a large incision.

A woman who thinks she may have endometriosis should be examined by a gynecologist. The sooner treatment begins, the better it is for the patients, says Breitkopf. "When we find them at an early stage, we can arrest the condition more easily and keep after it so it doesn't progress as far."

Doctors don't know why endometriosis only strikes certain women.

Some probably inherit it, says Breitkopf. "I've seen it in sisters, including identical twins, and in grandmother-mother-daughter situations."

According to Robert Badwey, M.D., a gynecologist in suburban Washington, D.C., "For whatever reason—greater incidence, better diagnostic techniques, or both—we're much more aware of endometriosis now than even a few years ago."

What's Happening In The Body?

Normally, an increased level of hormones each month triggers the release of an egg from the ovary. Finger-like tissues on one of the fallopian tubes grasp the egg, and tiny hair-like "cilia" inside the tube transport it toward the uterus. When the egg is not fertilized, the uterine lining breaks down and is shed during menstruation.

The abnormal implants of endometriosis are not in the uterus, but they respond to hormonal changes controlling menstruation. Like the uterine lining, these fragments build tissue each month, then break down and bleed. Unlike blood from the lining, however, blood from implants outside the uterus has no way to leave the body. Instead, it is absorbed by surrounding tissue, which can be painful.

As the cycle recurs month after month, the implants may get bigger. They may seed new implants and form scar tissue and adhesions (scarring that connects one organ to another). Sometimes, a collection of blood called a sac or cyst forms. If a cyst ruptures, it often causes excruciating pain.

Symptoms vary from patient to patient. Severity of symptoms frequently has little to do with the extent of the implants. For instance, some women with just a few implants have severe pain, while some with many implants have little or no pain.

For some, pain starts before or during menstruation and gets worse as the period progresses. Others report pain at a variety of times during the month. There may be a sharp pain at ovulation when the egg, trying to move into the fallopian tube, causes a cyst on the ovary to burst. (Many women normally feel a twinge of pain at ovulation. Pain caused by a ruptured endometriosis cyst is severe.)

♣ It's A Fact!!

The pain of endometriosis can be so severe that it causes sufferers to miss school or work, skip social events, and plan around their periods because they know they will be unable to function for a few days each month. The good news is that endometriosis can be treated in a number of ways, including medications or surgery.

Patients whose implants affect the bladder or intestines often report painful urination or bowel movements and, sometimes, blood in the urine or stool.

Endometriosis sometimes causes premenstrual staining and, as the period progresses, heavy menstrual flow.

Often, endometriosis remains hidden a long time. A symptom such as pain at menstruation may not be seen as unusual, explains Mary Lou Ballweg, executive director of the Endometriosis Association.

"Perhaps a young woman is told by Mom, who had the same problems, that menstrual pain is normal," Ballweg says. "So she just lives with it and doesn't see a doctor until the symptoms become unbearable. Some young women with endometriosis have apparently normal menstrual periods for years before having discomfort and pain. Others report they've nearly always had difficult periods."

As many as 30 percent of women who report infertility problems have endometriosis.

Severe endometriosis can lead to infertility in various ways. In the ovaries, it can produce cysts that prevent the egg's release. In the fallopian tubes, implants can block the passage of the egg. Also, adhesions can fix ovaries and tubes in place so that projections on the tubes can't grasp the egg and move it into the tube. The effect of mild endometriosis on infertility is less clear.

Women with endometriosis may have a higher rate of "ectopic" pregnancy, a potentially life-threatening condition in which the fertilized egg begins to develop outside the womb.

The most common way to see whether a woman has endometriosis is by surgical examination using laparoscopy, a fairly simple procedure usually done without an overnight hospital stay. The doctor makes a tiny incision and inserts a lighted, flexible, telescope-like device called a laparoscope that allows a close look at the pelvis and internal organs. However, sometimes the implants themselves can only be seen through microscopic evaluation of biopsy specimens.

Drug Treatment

Drugs for endometriosis should not be taken by women who are, or who may be, pregnant.

The earliest drug approved to treat endometriosis was Danocrine (danazol), a synthetic steroid related to the hormone testosterone. Taken orally, in pill form, Danocrine changes endometrial tissue, shrinking and eliminating implants in some cases. Side effects include fluid retention, weight gain, and masculinizing effects such as voice change, hairiness, and reduction of breast size. Other side effects include menstrual irregularities, hot flashes, and vaginal dryness.

Other drugs, related to gonadotropin-releasing hormone (GnRH), act in a different way to decrease the hormones that make abnormal implants grow. One version is a nasal spray called Synarel (nafarelin acetate). In clinical studies, Synarel, at 400 or 800 micrograms a day (within the prescribed dosage range), was comparable to Danocrine at 800 milligrams a day (the recommended dosage) in relieving the clinical symptoms of endometriosis (such as pain) and in reducing the size of implants. Side effects include non-menstrual vaginal bleeding or ovarian cysts during the first two months of use, cessation of menstruation, hot flashes, headaches, decreased sex drive, vaginal dryness, acne, reduction in breast size, and a small loss in bone density. In clinical trials, about 10 percent of the patients experience nasal irritation from the spray. Lupron (leuprolide) is also commonly used for endometriosis, and works in the same manner as Synarel. However, Lupron is given by injection, usually every three months. Zoladex (goserelin acetate implant) is also injected under the skin of the upper abdomen. These drugs do not cause nasal irritation, but otherwise generally have the same side effects as Synarel.

Women taking endometriosis drugs need to watch for problems such as difficulty breathing or chest or leg pain, which may indicate a blood clot and should be reported to the doctor immediately. Other possible severe side effects include irregular heart rhythms. Frequent checkups are needed to monitor effects such as possible thinning of the bones. A patient should immediately report any new or worsened symptoms to the doctor. However, it's normal for endometriosis symptoms to temporarily worsen when a woman begins taking medicine.

Surgery

Sometimes medicine is not enough. Surgery may be needed to remove diseased tissue or to correct misaligned organs.

One method to remove diseased tissue combines laparoscopy with laser surgery. The laser is connected to the laparoscope and positioned so that its intense light beam is directed through the laparoscope onto the tissue to destroy it. The procedure usually is done without an overnight hospital stay and requires only about a week's recovery time at home.

Recurrence rates after treatment need further study, Ballweg says.

The monthly pain and heavy menstrual periods of chronic endometriosis can be frustrating and painful, and can lead to conceiving and infertility problems. But today, with prompt diagnosis and treatment, a young woman's life can often return to normal.

Chapter 15

Vaginal Infections

Have you heard about bacterial vaginosis? How about yeast infections? Do you know about normal vaginal discharge? While most women have heard about yeast infections, many women have not heard about or do not know much about bacterial vaginosis. Vaginal infections happen to women of all ages, to sexually active women and to women who aren't sexually active. Most women have a vaginal infection at least one time during their lives. Vaginal infections are actually the number one reason that adult women see their health care providers.

Most girls notice a yellow or white stain on their underwear after they go through puberty. This is a normal fluid that helps clean and moisten your vagina. You are completely healthy and normal if your discharge:

About This Chapter: Text in this chapter is from "Vaginal Infections (Vaginitis): A Guide for Teens," by Lara Hauslaib, B.A., Leadership Education in Adolescent Health (LEAH) Training Program Coordinator, AOL Youth Web Advisory Program Coordinator and CYWH Health Education Writer, from the Center for Young Women's Health website (www.youngwomenshealth.org). This information is reprinted with permission from the Center for Young Women's Health, Children's Hospital of Boston, 333 Longwood Avenue, 5th floor, Boston, MA 02115, 617-355-2994 (phone), 617-232-3136 (fax), cywh@tch.harvard.edu (E-mail). For additional information, visit the Center's website at www.youngwomenshealth.org, © 2002 Center for Young Women's Health.

- is cloudy white

- has no odor or has a slightly salty odor

- increases and becomes stringy (like egg whites) during the middle of your menstrual cycle when you are ovulating

If you find that your normal discharge is annoying, you can wear panty liners/shields on your underwear. Also, to keep your vaginal discharge under control, make sure you wear cotton underwear (which absorbs moisture and lets air circulate). Take daily showers or baths and make sure that you wash outside your vaginal area every day with mild soap, and then rinse and dry yourself. Don't use deodorized panty liners or deodorant sprays in your vaginal area.

If your discharge changes, it may be a sign that you have a vaginal infection and you need to see your health care provider.

What Is A Vaginal Infection?

A vaginal infection is known medically as vaginitis. The 3 most common causes of vaginal infections are yeast infections, bacterial vaginosis, and trichomoniasis. Vaginal discharge may also occur if you have an infection in

✎ Weird Words

Acidophilus: The bacteria contained in yogurt which can be helpful in preventing yeast infections.

Bacterial Vaginosis: A vaginal infection caused by an overgrowth of normally occurring organisms in the vagina.

Candida: A type of fungus that occurs naturally in the vagina; overgrowth of Candida causes yeast infections.

Gardnerella: The organism that, along with anaerobic bacteria, causes bacterial vaginosis.

Lactobacilli: A "good" bacteria found in the vagina which helps to keep organisms at a healthy balance.

Leukorrhea: Normal, healthy vaginal discharge.

Trichomoniasis: A sexually transmitted infection caused by a parasite called a trichomonad.

Yeast Infection: A common vaginal infection caused by an overgrowth of normal yeast in the vagina.

your cervix with gonorrhea or chlamydia. There are other causes of vaginal infections that are less common. Each type of vaginitis is caused by a different type of germ or organism, so each type must be treated differently.

What Are The Signs/Symptoms Of A Vaginal Infection?

If you have a vaginal infection, you may have any of the following:

• Vaginal odor

• Vaginal itching

• Vaginal burning

• Pain or irritation with urination or sexual intercourse

• Discharge different than normal

However, some women may not have any symptoms. Some women may not even notice any of these symptoms if they aren't too bad. A health care provider may notice signs of a vaginal infection, such as discharge or an odor, during a gynecologic examination and then may do a test of the vaginal fluid to see if an infection is present. It is important to have regular checkups with a health care provider so if you miss something about your health, he/she may discover it.

What Do I Do If I Think I Have A Vaginal Infection?

If you have any of the symptoms of a vaginal infection, you should see your health care provider right away. Each type of vaginal infection has different symptoms, so you may think you know what type of vaginal infection you have. However, you may confuse the symptoms since sometimes the outward symptoms (symptoms you are able to notice) of vaginal infections can appear the same. Sometimes you can have more than one type of vaginal infection at a time. It's also a good idea to go to your health care provider if you notice symptoms of a vaginal infection, because you might have something more serious, like a sexually transmitted disease. It is possible to confuse vaginal infections with the STDs gonorrhea or herpes, since they can have similar symptoms to vaginal infections. Only health care providers can find out if you definitely have a vaginal infection, and if you do, exactly what type you have. You should be completely honest with your health care provider about what symptoms you have, such as odor, burning, or strange vaginal discharge, even if it is embarrassing. This way, your health care provider can make a correct diagnosis as to what type of vaginal infection you have. This is very important, because how you treat a vaginal infection depends on what type of vaginal infection you have.

For example, anti-yeast medications only help to cure yeast infections. They do not work against other kinds of vaginal infections, like bacterial vaginosis, that need prescription medications. Also, if you use anti-yeast medications when you actually have bacterial vaginosis, it may make it harder for your health care provider to give you a correct diagnosis.

Once your health care provider gives you a diagnosis, he/she can then give you medications or a prescription for medications to fight the infections. There are also medications for yeast infections that you can buy in drugstores without a prescription.

Can I Douche If I Have A Vaginal Infection?

You should never douche. Douching can cause infections by changing the normal balance of organisms in your vagina. Douching can also make an infection worse if you already have one, push the infection up into your reproductive area, or hide symptoms of a vaginal infection so it is harder to diagnose it and treat it. Other things that can cause vaginal infections are scented tampons, deodorant spray, and harsh soaps. You do not need any of these things to clean your vagina. Your vagina cleans itself best when you don't use any of these things.

How Can A Health Care Provider Definitely Tell If I Have A Vaginal Infection?

Your health care provider will use a cotton swab to take a sample of your vaginal discharge to look at it under a microscope and to check with pH paper. This may mean just an external exam with Q-tip samples, or it may mean a vaginal exam with a speculum (a metal or plastic instrument inserted into your vagina and then opened up in order to get a better look at your vagina and cervix). Ask your health care provider which is best for you to find out if you have a vaginal infection. The tests are very simple and quick.

Does My Health Care Provider Check To See If I Have A Vaginal Infection When He/She Does My Pap Smear?

An annual Pap smear is very important to see if there are changes in the cells of your cervix that can lead to cervical cancer. If the outward symptoms, like discharge or odor, are obvious enough, your health care provider will do some tests to see if you do have a vaginal infection. You need to make sure to tell your health care provider if you are having some symptoms of a vaginal infection.

What Can I Do To Prevent Vaginal Infections?

The best way to prevent vaginal infections is to practice good feminine hygiene. Vaginal infections can happen more than once. You should always follow this advice:

• Keep your vaginal area clean and dry. You should wash outside your vaginal area every day with mild soap, and then rinse and dry yourself well.

• Do not douche. Douching can upset the normal balance of organisms in your vagina, which can cause a vaginal infection, make an infection worse, or spread the infection further up into your reproductive area (into your uterus or fallopian tubes).

• Do not use perfumed soaps, perfumed bubble bath or gel, scented tampons, vaginal powders, or vaginal deodorant sprays. They can irritate your vagina and cause a vaginal infection. If your vaginal area is already irritated, you should not use scented toilet paper, spermicides, or harsh soaps.

• Make sure you wipe yourself from front to back after going to the bathroom, so that the bacteria normally present in your rectum doesn't get spread to your vaginal area.

• Don't wear tight or damp clothing, because they can keep moisture in and irritate your vagina. This can cause bad bacteria to grow. If you do have to wear tight clothing, don't wear it for a long time.

- Wear white cotton underwear. Avoid nylon and Lycra. Cotton helps to absorb moisture and allows air to circulate. Never wear pantyhose without wearing cotton underwear underneath.

- Practice safer sex. You shouldn't have sex with someone with a sexually transmitted disease. But no matter what, you should always use latex (or polyurethane) condoms to lessen your chance of getting sexually transmitted diseases.

- Keep your stress level down.

- If you use diaphragms, cervical caps, or any medication applicators, you need to make sure you clean them with warm water and soap and dry them well.

Vaginal Yeast Infections (Candidiasis)

You probably have heard a lot about yeast infections because of all the ads on TV and in magazines. Most women get at least one yeast infection during their lifetime. Some women have many yeast infections. Women of all ages can get yeast infections.

What causes yeast infections?

Yeast infections are caused by an overgrowth of a type of fungus called Candida, also known as yeast. Small amounts of yeast and other organisms are normally found in your vagina, as well as in your mouth and digestive tract. Yeast infections occur when the balance of organisms in your vagina is upset and the amount of yeast in your vagina overgrows, causing an infection. Yeast infections are most likely to act up just before or just after your menstrual period. Different things can change this balance of organisms in your vagina and include:

- Antibiotics (for acne, throat, and ear infections or even vaginal infections) because they can kill the normal bacteria in your vagina and let the yeast grow

- Being overweight

- Diabetes

- Pregnancy

- HIV infection

- Steroids

- Poor feminine hygiene

- Too much exposure to moisture (occurs a lot when there is an increase in temperature or humidity, especially in the summer)

- Tight underwear made of material like nylon or Lycra that traps moisture and heat. (You should wear cotton underwear because it absorbs moisture better.)

What are the signs/symptoms of a yeast infection?

The outward signs of a yeast infection may include vaginal discharge that is thicker than normal and is white and curd-like (almost like cottage cheese). The discharge will be odorless. Other signs are itching, burning, redness, and irritation of the vaginal area. Severe yeast infections may cause swelling of the lips of the vagina. Sometimes, women have painful and/or frequent urination because of inflammation of the urinary opening.

Sexual intercourse may also be painful for women because of inflammation of the vagina.

How can a health care provider tell if I definitely have a yeast infection?

A health care provider will use a cotton swab to take a sample of your vaginal discharge. The sample is put on a slide along with a drop of a special chemical. He/she will then look at your vaginal discharge under a microscope to see if you have an overgrowth of yeast.

How are yeast infections treated?

Yeast infections are treated with a pill that you swallow or with a vaginal cream or vaginal suppository (a partially solid material that you insert into your vagina, where it dissolves and releases medicine). Your health care provider will explain to you what your choices are and if one is better than another for you. The pill is especially good if you don't want to put a cream up inside of your vagina. Some anti-yeast vaginal creams are sold over-the-counter (without a prescription) in drug stores. Other anti-yeast vaginal creams need a prescription. If you use a cream, then you should not use tampons during the treatment since it will absorb the medication and make it less effective.

Some anti-yeast medications may weaken latex condoms and diaphragms, so they are more likely to break. Talk to your health care provider about which types of anti-yeast medications do this. If you are using anti-yeast medications that weaken latex condoms or diaphragms, either use a polyurethane condom or don't have sex.

Remember, do not use anti-yeast medications without seeing your health care provider, unless you have been diagnosed by a health care provider with a yeast infection more than once so you are really sure of the symptoms and signs. They do not work against other kinds of vaginal infections, like bacterial vaginosis, that need prescription medications.

What serious health problems can yeast infections cause?

Yeast infections are not known to cause any serious health problems. But the yeast infection itself can be very unpleasant, so you want to get it diagnosed and treated as soon as possible.

Is there anything else I can do to prevent yeast infections that is not listed above?

It is possible that eating one cup of yogurt (which contains acidophilus bacteria) a day is helpful in preventing yeast infections. However, realize that eating yogurt alone will not cure or prevent vaginal yeast infections.

If you have to take antibiotics and are getting lots of yeast infections, talk to your health care provider about using anti-yeast cream.

What if I get yeast infections all the time?

Some women get yeast infections every month around the time of their menstrual periods, because of changes in the pH of the vagina. If you have this problem, definitely talk to your health care provider. He/she may tell you that you need to self-treat yourself every month before you get the yeast infection, so you can stop the symptoms from developing. This means that you will need to use anti-yeast medication that you buy in a drugstore without a

---

✦ It's A Fact!!

The most common forms of vaginitis are:

- yeast infections,

- bacterial vaginosis, and

- trichomoniasis.

Yeast infections and bacterial vaginosis can occur without any sexual contact, but trichomoniasis is considered a sexually transmitted disease.

---

prescription. Or you may be told that you need to take or use oral pills or vaginal creams for longer. But do not start self-treating yourself until your health care provider tells you.

Getting yeast infections every month could also mean that you have a more serious problem, like diabetes. So it's very important to talk with your health care provider if you have this problem.

Bacterial Vaginosis

Bacterial vaginosis is the most common type of vaginal infection, although you may not have heard as much about it as you have heard about yeast infections. Bacterial vaginosis can also be the most serious type of vaginal infection.

What causes bacterial vaginosis?

Bacterial vaginosis is caused by an overgrowth in your vagina of anaerobic bacteria (meaning that they don't need any oxygen to survive or grow) and an organism called *Gardnerella*. Small amounts of these anaerobic bacteria and *Gardnerella* can normally be found in your vagina. Bacterial vaginosis occurs when the balance of organisms in your vagina is upset and the anaerobic bacteria and *Gardnerella* overgrow. The good, protective bacteria *Lactobacilli* is then outnumbered and is not able to do its normal job, which is to produce a natural disinfectant (like hydrogen peroxide) which helps keep organisms at the normal, healthy balance in your vagina. An infection then occurs.

The exact reasons that bacteria overgrow are not known. It is not clear if bacterial vaginosis is sexually transmitted, but it is more common in women with multiple sexual partners. Many times, bacterial vaginosis develops after sexual intercourse with a new partner. However, women who are not sexually active can also get bacterial vaginosis. It is also possible that douching, a change in sexual partners, multiple sexual partners, and poor feminine hygiene may increase your chances of getting bacterial vaginosis.

What are signs/symptoms of bacterial vaginosis?

The outward signs of bacterial vaginosis may include a foul or fishy vaginal odor and a clear, milky-white, or gray vaginal discharge. The discharge may be light or heavy. The odor may get worse around the time of menstruation or after unprotected sexual intercourse. When semen (male sperm) mixes with vaginal secretions, the odor becomes stronger. The vagina may also be itchy and/or may burn.

However, many women have bacterial vaginosis but don't have any outward symptoms. The health care provider may notice vaginal discharge or odor during a physical examination and do a test of the vaginal fluid and then recommend treatment. So always get regular checkups with a health care provider so you catch and treat bacterial vaginosis.

How can a health care provider tell if I definitely have bacterial vaginosis?

A health care provider will use a cotton swab to take a sample of your vaginal discharge. He/she can then measure the acidity of the discharge with pH paper. If your vagina is less acid than it should be (pH of more than 4.5), this is a sign that you may have bacterial vaginosis. Your health care provider can look at the sample under a microscope. If the normal bacteria (*Lactobacilli*) are not there, or if numerous "clue" cells (cells from the vaginal lining that are coated with vaginosis bacteria) are present, then you have bacterial vaginosis.

How is bacterial vaginosis treated?

If you have bacterial vaginosis, your health care provider will either give you a prescription for pills that you take by mouth, or a prescription for a cream or gel that you insert into your vagina with an applicator. (You should let your health care provider know about any other medications that you are taking.) If you use a cream, then you should not use tampons during the treatment since it will absorb the medication and make it less effective. The antibiotics work against the overgrowth of the anaerobic bacteria and Gardnerella. The medication works pretty quickly to cure bacterial vaginosis, but you need to make sure that you take all of the medication for it to be the most effective.

You should not use douches or deodorant sprays that cover up your vaginal odor to treat bacterial vaginosis. Although they may help mask the odor, they will not help cure the infection, and they might make your infection worse.

Even though bacterial vaginosis is more common in young women who have sexual intercourse, treatment of a male partner does not seem to prevent re-infection of a woman with bacterial vaginosis.

Can I get bacterial vaginosis again?

Unfortunately, bacterial vaginosis often comes back, even if you take all of your medication and follow all advice. If your symptoms come back, see your health care provider and get treated again.

What serious health problems can bacterial vaginosis cause?

Bacterial vaginosis can increase your chance of getting a serious pelvic infection, pelvic inflammatory disease (PID), or an infection after a vaginal or uterus operation. It can also increase your chance of having problems with pregnancy. Problems with pregnancy can include low-birth weight babies or premature delivery (delivery before the normal 9 months). It is very important to talk to your health care provider if you think you have a vaginal infection and you are pregnant or thinking about getting pregnant. Treatment is important in pregnant women who have had premature babies in the past.

If bacterial vaginosis is caught early and treated, the risks of getting any of these health problems are low.

Trichomoniasis (Trichomonal Vaginitis)

Trichomoniasis is another common form of vaginitis. It occurs in both adolescents and adults. Trichomoniasis is caused by a single-cell parasite called a trichomonad. Unlike yeast infections, you get trichomoniasis through sexual intercourse, so it is a sexually transmitted disease. Trichomoniasis lives and multiplies in men but hardly ever causes symptoms in men. Therefore, women are often continuously re-infected by their partner since they are not aware that their sexual partner is infected. Women may not know they have trichomoniasis for days or months because the parasite can live inside the woman without causing any symptoms. Then suddenly, the parasite rapidly multiplies and causes very unpleasant symptoms. The parasite affects the vagina, urethra (the canal that carries urine from the bladder to outside the body), and bladder (a sac where urine is held) of women. Since the parasite lives in both males and females, both sexual partners need treatment.

☞ **Remember!!**

If you have any unusual or uncomfortable symptoms such as vaginal discharge, itching, burning, or pain, see your health care provider to be checked for a vaginal infection. Even if you have no problems, it is important to have regular pelvic exams, especially if you are sexually active, because infections do not always cause noticeable symptoms.

If a woman has more than one sexual partner, her chance of getting trichomoniasis is much higher. Very rarely, the parasite can be passed on by wet towels, washcloths, and bathing suits.

What are some signs/symptoms of trichomoniasis?

The outward signs of trichomoniasis may include a yellow-gray-green, frothy vaginal discharge with a foul or fishy odor. The vagina may be sore and red and may burn and itch. It may be painful to urinate or have sexual intercourse. However, some women with trichomoniasis may not have any symptoms.

How can a health care provider definitely tell if I have trichomoniasis?

A health care provider will use a cotton swab to take a sample of your vaginal discharge and do some simple tests on it. Your health care provider knows that you have trichomoniasis if your vaginal pH level is higher (less acidic) than 4.5, and if the trichomonad parasite can be seen under the microscope. Sometimes, a health care provider can diagnose you with trichomoniasis by a Pap smear or culture.

How is trichomoniasis treated?

If you are diagnosed with trichomoniasis, your health care provider will give you a prescription for a specific antibiotic (called metronidazole) for both you and your partner. (You and your partner should let your health care provider know about any other medications that you are taking.) Both of you need to be treated since trichomoniasis is a sexually transmitted disease.

Medication for trichomoniasis is only available by prescription. You and your partner need to take the whole dose of the medication for it to be the most effective. Do not drink alcohol while you are taking the medication, or you will have vomiting. If you take all of the antibiotic dose, trichomoniasis is usually cured. You and your partner should avoid sexual intercourse until both of you are completely cured.

Other Causes Of Vaginal Infections

There are other causes of vaginal infections besides the 3 most common causes, yeast infections, bacterial vaginosis, and trichomoniasis. These causes may include sexually transmitted diseases (STDs), a tampon you left in by accident, a congenital (something you have since birth) vaginal or uterus problem (very rare), or an allergy to or irritation from:

- Spermicides
- Vaginal hygiene products
- Detergents
- Fabric softeners

These products can cause irritation to the vagina. But when a health care provider does tests on your vaginal discharge, he/she can figure out if your infection is one of the 3 more common ones or is different. If it's different, your health care provider will have to treat it depending on what caused it. So you should always see your health care provider when you notice symptoms of a vaginal infection to make sure that you get it diagnosed and treated correctly.

Chapter 16

Yeast Infections

It's an itchy feeling you might hardly notice at first.

Maybe, you muse, it's just that your jeans are too tight.

Actually, tight jeans may have something to do with it. But if the itch keeps getting itchier, even when your jeans have been off for a while, then there's something else involved.

That something else could very well be a fungus whose technical name is Candida, and which causes what is often called a "yeast" infection. Such infections are most common in teenage girls and women aged 16 to 35, although they can occur in girls as young as 10 or 11 and in older women (and less often, in men and boys as well). You do not have to be sexually active to get a yeast infection.

The Food and Drug Administration now allows medicines that used to be prescription-only to be sold without a prescription to treat vaginal yeast infections that keep coming back. But before you run out and buy one, if you've never been treated for a yeast infection you should see a doctor. There are other kinds of vaginal infections which may be mistaken for yeast infections;

About This Chapter: Text in this chapter if from "Getting Rid of Yeast Infections," by Judith Levine Willis, *FDA Consumer,* April 1996, Publication No. 97-2301. Reviewed and updated in January 2003, by Dr. David A. Cooke, MD, Diplomate, American Board of Internal Medicine.

a pelvic exam may be necessary to distinguish them. Your doctor may advise you to use one of the over-the-
counter products. In some cases, a
single oral dose of a medication
called fluconazole (brand name
Diflucan) may be prescribed.

> ♣ **It's A Fact!!**
> Yeast infections are most
> common in teenage girls
> and women aged 16 to 35, al-
> though they can occur in girls as
> young as 10 or 11 and in older
> women (and less often, in men
> and boys as well). You do not
> have to be sexually active
> to get a yeast infection.

Though itchiness is a main
symptom of yeast infections, if
you've never had one before, it's
hard to be sure just what's causing
your discomfort. After a doctor makes
a diagnosis of vaginal yeast infection, if
you should have one again, you can more
easily recognize the symptoms that make it different from similar problems.
If you have any doubts, though, you should contact your doctor.

In addition to intense itching, another symptom of a vaginal yeast infection is a white curdy or thick discharge that is mostly odorless. Although
some women have discharges midway between their menstrual periods, these
are usually not yeast infections, especially if there's no itching.

Other symptoms of a vaginal yeast infection include:

• soreness

• rash on outer lips of the vagina

• burning, especially during urination

It's important to remember that not all girls and women experience all these
symptoms, and if intense itching is not present it's probably something else.

Candida is a fungus often present in the human body. It only causes problems when there's too much of it. Then infections can occur not only in the
vagina but in other parts of the body as well—and in both sexes. Though
there are four different types of Candida that can cause these infections,
nearly 80 percent are caused by a variety called *Candida albicans*.

Many Causes

The biggest cause of Candida infections is lowered immunity. This can happen when you get run down from doing too much and not getting enough rest. Or it can happen as a result of illness.

Though not usual, repeated yeast infections, especially if they don't clear up with proper treatment, may sometimes be the first sign that a woman is infected with HIV, the virus that causes AIDS.

FDA requires that over-the-counter (OTC) products to treat yeast infections carry the following warning: "If you experience vaginal yeast infections frequently (they recur within a two-month period) or if you have vaginal yeast infections that do not clear up easily with proper treatment, you should see your doctor promptly to determine the cause and receive proper medical care."

✔ Quick Tip

How To Avoid Infection

Here are some steps young women can take to make vaginal yeast infections less likely:

- Wear loose, natural-fiber clothing and underwear with a cotton crotch.

- Limit wearing of panty hose, tights, leggings, nylon underwear, and tight jeans.

- Don't use deodorant tampons and feminine deodorant sprays, especially if you feel an infection beginning.

- Dry off quickly and thoroughly after bathing and swimming—don't stay in a wet swimsuit for hours.

- It's better not to have sex in your teens, but if you're sexually active, always use a latex condom.

Repeated yeast infections can also be caused by other, less serious, illnesses or physical and mental stress. Other causes include:

- use of antibiotics and some other medications, including birth control pills

- significant change in the diet

- poor nutrition

- diabetes

- pregnancy

✎ **Weird Words**

Butoconazole Nitrate, Clotrimazole, Miconazole, and Tioconazole: The active ingredients in four different antifungal drugs used to treat yeast infections.

Diflucan: A prescription drug used to treat yeast infections. Diflucan is easier to use than vaginal cream treatments because it is a pill that is taken orally in just one dose. However, it can interact with some medications, and can be dangerous in people with liver disease.

Thrush: A yeast infection in the mouth.

Some women get mild yeast infections towards the end of their menstrual periods, possibly in response to the body's hormonal changes. These mild infections sometimes go away without treatment as the menstrual cycle progresses. Pregnant women are also more prone to develop yeast infections.

Sometimes hot, humid weather can make it easier for yeast infections to develop. And wearing layers of clothing in the winter that make you too warm indoors can also increase the likelihood of infection.

"Candida infections are not usually thought of as sexually transmitted diseases," says Renata Albrecht, M.D., of FDA's division of anti-infective drug products. But, she adds, they can be transmitted during sex.

The best way not to have to worry about getting yeast infections this way is not to have sex. But if you do have sex, using a condom will help prevent transmission of yeast infections, just as it helps prevent transmission of more commonly sexually transmitted diseases, including HIV infection, and helps prevent pregnancy. Teens should always use a latex condom if they have sex, even if they are also using other forms of birth control.

If one partner has a yeast infection, the other partner should also be treated for it. A man is less likely than a woman to be aware of having a yeast infection because he may not have any symptoms. When symptoms do occur, they may include a moist, white, scaling rash on the penis, and itchiness or redness under the foreskin. As with females, lowered immunity, rather than sexual transmission, is the most frequent cause of genital yeast infections in males.

OTC Products

The OTC products for vaginal yeast infections have one of four active ingredients: butoconazole nitrate (Femstat), clotrimazole (Gyne-Lotrimin and others), miconazole (Monistat and others), and tioconazole (Vagistat). These drugs are in the same anti-fungal family and work in similar ways to break down the cell wall of the Candida organism until it dissolves. They differ from each other mainly in the duration of treatment (one to seven days, depending on the drug) and the form of the medication (cream, vaginal suppositories, vaginal tablets).

When you visit the doctor the first time you have a yeast infection, you can ask which product may be best for you and discuss the advantages of the different forms the products come in: vaginal suppositories (inserts) and creams with special applicators. Remember to read the warnings on the product's labeling carefully and follow the directions.

Symptoms usually improve within a few days, but it's important to continue using the medication for the number of days directed, even if you no longer have symptoms.

Contact your doctor if you have the following:

• abdominal pain, fever, or a foul-smelling discharge

• no improvement within three days

• symptoms that recur within two months

OTC products are only for vaginal yeast infections. They should not be used by men or for yeast infections in other areas of the body, such as the mouth or under the fingernails.

Candida infections in the mouth are often called "thrush." Symptoms include creamy white patches that cover painful areas in the mouth, throat, or on the tongue. Because other infections cause similar symptoms, it's important to go to a doctor for an accurate diagnosis.

Wearing artificial fingernails increases the chance of getting yeast infections under the natural fingernails. Fungal infections start in the space between the artificial and natural nails, which become discolored. Treatment for these types of infections—as well as those that occur in other skin folds, such as underarms or between toes—require different products, most of which are available only with a doctor's prescription.

Knowing the causes and symptoms of yeast infections can help you take steps—such as giving those tight jeans a rest—to greatly reduce the chances of getting an infection.

And, if sometimes prevention isn't enough, help is easily at hand from your doctor and pharmacy.

Chapter 17

Pelvic Inflammatory Disease

What Is PID?

PID is an infection of the reproductive organs (the fallopian tubes, uterus, and ovaries). It is usually caused by a STD.

Who Gets PID?

Any woman can get PID, but women who have multiple sexual partners and practice unsafe sex are most likely to get a STD, which can lead to PID.

How Does Someone Get PID?

PID usually begins with an infection of the cervix (the opening to the uterus), such as gonorrhea or Chlamydia. If the infection of the cervix is not treated with antibiotics, it can spread to the endometrium (lining of the

About This Chapter: Text in this chapter is from "Pelvic Inflammatory Disease (PID)," by Lara Hauslaib, B.A., Leadership Education in Adolescent Health (LEAH) Training Program Coordinator and CYWH Health Education Writer, from the Center for Young Women's Health website (www.youngwomenshealth.org). This information is reprinted with permission from the Center for Young Women's Health, Children's Hospital of Boston, 333 Longwood Avenue, 5th floor, Boston, MA 02115, 617-355-2994 (phone), 617-232-3136 (fax), cywh@tch.harvard.edu (E-mail). For additional information, visit the Center's website at www.youngwomenshealth.org, © 2002 Center for Young Women's Health.

uterus), and then to the fallopian tubes, uterus, ovaries, and abdomen. PID is an infection of these reproductive organs.

PID rarely can occur after having certain surgical procedures, such as an abortion, or after treatment for an abnormal Pap smear.

What Are The Symptoms Of PID?

A woman with PID may not always have symptoms. However, the symptoms of PID can include:

- Lower abdominal pain and/or lower back pain

- Longer and/or heavier menstrual periods

- Cramps or spotting throughout the month

- Unusual vaginal discharge (change in smell, color, or amount)

- Tiredness, weakness

- Fever

- Vomiting, nausea

- Pain during sex

- Pain or burning when urinating

- Pain or belly tenderness when your health care provider moves your cervix or examines your ovaries

> ## ✎ Weird Words
>
> Abortion: A surgical method for ending a pregnancy; can lead to pelvic inflammatory disease.
>
> Chlamydia: A sexually transmitted disease that can lead to PID.
>
> Ectopic Pregnancy: A pregnancy in which the fertilized egg begins to grow outside of the uterus, usually in one of the fallopian tubes. Ectopic pregnancy can be caused by scarring in the fallopian tubes from a PID infection.
>
> Endometrium: The lining of the uterus.
>
> Gonorrhea: A sexually transmitted disease that can lead to PID.

As soon as you notice symptoms, you should see your health care provider right away. The infection can spread higher and cause worse pain and damage to your body in just a day or two.

How Is PID Diagnosed?

Your health care provider can tell if you have PID based on your symptoms, a pelvic exam, and blood tests. Sometimes a laparoscopy (a minor surgery to look at your reproductive organs) will be needed to correctly diagnose PID if you are not getting better.

How Is PID Treated?

Depending on how sick you are, you may be treated either in a hospital or as an outpatient (just come in for appointments). Most teens are treated in the hospital. You will receive intravenous (IV) and oral antibiotics until the symptoms get better. After leaving the hospital, you have to take oral antibiotics for another 2 weeks.

If you are treated as an outpatient, you will need to follow your health care provider's directions on taking oral antibiotics. You need to take all of the pills, or else you could get sicker and will need to go to the hospital. A few days after you start taking medicine, you will need to see your health care provider again. If you don't get better, you may need to stay in a hospital to get stronger medicine.

If you find out you have PID, you need to make sure your partner gets tested for a STD and treated if needed. Unless your partner is treated at the same time as you, you may get infected again.

Is PID Dangerous?

PID can be dangerous if not treated early. Scar tissue can form in the fallopian tubes and inside the abdomen. These scars can block the fallopian tubes, which can cause difficulty getting pregnant or infertility (meaning you can't have children). If the tubes are partly blocked, fertilized eggs may not reach the uterus and the pregnancy can form in the fallopian tubes (known as a tubal or ectopic pregnancy). Scarring can cause pain that lasts for months or even years. If the effects of PID are very severe, surgery may be needed to remove pus, scar tissue, or damaged organs. PID is more likely to come back if you get a STD again. Also, the more times you have PID, the more likely you are to have problems and more damage to your body.

How Can PID Be Prevented?

To prevent PID, you need to avoid getting a STD. The best ways to do this are:

- Don't have sex, including vaginal, anal, and oral sex

- If you do have sex, use a latex condom (polyurethane if allergic to latex) correctly every time

- Limit the number of sexual partners you have

- Don't use douches—douches can spread the bacteria further up the vagina

- Don't smoke cigarettes

- Finish all your antibiotics if you are being treated for a cervical infection or PID

- Make sure all your partners get treated for STDs

If you have any symptoms of a STD or PID, see your health care provider right away. Stop having sexual contact until you have finished treatment and your health care provider says it's okay.

☞ **Remember!!**

Pelvic inflammatory disease can spread quickly, causing damage to your body in just a day or two, so if you have any of the symptoms of PID, see your health care provider right away.

Chapter 18

Breast Cancer: Early Detection

Early Signs

- A lump is detected, which is usually single, firm, and most often painless.

- A portion of the skin on the breast or underarm swells and has an unusual appearance.

- Veins on the skin surface become more prominent on one breast.

- The breast nipple becomes inverted, develops a rash, changes in skin texture, or has a discharge other than breast milk.

- A depression is found in an area of the breast surface.

Women's breasts can develop some degree of lumpiness, but only a small percentage of lumps are malignant.

While a history of breast cancer in the family may lead to increased risk, most breast cancers are diagnosed in women with no family history. If you have a family history of breast cancer, this should be discussed with your doctor.

About This Chapter: Text and graphics in this chapter is from "Early Detection," © 2002 National Breast Cancer Foundation website (www.nationalbreastcancer.org). Reprinted with permission. Available online at http://www.nationalbreastcancer.org/index_ie.htm.

Figure 18.1. How To Do A Breast Self-Examination

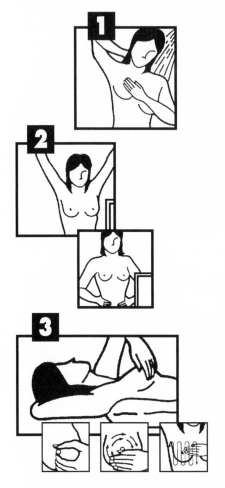

1. In The Shower: *Fingers flat, move gently over every part of each breast. Use your right hand to examine left breast, left hand for right breast.*

Check for any lump, hard knot or thickening. Carefully observe any changes in your breasts.

2. Before A Mirror: *Inspect your breasts with arms at your sides. Next, raise your arms high overhead.*

Look for any changes in contour of each breast, a swelling, a dimpling of skin or changes in the nipple. Then rest palm on hips and press firmly to flex your chest muscles. Left and right breasts will not exactly match—few women's breasts do.

3. Lying Down: *Place pillow under right shoulder, right arm behind your head. With fingers of left hand flat, press right breast gently in small circular motions, moving vertically or in a circular pattern covering the entire breast. Use light, medium and firm pressure. Squeeze nipple; check for discharge and lumps. Repeat these steps for your left breast.*

Facts

- Every three minutes a woman is diagnosed with breast cancer.

- This year 182,000 new cases of breast cancer are expected in the United States.

- One woman in eight who lives to age 85 will develop breast cancer during her lifetime.

- Breast cancer is the leading cause of death in women between the ages of 40 and 55.

- Seventy percent of all breast cancers are found through breast self-exams. Not all lumps are detectable by touch. We recommend regular mammograms and monthly breast self-exams.

- Eight out of ten breast lumps are not cancerous. If you find a lump, don't panic—call your doctor for an appointment.

- Mammography is a low-dose X-ray examination that can detect breast cancer up to two years before it is large enough to be felt.

- When breast cancer is found early, the five-year survival rate is 96%. This is good news. Over 2 million breast cancer survivors are alive in America today.

Detection Plan

An early detection plan should include:

- Clinical breast examinations every three years from ages 20-39, then every year thereafter.

- Monthly breast self-examinations beginning at age 20. Look for any changes in your breasts.

- Baseline mammogram by the age of 40.

- Mammogram every one to two years for women 40-49, depending on previous findings.

- Mammogram every year for women 50 and older.

- A personal calendar to record your self-exams, mammograms, and doctor appointments.

- A low-fat diet, regular exercise, and no smoking or drinking.

✎ **Weird Words**

Clinical Breast Exam: A breast examination that is done by a health care provider.

Malignant: Cancerous. Most breast lumps are not malignant.

Mammogram: A type of x-ray performed on the breasts to look for early signs of breast cancer.

Part 3
Reproductive Health For Boys

Chapter 19

Sexual Health Is Important For Boys Too

Men are less aware than women about sexual health issues because of a flawed information network, says a new study on male reproductive health.

There are "significant gaps" in the way the nation meets men's sexual health needs, says David J. Landry, a lead researcher of "In Their Own Right: Addressing the Sexual and Reproductive Health Needs of American Men," published this week by the Alan Guttmacher Institute (AGI).

Women, researchers explain, are compelled by biology, pregnancy and public health campaigns to seek regular medical attention, where they are routinely asked about their sexual history. Women also have the advantage of thousands of federally funded and private clinics waiting to serve them.

Men, meanwhile, are not required to see a doctor except for sports or employment physical exams and may not be asked about their sexual activity even at these appointments, said AGI researchers, who looked at dozens of national surveys on the sexual health of men aged 15-49.

Moreover, sexual and reproductive health has been feminized. The typical family planning clinic features pink walls, posters of gigantic ovaries and a mostly female staff.

About This Chapter: Text in this chapter is from "Anatomy Lesson," by Cheryl Wetzstein, from the *Washington Times*, March 7, 2002. Copyright © 2002 New World Communications, Inc. Reprinted with permission of *The Washington Times*.

The result appears to be that men know less about sexual health, reproduction and sexually transmitted diseases (STDs) than they should, AGI researchers said. Men begin to pay more attention to this aspect of personal health later in life, when prostate cancer becomes a possibility.

Two consequences of this ignorance, they added, are "alarmingly high" STD rates among young men and rising rates of men with AIDS who were infected through heterosexual contact.

It's like trying to fight unintended pregnancy and STDs "with one hand tied behind our back," said Sara Seims, AGI president and chief executive officer.

♣ **It's A Fact!!**

Teenage boys and young men are much less informed about their sexual health than teen girls and women. The Los Angeles chapter of Planned Parenthood reports that only 5 percent of its clients are male, indicating that men look for advice on sexual health much less often than women.

"We must pay more attention to men, who have sexual and reproductive health needs in their own right as well as in their roles as partners and fathers," she said.

The dearth of sexual health services for men was identified several years ago.

"There is no traditional medical or public health infrastructure oriented to the sexual and reproductive needs of men," said an Urban Institute report on young men's health, issued in December 2000.

The AGI report is an important milestone in the issue because it looks at men's sexual health from the teen years into middle age and comes from the nation's premier reproductive research organization, said researcher Freya L. Sonenstein, who worked on the Urban Institute study.

Saying that men deserve good sexual health care "in their own right" and not just because they are women's partners is a critical symbolic shift, she said.

Ms. Sonenstein also applauded the Bush administration's "great interest" in fostering strong families and fathers' connections to their children.

"I would hope that [the administration's] efforts to strengthen relationships between men and women, and to strengthen families with children, would [recognize] that we need to address sexual and reproductive health needs of both women and men," she said.

While identifying problems regarding men's sexual health and education is a giant step forward, those who work with teen boys and young men said a lot of work remains to be done. In Los Angeles, for instance, Planned Parenthood clinics try to attract men with an outreach program, male voices in radio ads and male staff in the clinics.

"We see lots of men in our clinic, but they're usually hanging out in the waiting room or on the street in their cars, waiting for their partners while they're in the clinic," said Nancy Sasaki, president of Planned Parenthood Los Angeles.

"Our goal is to get more of them out of our waiting rooms and into an exam room for their own health care," she said, adding that 5 percent of their clients are men.

Men's need for sexual and health education is huge, said German Rodrigues and Caesar Castro, who are part of Planned Parenthood's male outreach program.

"So many guys we work with have no idea about how their bodies work or even their partners' [bodies]," Mr. Rodrigues said. Many men

☞ Remember!!

Sexually transmitted diseases often have no visible symptoms, so you can't tell just by looking at a person whether or not they are "safe" to have sex with. This is one reason why it's important to never have unprotected sex.

still think "you can't get a woman pregnant the first time you have sex or get a disease from oral sex," he said.

Old-fashioned macho attitudes also block men from taking a more active role in preparing for a child or taking care of themselves.

"Typically, a guy will think that once he gets a girl pregnant, he's pretty much done," said Mr. Rodrigues, the outreach program coordinator.

"Men don't get the same message that women tend to get, which is be careful, take care of yourself, get checked," said Mr. Castro, an outreach worker. "Men would rather play Russian roulette with sex."

Jeff Rodrigues, who taught sex education to young men in Texas during the 1990s, said in his experience, guys aren't overly interested in their own "plumbing."

"They're more interested in the girls," partly because they want to be good lovers, he said.

However, the STD crisis generates intense interest in sexual health among both boys and girls, said Mr. Rodrigues, who now teaches the "Up Close" sex education program in high schools in Fort Worth, Texas.

"As we say in class, no one has sex with someone who they think is going to give them an STD. They pick someone who is 'safe,'" he said. But unfortunately, "you can't tell if someone has a disease by looking at them, even intimately," said Mr. Rodrigues, noting that many incurable STDs are asymptomatic.

> **✔ Quick Tip**
>
> STD symptoms can come and go, making you think that whatever was wrong went away on its own. If you have any of the symptoms of an STD, even if they seem to go away, you should still see your health care provider to make sure you don't have an infection.

He said many teens are confused by STDs' mysterious behavior. "Sometimes our students think the STD will go away like a cold does," said Mr. Rodrigues. A syphilis sore, for instance, "does clear up and go away, and the discharge from chlamydia, if there is one, can come and go. So they can think, 'Well, whatever it was went away.'"

Sadly, this kind of attitude is contributing to the 15 million new STD cases a year, with 3 million among teens, he added.

Scott Phelps, co-author of "A.C. Green's Game Plan" abstinence education program, said they chose the sports motif, in part, to reach young males.

The program, which is distributed by Project Reality in Golf, IL, calls for "making a game plan for your life," setting boundaries, "avoiding the penalties," choosing good "teammates" and viewing marriage as "the prize" that's worth winning.

"We try to get [teens] to look at the long term," said Mr. Phelps. "And we say that the same self-control and self-discipline that's required for abstinence is the same self-control and self-discipline that is going to help them accomplish their goals and dreams."

Game Plan also features male role models, such as soon-to-be-married basketball star A.C. Green,[1] who is known for his premarital sexual abstinence and "Iron Man" reputation for not missing any games.

—by Cheryl Wetzstein

Note

1. A. C. Green was married on April 20, 2002. His wife's name is Veronique.

Chapter 20

Circumcision

What Is Circumcision?

Boys are born with a hood of skin, called the foreskin, covering the head (glans) of the penis. In circumcision, the foreskin is surgically removed, exposing the end of the penis. Parents who choose circumcision often do so based on religious beliefs, concerns about hygiene, or cultural or social reasons, such as the wish to have their son look like other men in the family.

Approximately 65% of all newborn boys—about 1.2 million babies—are circumcised annually in the United States. According to the National Center for Health Statistics, there have been several notable trends in recent years. One is the closing of the gap between circumcision rates among white babies and black babies (in the past white babies were about 13% more likely to be circumcised than black babies). Another is a sharp difference in the rates of circumcision around the country—most notably, a 25% decrease in the West between 1980 and 1999. Researchers speculate that this might be due to an increase in the Asian and Latino populations in that region—two groups that are culturally less likely to opt for circumcision. Circumcision is

About This Chapter: This information was provided by KidsHealth, one of the largest resources online for medically reviewed health information written for parents, kids, and teens. For more articles like this one, visit www.KidsHealth.org, or www.TeensHealth.org. © 2000 The Nemours Center for Children's Health Media, a division of the Nemours Foundation.

much more widespread in the United States, Canada, and the Middle East than in Asia, South America, Central America, and most of Europe, where it's not common.

Circumcision is usually performed during the first 10 days of life, either in the hospital or, for some religious ritual circumcisions, at home. If you decide to have your son circumcised at the hospital, a doctor will perform the procedure before you bring your baby home. In preparation, the baby will be placed in a padded restraint chair and given local anesthesia. Then the doctor will slit the foreskin and insert a device under the foreskin to hold it away from, and protect, the glans. When the instrument has been in place for a few minutes, the doctor quickly cuts off the foreskin, removes the device, and covers the incision with an antibacterial ointment and gauze coated with petroleum jelly.

Pros And Cons Of Circumcision

Although circumcision appears to have some medical benefits, it also carries potential risks—as does any surgical procedure. These risks are small, but you should be aware of both the possible advantages and the problems that can be associated with the procedure before you make your decision.

Complications of newborn circumcision are uncommon, occurring in between one in 200 and one in 500 cases. Of these, the most frequent are minor bleeding and local infection, both of which can be easily treated by your child's doctor. Even rarer are instances where either too little or too much skin is removed. The former requires a repeat circumcision, whereas the latter can take longer to heal or, occasionally, may lead to reconstructive penile surgery (this extreme measure is only necessary if a significant amount of skin is mistakenly cut, which happens very infrequently in the hands of an experienced circumciser).

Pain is another consideration. Although the procedure is painful, local anesthesia can greatly reduce your baby's discomfort. If you decide to circumcise your son, talk with your child's doctor about anesthesia options.

Some people also claim that circumcision either lessens or heightens the sensitivity of the tip of the penis, decreasing or increasing sexual pleasure later in life. But neither of these subjective findings has been proven to be true.

On the plus side, studies indicate that circumcised infants are less likely to contract a urinary tract infection (UTI) in the first year of life. About one out of every 1,000 circumcised boys has a UTI in the first year, whereas the rate is one in 100 for uncircumcised infants. Circumcised men may also be at lower risk for penile cancer, although the disease is rare in both circumcised and uncircumcised males. The procedure might offer an additional line of defense against sexually transmitted diseases (STDs), particularly HIV, but the results of studies in this area are conflicting and difficult to interpret. It's also easier to keep a circumcised penis clean, although uncircumcised boys can learn how to clean beneath the foreskin once the foreskin becomes retractable (usually some time before age 5). However, some uncircumcised boys do end up with infected foreskins as the result of poor hygiene.

Making A Circumcision Decision

Despite the possible benefits and risks, circumcision is neither essential nor detrimental to a boy's health. Indeed, the American Academy of Pediatrics (AAP) does not find sufficient evidence to medically recommend circumcision or argue against it. As a parent, you need to choose what is right for your child.

In addition to the medical issues discussed above, religious and cultural beliefs often figure into the circumcision decision. If these are important to you, they deserve to be considered seriously. You might also ask yourself if it will matter whether your son looks like other men in the family or maybe even his peers someday.

Perhaps one of the hardest parts of this decision is accepting that circumcision can be painful. The AAP recommends the use of pain relief measures

♣ It's A Fact!!

Report Says Circumcision Isn't As Helpful—Or As Horrible—As You Might Have Heard

As if parents didn't have enough to feel guilty about. Some advocacy groups are trying to convince them that circumcision—the cutting away of the foreskin of the penis—is the most barbaric thing they can do to a newborn boy. Others believe circumcision will make a boy healthier and happier all his life. The truth is far less dramatic. According to a review of 40 years of data published by the American Academy of Pediatrics, circumcision does provide some potential medical benefits, but they are not so overwhelming that parents should feel compelled to have it done.

If you want to circumcise your son for religious, personal or cultural reasons, fine. If you don't, that's fine too. The pediatricians' group is adamant, however, in saying no boy should be circumcised without adequate pain relief. Perhaps 45% of U.S. circumcisions are still carried out without analgesia.

Circumcision is, of course, nothing new. Egyptian priests practiced it as a purification rite more than 4,500 years ago. To this day, it is an important religious ritual in Islamic and Jewish communities worldwide. Circumcision became popular in the U.S. in the early 1900s, in the belief that it promoted good hygiene and discouraged masturbation. World War II veterans swore by its health benefits in unsanitary tropical conditions. Currently, more than two-thirds of U.S. infant boys are circumcised.

What are the medical benefits? According to the pediatricians' review, boys who are not circumcised are at least four times as likely to develop urinary-tract infections in their first year of life. These infections occasionally lead to kidney problems. But the rate of urinary-tract infections among uncircumcised infants in the U.S. is still no more than 1%. Intriguingly, uncircumcised boys who are breast-fed suffer fewer such problems than uncircumcised boys who are bottle-fed.

Uncircumcised men are three times as likely to develop penile cancer, but, again, the absolute risk is quite low. Only about 9 U.S. men out of 1 million ever develop the disease. Circumcised men are one-third to one-half as likely to become infected after exposure to HIV or other sexually transmitted diseases. But they are not by any means immune, and the difference in infection rates would probably diminish among men who use condoms and practice safer sex.

The pain that circumcision inflicts on babies, usually during their first days of life, can be dulled by an analgesic cream or shots of local anesthetic. Amid all the other shocks and discomforts of adjusting to life outside the womb, it's unlikely the procedure would leave a boy with lifelong trauma. Complications are uncommon and generally minor, involving a little bleeding or inflammation (and not accidental amputation). Older boys who undergo circumcision are typically given general anesthesia.

In short, medical considerations shouldn't be the parents' primary concern when deciding whether or not to circumcise their son. Health benefits do exist, but they aren't great enough to override any personal preferences.

Take It, or Leave It?

Circumcision has both pros and cons.

PRO:

- Fewer urinary-tract infections
- Smaller risk of penile cancer
- Lower rate of sexually transmitted diseases

CON:

- Often painful introduction to life
- Not essential to a boy's well-being
- Loss of sensation at the tip of the penis

Source: "Unkindest Cut? A New Report Says Circumcision Isn't As Helpful—Or As Horrible—As You Might Have Heard," by Christine Gorman, from *Time*, 3-15-1999, p. 100. © 1999 *Time*, Inc. Reprinted with permission.

for the procedure. Most doctors use one of three types of local anesthesia—a topical cream, a nerve block via injection at the base of the penis, or a nerve block via injection under the skin around the penis shaft—to make the operation less painful. Besides anesthesia, securing your child in the padded restraint chair and giving him a sugar-dipped pacifier can help reduce his level of stress (and yours). Used together, these methods can decrease discomfort by more than 50%.

♣ It's A Fact!!
Male Circumcision Linked To Lower Cervical Cancer Risk

Women whose sexual partners are circumcised are less likely to develop cervical cancer than the partners of uncircumcised men, concludes a recent report.

The difference was statistically significant only in the partners of men considered to be at high risk for infection with human papillomavirus, or HPV, according to the study in *The New England Journal of Medicine*. Such men had had at least six sexual partners in their lifetime, beginning before age 17.

HPV causes genital warts in men and women, and certain strains cause virtually all cervical cancers. HPV also has been linked to cancers of the vagina, anus and penis.

The new report is based on 1,913 couples in five countries. All were married or in a stable relationship for at least six months. Half of the women had cervical cancer, and 370 of the men were circumcised. Worldwide, an estimated one in four men are circumcised.

Researchers interviewed all of the men and got samples of penile cells from 1,524. The scientists tested the samples for HPV.

After accounting for such factors as age at first intercourse and lifetime number of sexual partners, circumcised men were only about a third as likely as uncircumcised men to test positive for HPV. The authors speculate that circumcision, which involves removal of the foreskin, minimizes the area of the penis vulnerable to HPV infection.

If you do opt for circumcision, it's best to perform the operation within the first 2 to 3 weeks of life, as circumcision can become more complicated as a child gets older.

In some instances, though, the doctor may decide to delay the procedure or forgo it altogether. Premature or medically unstable babies are not circumcised until they are ready to leave the hospital. And babies born with

---

On the whole, partners of circumcised men were about 25% less likely to have cervical cancer than partners of uncircumcised men, a difference that was not statistically significant. But among women in relationships with men at high risk for HPV, those with circumcised partners were 80% less likely to have cervical cancer.

Co-author Keerti Shah, a virologist at the Johns Hopkins Bloomberg School of Public Health in Baltimore, notes that other research suggests that circumcision also reduces men's risk of infection with HIV, the virus that causes AIDS.

"This may be something that may be true for many sexually transmitted infections," Shah says.

He and his co-authors write that more research is needed to determine whether routine circumcision could reduce the risks of HIV, HPV and other sexually transmitted diseases.

In 1999, an American Academy of Pediatrics task force concluded that the medical benefits "are not sufficient to recommend routine neonatal circumcision."

From 1979 to 1999, the proportion of circumcised U.S. newborns remained around 65%.

Anti-circumcision groups argue that the procedure causes unnecessary pain in newborns and adversely affects men's sexual sensations.

Source: "Male Circumcision Linked to Lower Cervical Cancer Risk," by Rita Rubin, from *USA Today*, 4-11-2002, p. 10D. © 2002, *USA Today*. Reprinted with permission.

physical abnormalities of the penis that need to be corrected surgically are often not circumcised at all because the foreskin may eventually be used as part of a reconstructive operation.

Caring For The Penis

Whether you choose circumcision or not, keeping your son's penis clean is important. Regardless of your son's circumcision status, wash his penis with soap and warm water when you bathe him. You do not need to use cotton swabs, astringents, or any special bath products.

With an uncircumcised boy, never forcibly pull back the foreskin to clean beneath it. Instead, gently tense it against the tip of the penis and wash off any smegma (the whitish "beads" of dead skin cells mixed with the body's natural oil). Over time, the foreskin will retract on its own so it can be pulled away from the glans toward the abdomen. This happens at different times for different children, but most boys can retract their foreskins by the time they are 5 years old.

As your son grows up, teach him to wash beneath the foreskin by gently pulling it back from the glans, rinsing the glans and the inside of the foreskin with soap and warm water, then pulling the foreskin back over the head of the penis.

There are no special washing precautions with newly circumcised babies, other than to be gentle. If your son has a bandage on his incision, you might need to apply a new one whenever you change his diaper for a day or 2 after the procedure (put petroleum jelly on the bandage so it will not stick to his skin). It usually takes between 7 to 10 days for a penis to heal.

Until it does, the tip may seem raw or yellowish in color. Although this is normal, certain other symptoms are not. Watch for persistent bleeding, redness around the tip of the penis that gets worse after 3 days, fever, or signs of infection such as the presence of pus-filled blisters. If you notice any of these, or if your baby does not urinate normally within 6 to 8 hours after the circumcision, call your child's doctor right away. With quick intervention, almost all circumcision-related problems are easily treated.

Chapter 21

Testicular Self-Exams

The Simple Test That Could Save A Man's Life

For Bruce Wilson, the trouble started during a ball game. When the O'Fallon, MO, engineer felt a pain in his scrotum, he thought maybe he'd hurt himself playing softball. His doctor diagnosed the problem as an infection. Wilson took some antibiotics and seemed to get better. But he still noticed some discomfort off and on. Months passed.

Almost a year later, Wilson was still having problems, only now one of his testicles was enlarged. This time his doctor ordered an ultrasound. The scan revealed a growth on his enlarged testicle. The diagnosis: testicular cancer.

"Up until that time, I'd never examined myself for signs of testicular cancer. In fact, I can't recall even hearing about testicular cancer before then," Wilson says. But if he had, it's likely he would have viewed it in the same dismissive light in which many doctors and health care professionals regard it: as a rare cancer that strikes only young men.

About This Chapter: Text in this chapter is from "The Simple Test that Could Save a Man's Life," by *Prevention* Senior Staff Editor Stephen C. George, from *Prevention*, Vol. 53, No. 6, 6-1-2001, p. 130. Reprinted by permission of *Prevention Magazine.* © 2001 Rodale, Inc. All Rights Reserved; And "How To Do A Testicular Self-Examination," © 2002 Testicular Cancer Resource Center website (www.tcrc.acor.org), reprinted with permission. Available online at http://www.acor.org/TCRC/tcexam.html.

> ✎ **Weird Words**
>
> Epididymis: The soft, tubelike structure behind each testicle which collects and carries sperm.
>
> Scrotum: The pouch of skin that holds the testicles.
>
> Testicles: The two oval-shaped organs that produce sperm. The testicles are enclosed in the scrotum, behind the penis.
>
> Urologist: A doctor who specializes in disorders of the urinary system and the male reproductive organs.

It's true that testicular cancer is the most common cancer among men ages 15 to 40. But it's also true that testicular cancer can and does strike at any age: Bruce Wilson was 47 when he got his diagnosis.

The Earlier, The Better

Overall, testicular cancer may be rare, accounting for only 1% of all cancers in men and about 300 deaths last year. It also has an estimated 5-year survival rate of 95%. (Three years after his initial diagnosis, Bruce Wilson is cancer free and likely to remain so.)

But as curable as it is, more men are getting it; over the past 50 years, the number of cases per year has doubled. And studies suggest it's not being caught as early as it could be.

In one review of testicular cancer diagnoses, Judd W. Moul, MD, a urologic oncologist and army colonel at Walter Reed Army Medical Center in Washington, DC, found that men with cancer symptoms may wait as long as 6 months before seeing their doctor. That's plenty of time for the more aggressive forms of testicular cancer to spread to the abdomen, the lungs, and even the brain.

What's worse, many family physicians who seldom see a case of testicular cancer in their practice misdiagnose the problem as a simple infection, allowing the cancer to grow unchecked.

"Obviously, the cure rate improves most dramatically the earlier the cancer is caught," says Eric A. Klein, MD, head of the section of urologic oncology at the Urological Institute of the Cleveland Clinic in Ohio. But Dr. Klein says that most men still don't know nearly enough about testicular cancer risks, or about a simple self-test that could spot the danger signs of testicular cancer long before it becomes life threatening.

What's Your Risk?

Although there are effective ways of treating testicular cancer, ranging from chemotherapy to surgery, very little is known about its causes. "We can't really link it to specific habits or environmental influences, the way we can with some other cancers," says Dr. Moul. But there are factors that may raise a man's risk of testicular cancer.

Undescended Testicle

Some boys are born with cryptorchidism, medical parlance for an undescended testicle. "In many cases, the testicle eventually descends as you get older, but surgery may be required to descend it or sometimes remove it," says Dr. Klein. If you had an undescended testicle, your risk for testicular cancer is at least three times higher than that of other men.

Family History

If your father or a brother had testicular cancer, your risk of developing it could be as much as 10 times higher than that of men with no family history.

Racial Background

In general, Caucasian men have a higher risk of developing this cancer than men of other racial backgrounds. For example, Caucasians have a fourfold greater risk for developing testicular cancer than African-Americans.

Infertility

Roughly half of the men diagnosed with testicular cancer do turn out to have fertility problems. If you have a history of fertility problems, this doesn't mean you're at greater risk of developing testicular cancer, says Dr. Moul. But it's one more reason to remain vigilant about cancer signs.

But Not Injury

At one time, doctors believed that trauma to the testicles increased the risk of developing cancer. "A guy would take a hit, then he'd notice something was wrong. Or the pain might take him to the doctor, who would notice an abnormality," explains Dr. Moul. "But in fact, what was probably happening was that the injury only brought attention to a cancer that was already present. More recent studies have not shown any real link between injuring your testicles at any point in your life and increasing your risk of developing cancer from that injury. Bicycling or horseback riding also does not increase your risk. Taking a shot to the groin does not increase your risk."

The More You Know

While there aren't yet any specific guidelines for reducing your risk of developing testicular cancer, there are some steps you can take to catch it early.

> ❖ **It's A Fact!!**
> Testicular cancer is the most common cancer among Men ages 15 to 40.

Listen to her. Dr. Moul says in many cases, men see their doctor because their wife or girlfriend insisted they make an appointment. In many cases, it was the woman who detected the abnormality.

Stay informed. Although testicular cancer doesn't get a lot of press, there are some sources you can use to stay up-to-date. One of the best is the Testicular Cancer Resource Center, an Internet site run by testicular cancer survivors. In addition to hard-core medical information, the site also has support areas and survivor stories. Some nonprofit organizations, such as the Cancer Alliance for Research, Education, and Survivorship (C.A.R.E.S.) founded by champion skater and testicular cancer survivor Scott Hamilton, or Cycle of Hope, Tour de France winner Lance Armstrong's cancer-awareness campaign, also have information resources. Call toll-free 877-717-4673 for information on Cycle of Hope, or 800-440-4140, for C.A.R.E.S., or go to www.prevention.com/links for a direct link to all the Web sites.

And most important, do the test. "If men were performing regular monthly testicular self-exams (TSE) much the same way women have been encouraged to perform self-exams for breast cancer, there would be a much higher awareness level of testicular cancer and faster treatment with fewer risks of side effects and complications," says Dr. Klein. "There are experts in this field who don't think men should be doing TSEs. Their view is that regular self-exams would lead to a lot of anxiety and false alarms. I would much rather see my doctor and find out nothing's wrong than miss spotting a cancer that could have been diagnosed early and treated decisively."

Moreover, Dr. Klein says, as men perform TSEs regularly, they'll learn what the various structures in the scrotum feel like and, therefore, be more likely to spot abnormalities.

How To Do A Testicular Self-Exam

It is common knowledge that a monthly breast self-exam for women is an effective part of early breast cancer detection. For men, starting at age 15, monthly self-exams of the testicles are also an effective way of getting to know this area of your body and thus detecting testicular cancer (TC) at an early—and very curable—stage.

The self exam for TC is best performed after a warm bath or shower. (Heat relaxes the scrotum, making it easier to spot anything abnormal.)

The National Cancer Institute recommends following these steps every month:

• Stand in front of a mirror. Check for any swelling on the scrotal skin.

• Examine each testicle with both hands. Place the index and middle fingers under the testicle with the thumbs placed on top. Roll the testicle gently between the thumbs and fingers—you shouldn't feel any pain when doing the exam. Don't be alarmed if one testicle seems slightly larger than the other, that's normal.

• Find the epididymis, the soft, tubelike structure behind the testicle that collects and carries sperm. If you are familiar with this structure, you won't mistake it for a suspicious lump. Cancerous lumps usually are found on the sides of the testicle but can also show up on the front. Lumps on the epididymis are not cancerous.

• If you find a lump, see a doctor, preferably a urologist, right away. The abnormality may not be cancer, it may just be an infection. But if it is testicular cancer, it will spread if it is not stopped by treatment. Waiting and hoping will not fix anything. Please note that free floating lumps in the scrotum that are not attached in any way to a testicle are not testicular cancer. When in doubt, get it checked out—if only for peace of mind.

♣ **It's A Fact!!**

Is It Cancer?

If you perform a regular monthly testicular self-exam, you may notice a lump, bump, or other irregularity. That doesn't mean its cancer, but it could be one of these common testicular problems:

Epididymitis: An infection that causes pain and swelling of the epididymis, the tubal structure that carries sperm from the testicle. Antibiotics can clear up the problem, but if symptoms continue after 2 weeks or come back after you've finished the antibiotics, see your doctor immediately.

Hernia: A tear in the muscle wall of your abdomen can cause part of your intestines to protrude into your scrotum. If you feel a mass in your scrotum, especially one accompanied by pain or tenderness, see your doctor at once. You may need immediate surgical treatment.

Hydrocele: This collection of fluid around the testicle can develop as a result of injury or infection and is more common in older men. Symptoms include a painless but obvious swelling as well as a sense of heaviness in the scrotum. Although often harmless and easily treated, hydrocele can be a sign of testicular cancer, so call your doctor if you detect one.

Spermatocele: This painless cyst, composed of dead sperm, sometimes develops near the testicle, but not on or in it. While your doctor should check it out, it's harmless and doesn't usually require any treatment.

Other signs of testicular cancer to keep in mind are:

- Any enlargement of a testicle

- A significant loss of size in one of the testicles

- A feeling of heaviness in the scrotum

- A dull ache in the lower abdomen or in the groin

- A sudden collection of fluid in the scrotum

- Pain or discomfort in a testicle or in the scrotum

- Enlargement or tenderness of the breasts

☞ **Remember!!**

Well-known athletes Lance Armstrong and Scott Hamilton are both survivors of testicular cancer. Each has created a source for more information on this disease. Call Armstrong's Cycle of Hope at 877-717-4673 or Hamilton's Cancer Alliance for Research, Education, and Survivorship (C.A.R.E.S.) at 800-440-4140.

I hesitate to mention the following list, since anything out of the ordinary down there should prompt a visit to the doctor, but you should be aware that the following symptoms are not normally signs of testicular cancer:

- A pimple, ingrown hair or rash on the scrotal skin

- A free floating lump in the scrotum, seemingly not attached to anything

- A lump on the epididymis or tubes coming from the testicle that kind of feels like a third testicle

- Pain or burning during urination

- Blood in the urine or semen

Remember, Only A Physician Can Make A Positive Diagnosis

For that matter, only a physician can make a negative diagnosis too. If you think something feels strange, go see the doctor.

Chapter 22

A Guy's Guide To Testicular Injuries

It's your nightmare if you're a guy. You're at sports practice, working hard to get ready for the next game. Just as you realize you forgot to put on your athletic cup, you take a hit to the testicles and drop to your knees in pain.

Ouch—you might be flinching just imagining it. No guy wants to experience testicular trauma, but you can prepare yourself by knowing the warning signs of a serious problem and when to call the doctor. Keep reading so you'll be ready if you're caught without a cup.

What Are Testicular Trauma And Torsion?

Because the testicles hang in a sac outside the body, they are not protected by bones and muscles like the rest of the reproductive system. The location of the testicles makes it easier for them to be injured or hit, a painful sensation most guys have experienced at some time. Generally, because the testicles are loosely attached to the body and are made of a spongy material, they are able to absorb the shock of impact without permanent damage. It's common for guys to experience testicular trauma, which is when the testicles

About This Chapter: This information was provided by TeensHealth, one of the largest resources online for medically reviewed health information written for parents, kids, and teens. For more articles like this one, visit www.TeensHealth.org, or www.KidsHealth.org. © 2001 The Nemours Center for Children's Health Media, a division of The Nemours Foundation.

are struck, hit, kicked, or crushed. Almost all testicular injuries occur during sports.

Another common type of testicular problem that occurs suddenly is called testicular torsion, and it occurs frequently in guys between the ages of 12 and 18. Within the scrotum, the testicles are secured at either end. Sometimes, a testicle can become twisted, cutting off the blood vessels that supply blood to the testicle. Testicular torsion might occur as the result of trauma to the testicles, strenuous activity, or it might develop while a guy is sleeping. In the United States, testicular torsion occurs in one out of 4,000 guys younger than 25.

An extremely rare type of testicular trauma is called testicular rupture. This condition may occur when the testicle receives a direct blow or when the testicle is crushed by some object. The testicle is compressed against the pubic bone, crushing the testicle against the bone and the object, causing blood to leak into the scrotum.

What Are The Signs And Symptoms?

If you are kicked or struck in the genital area, you may experience nausea, lightheadedness, dizziness, and sweating in addition to pain. For minor testicular injuries, the pain should gradually subside in less than an hour and the other symptoms should go away.

✎ Weird Words

Hernia: A condition in which part of an internal organ pokes through the structure that is supposed to hold it in. A common type of hernia is one where a part of the intestine comes through a weak point in the abdominal wall.

Testicular Rupture: A serious injury in which the testicle is hit or crushed and begins to bleed into the scrotum. Testicular rupture is an emergency and requires immediate treatment.

Testicular Torsion: An emergency situation in which one of the testicles becomes twisted within the scrotum, causing extreme pain. Testicular torsion must be treated very quickly to avoid loss of fertility or the need to remove the testicle.

Urinary Tract Infection: An infection in organs involved in the production of urine, including the bladder, ureter, and urethra. Urinary tract infections may cause pain in the testicles.

The signs and symptoms of testicular torsion are more severe and usually affect only one testicle, usually the left testicle. A guy with testicular torsion might experience rapid swelling and extreme pain in the scrotum that does not go away, nausea, vomiting, and abdominal pain.

Testicular rupture also causes extreme pain and swelling in the scrotum, nausea, and vomiting.

What Do Doctors Do?

If you are experiencing pain in your testicles that has lasted an hour or longer, extreme swelling, discoloration, or if your testicle was punctured, you need to seek medical treatment immediately, either by going to the emergency room or telling your parent, doctor, coach, or physical trainer.

♣ **It's A Fact!!**

In the United States, testicular torsion occurs in one out of 4,000 guys younger than 25.

The first thing a doctor will do is look at how you're acting—he or she can often assess the severity of your pain by observing whether you're writhing in pain or lying comfortably, whether you can talk to friends and family, and whether you're able to walk around without extreme discomfort.

The doctor may examine your abdominal and groin area to rule out a hernia. In addition, the doctor will look at your scrotum for swelling, color, and thickening of the skin. Because it's important how long you've been experiencing symptoms, the doctor may ask you questions like, "How long have you had pain?" "Have you had any blows or kicks to your testicles?" and "Do you play any sports?" In addition, the doctor will examine the testicle itself to check for tenderness and swelling.

To check for testicular torsion, your doctor may check a reflex in your genital area. The doctor will stroke or gently pinch the skin of the upper thigh while watching the muscles of your scrotum. If you don't have this reflex, it may tell the doctor that you have testicular torsion.

Because infections caused by bacteria can also cause extreme testicular pain, your doctor may give you a urine test to rule out a urinary tract infection.

Ultrasounds are another tool doctors may use to look at your scrotum, however, because testicular torsion and rupture often require immediate surgery, your doctor may not do an ultrasound to save time and get you to the operating room.

Depending on the situation, the doctor may try to fix a twisted testicle by manually rotating the testicle. In most cases, though, surgery is the treatment for testicular torsion. A urologist (pronounced: you-RAH-leh-jist), a doctor who specializes in urinary and genital problems, will make a small incision in your scrotum. He or she will check to see if the testicle is healthy, untwist it, and surgically anchor it so twisting can't occur in the future.

In the case of testicular rupture, surgery by a urologist is also necessary to drain and repair the ruptured testicle.

Dealing With And Preventing Testicular Injuries

If you've suffered a testicular injury, there are a few things you can do to feel better. Lie down, gently support the testicles with supportive underwear, and apply ice packs to relieve swelling and pain.

If you have had surgery for testicular torsion or rupture, your recovery time will be a little longer. According to T. Ernesto Figueroa, M.D., a urologist who works with teens in Wilmington, Delaware, it can take weeks to months until a guy recovers from testicular surgery and can resume normal sports activities. Even then, Dr. Figueroa says, in teens "the genital area is more sensitive and prone to injury." Your doctor or urologist will give you specific instructions on pain relief and how to care for yourself after testicular surgery.

Do you have to worry that your sexuality or sperm production will be affected if you have a testicular injury? Your testicles, although sensitive, can bounce back pretty quickly and minor injuries rarely have long-term effects.

With treatment within 6 hours from the time pain starts, 80% to 100% of guys with testicular torsion do not have to have the testicle removed. However, after 6 hours, there is a much greater possibility that infertility and loss of the testicle could result, so that's why it's so important to get treatment immediately. If a testicle does have to be removed, a guy will still be able to have normal sexual function. And because both testicles produce sperm, a guy will probably still be able to have children someday, even if one testicle has been removed.

Reading this chapter probably has you wondering how you can keep these injuries from happening to you. Try these tips to keep testicular trauma away:

• Always wear an athletic cup and supporter when you are playing sports or doing strenuous activity. This is the single most important thing you can do to protect yourself from genital injury.

• Check your fit. Make sure the athletic supporter and cup you wear are the right size—safety equipment that is too small or too large won't protect you as effectively from injury.

• Keep your doctor informed. If you play sports, you probably have regular physical exams by a doctor. If you experience testicular pain even occasionally, talk to your doctor about it because you might be prone to genital injury.

• Be aware of the risks of your sport. Dr. Figueroa says that lacrosse and baseball are the sports that have the highest incidence of testicular injury. Horseback riding may also put you at risk. If you play a sport with a higher risk for injury, talk to your coach or doctor about additional protective gear.

Sports are a great way to stay fit and relieve stress. Make sure that using protective gear is part of your pre-practice and pre-game routine and you'll be able to play hard without fear of testicular injury.

☞ **Remember!!**

Testicular injuries are extremely painful and can be serious. Always wear an athletic cup while participating in sports.

Chapter 23

Nocturnal Emissions: "Wet Dreams"

Sometime around puberty, most boys will wake up one morning with wet bedclothes. If they're not expecting it, they may be worried, ashamed, or fearful that they have a disease. In fact, it's a very normal and natural event called a nocturnal emission (often called a "wet dream").

What Is A Nocturnal Emission ("Wet Dream")?

A wet dream is the release of fluids from the penis that occurs during sleep. The release of fluids is called an ejaculation. The fluid (called ejaculate, or semen) is grey to whitish in color, and usually has a somewhat sticky consistency. Semen is a mixture of sperm cells and fluid produced by the testicles, prostate gland, and seminal vesicles.

By definition, this occurs without a person's awareness or control. Often, nocturnal emissions occur during a dream, but they don't have to.

Why Do Nocturnal Emissions Happen?

Nocturnal emissions are a sign of sexual maturity. Sperm are produced in the testicles, and then move into the body, where they are stored. Seminal

About This Chapter: Text in this chapter is by David A. Cooke, M.D., Diplomate, American Board of Internal Medicine. © 2003 Omnigraphics, Inc.

fluids are also produced and stored in preparation for an ejaculation. While the body can store these supplies, there is a limit to how long they can remain inside the body. Eventually, the body has to release them to make room for the new sperm and fluids that are being produced. The result is a nocturnal emission.

Why Did This Happen To Me? Is There Something Wrong With Me?

Nocturnal emissions are normal, and most boys experience one sooner or later. It is not a sign of disease. Rather, it is a sign of puberty.

Puberty begins at different ages in different people. In boys, the first signs of puberty appear between the ages of ten and fourteen, on average. However, there is a great deal of variability, and some boys will enter puberty sooner than ten or later than fourteen.

Nocturnal emissions are a sign that the reproductive organs are maturing and starting to work. It simply means that you are developing normally. The first nocturnal emission occurs around age fourteen, on average, but once again, it may be considerably sooner or later.

I've Never Had A Wet Dream. Is There Something Wrong With Me?

There is tremendous variation in sexual development. The age at which a first nocturnal emission happens is quite different from person to person. If you have not had one yet, it probably means that your body's "clock" is on a slightly slower schedule than some other people your age. This is still normal; everyone catches up in the end.

♣ It's A Fact!!

Nocturnal emissions are a sign of sexual maturity. Sperm are produced in the testicles, and then move into the body, where they are stored. Seminal fluids are also produced and stored in preparation for an ejaculation. While the body can store these supplies, there is a limit to how long they can remain inside the body. Eventually, the body has to release them to make room for the new sperm and fluids that are being produced. The result is a nocturnal emission.

Some boys never have nocturnal emissions at all. Also, most boys start to masturbate sometime during puberty. Some boys discover masturbation early on, and if this happens, they may not have wet dreams because they are ejaculating during masturbation.

☞ Remember!!

Nocturnal emissions are normal, and most boys experience one sooner or later. It is not a sign of disease. Rather, it is a sign of puberty.

What Should I Do If I Have A Nocturnal Emission?

Nocturnal emissions are normal, and a sign of a healthy reproductive system. However, they sometimes can be messy. If you wake up after having a nocturnal emission, check your bedclothes and sheets. Semen can stain some fabrics. If some of your ejaculate has gotten on them, try to clean them off with cold water as soon as possible. A stain remover may also be helpful. You may need to change your clothes or sheets.

I Had A Very Weird Dream, And I Woke Up With Wet Sheets. Did This Dream Mean Something?

Probably not. Nocturnal emissions often occur during dreams, but they don't have to. Sometimes these dreams are sexual. Many times they aren't.

The dreams that accompany nocturnal emissions may not be any different from dreams that don't. If you usually have vivid or disturbing dreams, it shouldn't be a surprise if your dreams during nocturnal emissions are too.

Some people are very disturbed by what they dream about during a nocturnal emission. Some worry that their wet dreams may mean they are homosexual. Others may suspect that they are some kind of sexual deviant. There is no evidence that this is true. What you dream about during nocturnal emissions doesn't tell anything about you or your sexuality, any more than your "regular" dreams do.

What Can I Do To Stop From Having Wet Dreams?

Nocturnal emissions are a response to having too much stored up sperm and seminal fluids. Ejaculating regularly will clear out the excess. Most boys masturbate, and if done regularly, this will usually stop nocturnal emissions from happening. Later on in life, sexual intercourse will also prevent nocturnal emissions.

Chapter 24

Breast Enlargement In Adolescent Boys

Gynecomastia: When Breasts Form In Males

Gynecomastia is a condition in which firm breast tissue forms in males. The breast tissue is usually less than 1-1/2 inches across and is located directly under the nipple. Gynecomastia may be present on one side or on both sides. This condition may make the breast tender.

Some men and boys have fat on their chests that makes it look like they have breasts. This condition is called pseudogynecomastia (false gynecomastia). It is not the same thing as gynecomastia.

What Causes Gynecomastia?

Gynecomastia is usually caused by changes in hormones at puberty or as part of aging. Hormones are chemicals produced by the glands of the body, such as the thyroid gland, the testes and the ovaries. Gynecomastia may be caused by changes in the balance of 2 hormones, estrogen and testosterone. In rare cases, gynecomastia is caused by prescription drugs, over-the-counter medicines, illegal drugs, tumors or disease.

Are Tests Needed To Find The Cause Of Gynecomastia?

Sometimes tests are needed, and sometimes they're not. Your doctor will ask you questions about your symptoms, such as how long you've had the breast tissue, and whether or not the area is tender. Your doctor will also ask you about the illnesses you have had in the past, the medicines you take, and other matters relating to your health. Then you will have a physical examination.

Whether you need tests depends on your age and what your doctor learns from your history and physical examination. If you are a teenager, you probably will not need more tests, since gynecomastia is common in teenage boys. As many as 65% of 14-year-old boys have gynecomastia. The breast enlargement usually goes away on its own in 2 or 3 years. However, younger boys and adult men with gynecomastia may need to have some tests, because it is more possible that some kind of disease is causing the problem.

♣ It's A Fact!!

- As many as 65% of 14-year-old boys have gynecomastia.

- Gynecomastia may be caused by changes in the balance of 2 hormones, estrogen and testosterone. In rare cases, gynecomastia is caused by prescription drugs, over-the-counter medicines, illegal drugs, tumors or disease.

- In 90% of teenage boys, gynecomastia goes away in less than 3 years.

How Is Gynecomastia Treated?

In most cases, no treatment is needed. Your doctor will probably want to check the size of your breast tissue every few months. In 90% of teenage boys, gynecomastia goes away in less than 3 years.

Sometimes the problem can be solved if you stop taking a medicine that is causing gynecomastia or stop using an illegal drug that is causing the problem.

Occasionally, medicines may be used to treat gynecomastia, especially if tenderness is a problem. The medicine will make the extra breast tissue go away. Rarely, surgery may be necessary to remove the extra breast tissue.

Treatment is necessary if gynecomastia is caused by a disease or a tumor. If it is due to a disease, the disease itself will need to be treated.

Could The Breast Lump Be Cancer?

Probably not. Breast cancer is very rare in males. Your doctor will probably be able to tell whether the lump is cancer. Lumps caused by cancer are usually not underneath the nipple, but breast tissue from gynecomastia grows in this area. Breast cancer feels different than the breast tissue of gynecomastia. With cancer, there sometimes is dimpling of the skin or a bloody discharge from the nipple. If there is any question that you have cancer, you will need to have a mammogram and a biopsy.

Part 4

Sexuality And Social Issues

Chapter 25

Tips For Talking About Sexuality

Talking To Your Parents About Sex

How can you talk to your parents about sex? Kids and adults can learn to talk things out by asking the following questions or others you have on your mind to get your conversation started.

Which approach best describes your style?

- *The "To-The-Point" Approach*

    "Can we talk? I have a question about something we learned in sex ed class."

    "I think I am not developing as fast as my friends. Is something wrong with me?"

- *The "Round-About" Approach*

    "Did you see that billboard about being a virgin? Should that stuff be in public where little kids can see it?"

    "This talk show had some teens on who had babies and the girls were only 13 years old. Do you think teens can be good parents?"

About This Chapter: Reprinted with permission from *How to Talk to Your Parents About Sex*, a brochure produced and published by Campaign for Our Children, Inc. (CFOC). © 2000. For additional information, contact CFOC at 120 West Fayette Street, Baltimore, MD 21201, 410-576-9015, or visit their website at www.cfoc.org.

- *The "Wonder If" Approach*

    "I wonder if you think it is a good idea to learn about sex in school. Do you?"

    "I wonder if kids will like me better if I do things they do even if I am not ready. What did you do when your friends did something you did not want to do?"

✔ Quick Tip

Tips For Talking About Sexuality

Tip Number One. Take full responsibility for your choices. Know your own body, ideas and values. Know what feels comfortable or uncomfortable and what brings you pleasure. Be sure to watch for the effects of your words and actions on others.

Tip Number Two. Use a good decision making memory tool, like STAR: Stop, Think, Act and Respond. It is a simple way to make a careful and good decision. It will help you decide what you want to do next.

Tip Number Three. Practice what you want to say with a relative, close friend, or trusted adult, or practice in a mirror. Practice is the best way to build self-confidence.

Tip Number Four. Be clear about your goals and aim your expectations high. At the same time always set realistic limits for yourself.

Tip Number Five. When talking to a friend or possible sexual partner, speak clearly, be direct and firm, and use "I" messages. You may say something like, "Joel, I feel upset when you act that way and pressure me into doing something I do not feel ready to do with you."

Tip Number Six. Talk with a possible sexual partner about your sexual limits and protection before you begin to get involved in any physical touch. It's a lot harder to talk about it in the heat of the moment than before you start.

Tip Number Seven. Begin talking about sexuality in a neutral place, not the bedroom or in the car on a date. Try to find a place where you can have privacy and where you both can feel as comfortable as possible to say what you mean.

- *The "I've Heard That" Approach*

  "I heard that lots of kids have had sex by high school. Is that just a rumor?"

  "I've heard if you say no to sex, the person you like will break up with you. How do you say no to someone and not hurt their feelings?"

Tip Number Eight. Use entertainment to help talk about sexuality. Television shows, music videos, popular songs, books and magazines are a good way to begin to talk about sexuality with a friend, parent or possible dating partner.

Tip Number Nine. Be a good listener. Let the other person speak without interrupting them. Ask questions if you don't understand what he or she is saying. Keep eye contact and respond after they are done talking.

Tip Number Ten. Be a good communicator. Be clear about your feelings and limits, try to understand the other person's point of view, work to solve problems, and use a positive response like a smile or an OK touch.

Tip Number Eleven. Avoid communication breakdown. Try not to yell, or call people names. Stay away from negative messages like frowning and interrupting.

Tip Number Twelve. Avoid alcohol and/or other drugs. It is hard enough to talk about this stuff. Being drunk or high only makes it harder and might keep you from making healthy choices for yourself.

Tip Number Thirteen. Get the information you need to communicate about sexuality. It is important to talk about sexuality because you are worth it. Your life is worth it. Remember, if you do not feel ready to express your sexuality with a partner, don't do it.

Source: Reprinted with permission of SIECUS, the Sexuality Information and Education Council of the United States (SIECUS), 130 W. 42nd Street, Suite 350, New York, NY 10036-7802. Phone: 212-819-9770. E-Mail: siecus@siecus.org. Website: www.seicus.org. © 2002.

Still Think Talking To Your Parents Will Be Too Tough?

Try the following tips from kids your age:

- Try writing your questions down and give your parents the note.
- Read the question you wrote on paper out loud. That way you can hide your face behind the paper.
- Talk to an empty chair, or your pet first or talk into the mirror to practice.
- Make sure your little brother or sister is out of the house. You can't talk about serious stuff when someone else is listening.

♣ It's A Fact!!

What Is Sexuality?

This probably seems like a stupid question. Sexuality is more than what you do with another person sexually. That is, sexuality is not only about having sex, or taking part in sexual behaviors. Sexuality is also about how the person you feel you are, your body, how you feel as a boy or girl, man or woman, the way you dress, move and speak, the way you act and feel about other people.

These are all parts of who you are as a person, from your birth until you die—your whole lifetime long. Everyone has his or her own way of being or feeling sexual. In fact, many teens choose to wait until they are adults before they are ready to be in a sexual relationship. You are a sexual person just the same. Our sexuality is a natural and healthy part of who we are. It's not about what you do, it's about who you are and how you live.

Source: Reprinted with permission of SIECUS, the Sexuality Information and Education Council of the United States (SIECUS), 130 W. 42nd Street, Suite 350, New York, NY 10036-7802. Phone: 212-819-9770. E-Mail: siecus@siecus.org. Website: www.seicus.org. © 2002.

- Bring up the subject of sex when you and your mom or dad are watching a show where someone is wearing tight clothes or making out. Or if there is a soap opera on you'll have lots of opportunities then.

- Leave this book lying around. Your mom or dad just might get the hint.

"I was nervous to talk to my mom at first. You know, this stuff can be embarrassing. I just blurted out "Can we talk?" She said "Yes" right away. It was easier than I thought. Now my mom asks, "Is there anything you want to talk about?" It's nice to know I can get my questions answered."

News Flash!

Think you can only talk to your friends about tough topics like sex?

Think again!

Try talking to your parents to get the straight scoop. Studies show that kids who get their questions answered by adults in their life have less chance of getting pregnant or getting someone pregnant as teens.

Your parents may have things to say to you about sex, values and morals and may not know how to start the subject.

Someone has to make the first move. Why not you?

Chapter 26

What Is Sexual Orientation?

Expressing Yourself Sexually

Sperm determine the baby's gender.

Humans have two genders—male and female. Gender is determined when the egg is fertilized. Men ejaculate two types of sperm. One produces a boy, and the other produces a girl. Gender identity is the way each of us feels about being male or female and about what other people expect of us because we are female or male.

Sexual Orientation Is Different From Gender And Gender Identity

Whether people are gay, straight, or bisexual is usually established before puberty and before they begin having sex. Although sexual orientation may begin to develop before birth, it may shift throughout life. It is not something that people can decide for themselves, or for others.

People who have sexual desire for the other gender are called heterosexual or straight. People who have sexual desire for their own gender are called homosexual or gay.

About This Chapter: Text in this chapter is from "Expressing Ourselves Sexually," reprinted with permission from Planned Parenthood® Federation of America, Inc. © 2002 PPFA. All rights reserved. For additional information, visit www.planned parenthood.org, or www.teenwire.org.

Gay women are also called lesbians. People who have sexual desire for both genders are called bisexual. But sexual orientation is more complex and diverse than these simple labels. This kind of complexity and diversity is not limited to people. It occurs naturally throughout the animal kingdom.

It is normal for boys and girls to have sex play with friends of either gender. People may also have sexy dreams and feelings about either gender. This does not mean a person is gay or straight or bisexual.

Some People Fear Or Hate Others Who Are Gay, Lesbian, Or Bisexual

This is called homophobia. When gay, lesbian, and bisexual people have these feelings about themselves, this is called internalized homophobia. Friends, family, and religious authorities often encourage negative feelings about sexual orientation and gender identity.

What Is Sexual Orientation?   ♣ It's A Fact!!

Our sexual orientation is who we are attracted to—is not a choice we make. You may be bisexual, and attracted to people of both sexes. You may be heterosexual, and attracted to people of the other sex. You may be homosexual (often called lesbian or gay), that is, attracted to people of your same sex.

For many young people, exploring their sexuality with someone of the same sex is a natural part of growing up. These normal feelings may continue through your adult lives. If you are struggling with questions about your sexual orientation, be sure to speak with a trusted adult and/or gay or lesbian organization in your area.

A lot of people think that some sexual activities are just for heterosexual people, or that others are just for lesbians and gay men. The truth

Some teenage boys worry about being gay. They might act very "macho" to prove they are straight. They might try to be the boss in romantic relationships. Some teenage girls can act very girlish. They may think boys always should be in charge. Some people who act in these ways are uncomfortable about their sexual orientation or gender identity. They may try to hurt people who they think are lesbian, gay, or bisexual by calling them names or attacking them. This is called gay-bashing.

Self-acceptance about sexual orientation and gender identity is very important. The process of accepting and being open about sexual orientation and gender identity for gay and bisexual people is called coming out.

The first step is coming out to ourselves. It may happen when we are teenagers, but it may not happen until we are older. The next step involves coming out to our friends and family. The whole process builds self-esteem, but can be very stressful. Coming out often helps us feel closer to people we love, even though it can be risky.

is that all people, regardless of their sexual orientation, may do all things. The difference is that gay men and lesbians do these activities with people of the same sex as themselves. Bisexual people do these activities with people of either sex. Heterosexual people do these activities with people of the opposite sex.

Lesbian and gay relationships, like heterosexual relationships, can be fulfilling and can last a very long time. All of these sexual orientations are part of being human.

Source: Reprinted with permission of SIECUS, the Sexuality Information and Education Council of the United States (SIECUS), 130 W. 42nd Street, Suite 350, New York, NY 10036-7802. Phone: 212-819-9770, Fax: 212-819-9776, E-Mail: siecus@siecus.org, Website: www.siecus.org. © 2002.

✔ Quick Tip
Healthy Relationship Checklist

- *We respect each other:*
  We listen to each other's ideas and opinions.
  We are proud of one another.
  We accept each other as we are now.

- *We trust each other:*
  We're not jealous of each other's friendships.
  We never hurt each other on purpose.
  We don't invade each other's privacy.

- *We are honest with each other:*
  We admit when we are wrong.
  We keep each other's secrets.
  We are not afraid to tell the truth.

- *We are fair to each other:*
  We don't expect to get our way all the time.
  We understand that feelings can change.
  We forgive mistakes.

- *Our relationship is based on equality:*
  We both give and take equally.
  We make decisions about money together.
  We both work on the relationship.

- *We both accept responsibility:*
  We don't blame other people for our mistakes.
  We protect each other from harm.
  We think through our decisions.

- *We talk to each other:*
  We can talk openly about our relationship.
  We try to understand each other.
  We tell each other how we really feel.

Love And Sexual Desire Are Not The Same Thing

Love is a strong caring for someone else. It comes in many forms—love for close friends, for parents and children, for God, and for humankind.

Sexual desire is a strong physical excitement. It can be a fantasy we create, a crush, or just a flirtation. Sometimes we let ourselves have sex because of it. Sometimes we don't.

Love can exist without sexual desire, and vice versa. Many people are happiest when both love and sexual desire are shared between both partners. When it comes to love and sexual desire, it is normal for people to be different—in their feelings, needs, and behavior.

It Is Easy To Confuse Love With Infatuation

Sometimes we decide to have sex because we think we are in love, but it turns out to be just an infatuation—a sudden emotional and sexual attachment. Infatuation makes us want to have sex just to feel closer to our partners. Sometimes it leads to long-lasting love. Most of the time, it doesn't.

Healthy Relationships Are Based On Respect, Trust, Honesty, Fairness, Equality, Responsibility, And Good Communication

People in healthy relationships protect each other from unintended pregnancy and sexually transmitted infection. They don't use pressure, guilt, or force to have sex.

☞ Remember!!

At this age, romantic relationships can begin and get serious very quickly. We think they will last forever. But they rarely do.

We need to learn how to end relationships. Breaking up with someone we care about can be hard—for both people. But it never has to be cruel.

We May Want To "Go Steady" At An "Unsteady" Time

Our bodies and hormones rush through changes so fast that we can become confused. The surging hormones intensify our feelings—the highs and the lows. In the middle of so much confusion, we might think a romantic relationship will help us feel steady. We want it to be the one thing that does not change in our lives. But that might not be a realistic expectation.

Sometimes We Have To Break Off The Relationship

When we do:

- We are ready. We know for sure that the relationship must end—even if it hurts to break up.

- We tell our partners our feelings have changed. We don't ask someone else to do it for us.

- We are kind. We point out the problems with the relationship, not with our partners.

- We are considerate. We don't hurt our partners on purpose.

> ♣ **It's A Fact!!**
> Some people believe that sexual intercourse outside marriage is never OK. Other people think it is always OK. Most people believe something in between. Deciding whether to have sexual intercourse is often difficult—no matter how old we are.

When someone breaks up with us:

- We may feel rejected, but we accept what we have learned.

- We may be angry or depressed. But we don't hurt ourselves or others.

- We understand that we will feel better in time.

Some people believe that sexual intercourse outside marriage is never OK. Other people think it is always OK. Most people believe something in between. Deciding whether to have sexual intercourse is often difficult—no matter how old we are.

Sexual intercourse is just one way to "have sex" or express feelings for another person. It carries the highest risks of infection and pregnancy. We need to be aware of and think about these consequences when we make decisions about sex.

We all make decisions using the values we learn from our families as well as our own religious and moral beliefs. We need to make responsible choices and accept the consequences.

☞ Remember!!
Are You In Love?

- You know your partner very well.

- You are good friends.

- You trust each other.

- You both are interested in giving as well as receiving.

- You have time for others, such as family and friends.

Or Just Infatuated?

- You love the idea of being in love.

- You are focused on the sexual part of the relationship.

- You find yourself always giving or always getting.

- You rely on your partner for your happiness.

- You are jealous when your partner is away from you.

Chapter 27

Virginity: A Very Personal Decision

Sometimes it might seem like everyone in school is talking about who's a virgin, who isn't, and who might be. For both girls and guys, the pressure can sometimes be intense.

But deciding whether it's right for you to have sex is one of the most important decisions you'll ever have to make. Each person must use his or her own judgment and decide if it's the right time—and the right person.

This means considering some very important factors—both physical ones, like the possibility of becoming pregnant or getting a sexually transmitted disease—and emotional factors, too. Though a person's body may feel ready for sex, sex also has very serious emotional consequences. For many teens, moral factors are very important as well. Family attitudes, personal values, or religious beliefs provide them with an inner voice that guides them in resisting pressures to get sexually involved before the time is right.

About This Chapter: The first part of this chapter is from "Virginity: A Very Personal Decision." This information was provided by TeensHealth, one of the largest resources online for medically reviewed health information written for parents, kids, and teens. For more articles like this one, visit www.TeensHealth.org, or www.KidsHealth.org. © 2001 The Nemours Center for Children's Health Media, a division of The Nemours Foundation. The text beginning with the heading "Protecting Ourselves Sexually," is reprinted with permission from Planned Parenthood® Federation of America, Inc. © 2002 PPFA. All rights reserved. For additional information, visit www.planned parenthood.org or www.teenwire.org.

Peer Pressure Problems And Movie Madness

Nobody wants to feel left out of things—it's natural to want to be liked and feel as if you're part of a group of friends. Unfortunately, some teens feel that they have to lose their virginity to keep up with their friends or to be accepted.

It doesn't sound like it's all that complicated; maybe most of your friends have already had sex with their boyfriends or girlfriends and act like it isn't a big deal. But sex isn't something that's only physical; it's emotional, too. And because everyone's emotions are different, it's hard to rely on your friends' opinions to decide if it's the right time for you to have sex.

What matters to you is the most important thing, and your values may not match those of your friends. That's OK—it's what makes people unique. Having sex to impress someone or to make your friends happy or feel like you have something in common with them won't make you feel very good about yourself in the long run. True friends don't really care whether a person is a virgin—they will respect your decisions, no matter what.

Even if your friends are cool with your decision, it's easy to be misled by TV shows and movies into thinking that every teen in America is having sex. Writers and producers may make a show or movie plot exciting by showing teens being sexually active, but these teens are actors, not real people with real concerns. They don't have to worry about being ready for sex, how they will feel later on, or what might happen as a result. In other words, these TV and movie plots are stories, not real life. In real life, every teen can, and should, make his or her own decision.

Boyfriend Blues Or Girlfriend Gripes

Although some teens who are going out don't pressure each other about sex, the truth is that in many relationships, one person wants to have sex although the other one doesn't.

Again, what matters most differs from person to person. Maybe one person in a relationship is more curious and has stronger sexual feelings than the other. Or another person has religious reasons why he or she doesn't want to have sex and the other person doesn't share those beliefs. Whatever the situation, it can place stress and strain on a relationship—you want to keep your boyfriend or girlfriend happy, but you don't want to compromise what you think is right.

As with almost every other major decision in life, you need to do what is right for you and not anyone else. If you think sex is a good idea because a boyfriend or girlfriend wants to begin a sexual relationship, think again.

Anyone who tries to pressure you into having sex by saying, "if you truly cared, you wouldn't say no," or "if you loved me, you'd show it by having sex," isn't really looking out for you and what matters most to you. They're looking to satisfy their own feelings and urges about sex.

If someone says that not having sex after doing other kinds of fooling around will cause him or her physical pain, that's also a sign that that person is thinking only of himself or herself. If you feel that you should have sex because you're afraid of losing that person, it may be a good time to end the relationship.

Sex should be an expression of love—not something a person feels that he or she must do. If a boyfriend or girlfriend truly loves you, he or she won't push or pressure you to do something you don't believe in or aren't ready for yet.

Feeling Curious

You might have a lot of new sexual feelings or thoughts. These feelings and thoughts are totally normal—it means that all of your hormones are working properly. But sometimes your curiosity or sexual feelings can make you feel like it's the right time to have sex, even though it may not be.

Though your body may have the ability to have sex and you may really want to satisfy your curiosity, it doesn't mean your mind is ready. Although some teens understand how sex can affect them emotionally, many don't—and this can lead to confusion and deeply hurt feelings later. But at the same time, don't beat yourself up or be too hard on yourself if you do have sex and then wish you hadn't. Having sexual feelings is normal and handling them can sometimes seem difficult, even if you planned otherwise. Just because you had sex once doesn't mean you have to continue or say yes later on, no matter what anyone tells you. Making mistakes is not only human, it's a major part of being a teen—and you can learn from mistakes.

Why Some Teens Wait

Some teens are waiting longer to have sex—they are thinking more carefully about what it means to lose their virginity and begin a sexual relationship. For these teens, there are many reasons for abstinence (not having sex). Some don't want to worry about unplanned pregnancy and all its consequences. Others see abstinence as a way to protect themselves completely from sexually transmitted diseases (STDs). Some STDs (like AIDS) can literally make sex a life-or-death situation, and many teens take this very seriously.

Some teens don't have sex because their religion prohibits it or because they simply have a very strong belief system of their own. Other teens may recognize that they aren't ready emotionally and they want to wait until they're absolutely sure they can handle it.

When it comes to sex, there are two very important things to remember: one, that you are ultimately the person in charge of your own happiness and your own body; and two, you have a lot of time to wait until you're totally sure about it. If you decide to put off sex, it's OK—no matter what anyone says. Being a virgin is one of the things that proves you are in charge, and it shows that you are powerful enough to make your own decisions about your mind and body.

If you find yourself feeling confused about decisions related to sex, you may be able to talk to an adult (like a parent, doctor, older sibling, aunt, or uncle) for advice. Keep in mind, though, that everyone's opinion about sex is different. Even though another person may be able to share useful advice, in the end, the decision is up to you.

♣ It's A Fact!!

At least one in four people who has sex with other people gets a sexually transmitted infection.

Tips For Teens On Abstinence ✔ Quick Tip

1. You have a right to say no. But don't get tricked into giving excuses or reasons. They give the other person an opportunity to try to talk you out of your decision.

2. Safer sex doesn't protect you from feeling badly afterwards, or wishing you had waited. Safer sex doesn't even guarantee that you won't get involved in a pregnancy or a disease. That's why abstinence is a good choice for teens.

3. Distorted media images of men and women and how they behave when it comes to sex can mislead teens. Sex is used by the media to make money, not to instruct on healthy ways to handle sexual feelings. Don't be fooled.

4. You do not have the right to pressure another person to have sex. By talking about the decision to have sex, you may be able to understand the other person's point of view and why it is important to him or her to say no.

5. Boys often are pressured more about sex than girls. What to do? Don't confuse having sex with being a man. State your reasons for waiting. Remind others that decisions about sex are personal. Hang out with teens who respect your decision.

6. If you are pressuring yourself about sex, you can talk back to the voice inside you that's urging you on. Remind yourself of the risks and consequences. Turn your attention to something else so you won't hear the voice that's tempting you.

7. If having sex is what's needed to hold a relationship together, then it's probably not a very good one and will break up later anyway.

8. Single parents can be easily overwhelmed by all the responsibilities of raising a child by themselves. It can limit their ability to achieve personal goals other than being a parent. Waiting for marriage benefits children, parents, and society.

9. There are just as many good reasons for boys to avoid sexual involvement as there are for girls. Decide beforehand where you want to stop and stick to it.

continued on the next two pages

Tips For Teens On Abstinence, continued from p. 183

10. The consequences of sex—having children, for example—are much better handled within marriage. That's one reason why society expects school-age youth to wait until marriage before becoming sexually involved.

11. No one has a right to force you to do anything sexual that you do not wish to do. If someone has forced you to have sex tell someone you trust. Get help from a counselor. Understand it's not your fault.

12. Managing sexual pressures is easier if you know what you think and how you feel. Make decisions that are in your best interest. Stick to your values.

13. To avoid becoming a victim of date rape, go out only with someone you trust. Avoid going places where assault could occur. If you feel threatened, get out of the situation. Go where there are other people. Say no. Yell for help.

14. Teens who have decided to save sex for marriage can feel less good about themselves if they don't wait. Therefore, be clear with the other person about your desires to wait. Talk with the other person about the sexual pressures you both feel and ways to handle them. Avoid situations where you might be tempted to have sex.

15. The majority of high school students are NOT having sex. So, if you're not having sex, it doesn't mean there's anything wrong with you. You're just doing what most other teens are doing.

16. A teen who has sex is exposed to the diseases of the other people their sexual partner has had sex with. So, if you have sex with someone who has had sex with three other people, you have exposed yourself to the possible consequences of having sex with four people.

17. Saying no to sex can be the best way to say I love you. Most people know they are loved by caring words and actions, not by having sex.

18. Left untreated, sexually transmitted diseases can damage a boy's or girl's body so severely that they cannot have children naturally. Several STDs have no symptoms to tell you that you are infected.

19. It is never too late to stop and say no—even if you have gone pretty far, even if you feel you have led the other person on, even if you feel those urges to go further.

20. Marrying and remaining faithful to the other person, over time, has proven to be in most people's best interest and in the best interests of society.

21. An overwhelming number of teens who become involved in a pregnancy reported using drugs or alcohol when it happens. Alcohol or other drugs limit ability to think and make good decisions about having sex or protecting yourself from unwanted consequences.

22. Far more unmarried people are shown to be having great sex on television than are married people. But a national study showed those people most satisfied with their sex lives were married. Don't be misled by what you see.

23. Teens may confuse desires for touch and affection and feeling cared about with love. When teens feel they are in love, sex may seem more acceptable—but, sex and love are not the same thing at all. Guard against being misled about what true love is.

24. Television and movies don't give teens a true picture of the consequences of having sex. How many times have you seen or heard characters discuss the genital warts they got from sex?

25. Choosing abstinence allows you to be free from being used or exploited, or feeling that way; to be free to have an open relationship with your parents; to be free to respect yourself and others; to be free to get to know another person without the complication of sexual involvement.

26. Choosing abstinence allows you: to be free to pursue your life goals; to be free from the responsibilities of parenting; to be free from knowing that you have damaged your (or someone else's) reproductive health.

27. Being independent and self-sufficient before getting married and starting a family increases the chances of being financially and emotionally ready to take on those responsibilities.

Source: "Tips for Teens: Did you know . . . . ," an undated document from the State of Florida, Department of Health Abstinence Education Program, an HRSA Title V Grant Award recipient. Cited January 2003, from http://www.greattowait.com/why_wait/fs_tips.html. Reprinted with permission.

Protecting Yourself Sexually

The surest way to avoid pregnancy is not to have vaginal intercourse.

Couples can also decide to reduce their sexual health risks through safer-sex practices. Safer sex is anything we do to lower our risk of sexually transmitted infection. The basic rule for safer sex is—keep each others' fluids out of our bodies.

Having any kind of sex with other people has certain physical and emotional risks. We all must learn how to protect ourselves from unintended pregnancy, sexually transmitted infection, and relationships that are not good for us.

The safest way to avoid pregnancy and infection is not to have any kind of sex play. This is called abstinence. Many people abstain until they are past their teens. Some until they are married. Some abstain their whole lives.

Avoiding Pregnancy

People who decide to have vaginal intercourse but don't want to cause pregnancy use birth control.

Vaginal intercourse without birth control, even once, even the first time, can cause pregnancy. Of every 100 women who don't use birth control for vaginal intercourse for a whole year, 85 will become pregnant.

Although many methods of birth control are nearly 100 percent effective, no method is perfect. But women and men who use birth control can worry less about unplanned pregnancy. They can be more confident about the plans they have for their lives. Sharing the responsibility to prevent pregnancy also develops trust between partners.

There are many kinds of birth control. Most kinds are reversible. They allow women to get pregnant after couples stop using them. All reversible methods are available without a parent's permission.

Some kinds are permanent. Sterilization, however, is not recommended for young people. It does not allow them to have children.

✎ Weird Words

Abstinence: Not having sex.

Outercourse: Finding other ways for sexual pleasure besides intercourse that can help us learn how to give and receive pleasure.

Periodic Abstinence: Keeping very careful records to try to tell when pregnancy could happen, then abstaining from vaginal intercourse whenever there's a chance it could cause pregnancy.

Sexually Transmitted Infections: Germs that are passed from one person to another by vaginal, oral, or anal intercourse, or other intimate contact. The most serious are passed through sexual intercourse. Millions of teens are infected but have no symptoms and do not know it.

Sterilization: A permanent method of birth control, usually chosen by older people who are very sure they will not want any children in the future. Sterilization is a simple operation that keeps egg and sperm from meeting. The operation for men is simpler than the one for women.

Birth control works by preventing ovulation, fertilization of the egg, or implantation of the pre-embryo. Some kinds are available in drugstores without a prescription. Others must be prescribed or fitted by a doctor or clinician.

Most reversible birth control is designed for women to use. They may use different kinds at different times in their lives. To decide which kind to use, women consider what they like about the method, how safe it is, how well it works, how easy it is to use, and how their sex partners feel about it.

Limiting Sexual Contact

Both partners can decide to limit their sexual contact. Some couples decide not to have any sex play. This is called continuous abstinence. It is a good way to put off taking sexual health risks until we are mature enough to handle them.

Women who put off vaginal intercourse until their early 20s have other health advantages. They reduce their chances of becoming sterile or developing cervical cancer because they are less likely to get sexually transmitted infections than those who start younger. However, many people find it hard to abstain for long periods of time.

Some couples use periodic abstinence. They keep very careful records to try to tell when pregnancy could happen. They abstain from vaginal intercourse whenever they think there's a chance it could cause pregnancy.

Many couples have safer-sex play with outercourse. Finding other ways for sexual pleasure besides intercourse can help us learn how to give and receive pleasure. This is important because many teens get little satisfaction from sexual intercourse because their partners do not know how to give them

---

♣ It's A Fact!!
Know The Truth About Sexuality, Birth Control, And Pregnancy

There are lots of crazy stories about sexuality, birth control, and pregnancy. The truth is that a woman can get pregnant even if:

• She is having vaginal bleeding

• She doesn't have an orgasm

• She doesn't have vaginal intercourse very often

• She has vaginal intercourse standing up

• She urinates right after having vaginal intercourse

• She douches with Coke® or Sprite®, or anything else

• The man pulls his penis out of her vagina before he "comes"

• She jumps up and down after vaginal intercourse

• She hasn't had her first period yet

• She's under 12 years old

• It's her first time

The truth is:

• Men do not have stronger sex drives than women.

• The size of a man's penis does not depend on how much sexual intercourse he has.

• A man's sex drive does not depend on the size of his penis.

pleasure. Outercourse also protects against most serious sexually transmitted infections. One drawback—it may lead to a couple's desire to take a risk and have unprotected intercourse.

Many people use withdrawal when no other method is available—the man pulls his penis out of the vagina before he "comes." But many men become so sexually excited that they don't withdraw in time. Also, they leak a few drops of semen before they ejaculate. Even these few drops can cause pregnancy.

- Masturbation does not make a person gay or straight.
- Masturbation will not make a person blind or crazy or cause hair to grow on the palms of the hands.
- Men aren't harmed if they don't ejaculate when sexually aroused.
- When a woman or a man says "no," believe it.
- Women with larger breasts do not have stronger sex drives.
- Plastic wrap wrapped around the penis is not an effective contraceptive.
- Nobody has a right to touch anyone who does not want to be touched.
- The Pill does not prevent sexually transmitted infections.
- Having a sexually transmitted infection does not mean that someone is a bad person.
- Sometimes, it seems that having sexual intercourse is more important than anything else. It isn't.
- Sometimes, it seems that having sexual intercourse will solve all our problems. It won't.
- Sometimes, people have sexual intercourse before they're ready and when they don't really want to. It's not worth it.
- Having sex before we are ready can interfere with our dreams and plans for the future.

When we plan ahead and wait until we're ready, sex can be exciting, satisfying, caring, and rewarding. If we know what we're doing, and if we stay in charge, we can have happier, healthier, and more successful lives.

Birth Control Methods

Cervical caps, diaphragms, IUDs (intrauterine devices), and hormonal pills, injections, and implants are reversible methods that require a prescription.

Cervical caps and diaphragms are worn in the vagina for vaginal intercourse. IUDs are inserted into the uterus by a clinician and work continuously for years. Birth control pills contain hormones and are taken daily on a monthly schedule. Hormonal shots are injected every 12 weeks. Hormonal implants are inserted under the skin of the arm and last for five years.

Many teen women prefer hormonal injections because they are very private. However, there is debate about possible long-term health risks for teenagers. Although it has not been proven, some scientists believe using one type of hormonal injections for many years may decrease the bone strength in some young women.

Like other medicines, prescription birth control may have side effects and health risks for some women. They can also have other health benefits besides preventing pregnancy.

Clinicians can help women decide what method might work best for them. Sexually active women should have a gynecological checkup, Pap test, and screening for sexually transmitted

Emergency Contraception

- Is designed to prevent pregnancy after unprotected vaginal intercourse. It is also called "post-coital" or "morning-after" contraception.

- Is provided in two ways:

    emergency hormonal contraception (increased doses of the Pill)

    insertion of an IUD.

- Is used only if a woman is sure she is not already pregnant from a previous act of intercourse. It prevents pregnancy—it will not cause an abortion.

infections at least once a year. Clinicians may not test unless asked—so be sure to tell them that you want to be tested.

Condoms, female condoms, foams, creams, jellies, films, and suppositories are reversible methods that can be bought over the counter, without a prescription. They are easy to use and rarely cause side effects when used as directed.

Condoms are worn on the penis. The others are inserted into the vagina before vaginal intercourse.

Women who only have sex now and then may prefer over-the-counter methods to avoid the possible, ongoing side effects of prescription methods.

Sterilization is a permanent method usually chosen by older people who are very sure they will not want any children in the future. Sterilization is a simple operation that keeps egg and sperm from meeting. The operation for men is simpler than the one for women.

Sexually Transmitted Diseases

Sexually transmitted infections are germs that are passed from one person to another by vaginal, oral, or anal intercourse, or other intimate contact. The most serious are passed through sexual intercourse. Millions of teens are infected but have no symptoms and do not know it.

☞ **Remember!!**

If you have a sex partner and one of you even thinks you are infected, don't put off doing something about it. Even if the symptoms are gone, you may still be infected. Stop all sexual activity and see your health care provider.

Many sexually transmitted infections cause serious diseases or damage a person's health permanently without showing any symptoms. People who aren't treated and cured may never be able to have children. Certain infections can be passed to the fetus during pregnancy and birth. Some can cause a lifetime of health problems or even death. The most serious is HIV (human immunodeficiency virus)—it has no cure. It causes AIDS—the last stage of HIV disease. AIDS usually causes death.

Latex condoms and female condoms offer protection against most serious sexually transmitted infections, including HIV. All sexually active people who have had more than one partner—or whose partners have had more than one partner—should use condoms every time they have sexual intercourse. People allergic to latex can use condoms made of polyurethane or lambskin.

Some barrier methods offer limited protection against some infections. The Pill, injections, implants, IUDs, withdrawal, periodic abstinence, and sterilization do not protect against any. If you need protection against infection, use condoms as well.

Common signs or symptoms of sexually transmitted infections are sores and blisters on or near the sex organs or mouth; unusual discharges from the penis or vagina;

♣ It's A Fact!!
Masturbation

Touching yourself sexually, or masturbation, is something you may enjoy and feel good about. It is a perfectly healthy thing for boys and girls, men and women to do as a way of releasing tension and having physical pleasure. Because masturbation is something that is done without a partner, you can't get HIV or other STDs, you can't become pregnant and you can't get someone else pregnant. It is also just fine to never masturbate. Masturbation is just one possible choice.

Source: From "Masturbation," reprinted with permission of SIECUS, the Sexuality Information and Education Council of the United States (SIECUS), 130 W. 42nd Street, Suite 350, New York, NY 10036-7802. Phone 212-819-9770, Fax: 212-819-9776, E-Mail: siecus@siecus.org, Webite: www.siecus.org. © 2002.

itches, rashes, and bumps on the sex organs and other parts of the body; and burning pain during urination. HIV can be in a person's body for 10 years or more before symptoms appear. During that time people with HIV can infect their partners without knowing.

Don't let embarrassment become a health risk. Many people find sex and sexual health very difficult to talk about. Some even find it shameful because they think having an infection means they are not moral. But when shame gets in the way of common sense, it keeps people from taking good care of themselves and their partners.

All plants and animals that reproduce sexually can get sexually transmitted infections. Morality and shame have nothing to do with it. Keep yourself healthy by speaking frankly with a clinician about your sex life. Some of them won't ask—so take charge and speak up. Testing, examination, and treatment for sexually transmitted infections are confidential.

Sexual Abuse

Some people hurt us by trying to force us to have sex with them. This is sexual abuse. Most often sexual abusers are people we know. They may be our friends. They may even be in our own families.

Sexual abuse includes unwanted touching, fondling, watching, talking, and giving baths, douches, or enemas. And it includes people forcing us to look at their sex organs. It happens whenever our sexual privacy is not respected.

Forced sexual intercourse is called rape. If a husband, friend, or date forces sexual intercourse, it is called acquaintance rape. If the abuser is a family member, it is called incest. Sexual abuse, rape, acquaintance rape, or any kind of intercourse between an adult and a minor, including incest, are serious crimes. The victims of these crimes are not responsible for what happened to them.

The sexually abused can be helped by revealing the abuse to a trusted parent, friend, teacher, or advisor—even if they promised to keep it a secret. A parent, other relative, guidance counselor, clergy, clinician, teacher, or close

friend may be able to help stop the abuse. Abused people need to find someone who will believe them, know how to help them and keep them safe—
even if they've been threatened not to tell.

♣ It's A Fact!!

Sexual abuse includes unwanted touching, fondling, watching, talking, and giving baths, douches, or
enemas. And it includes people forcing us to look at
their sex organs. It happens whenever our
sexual privacy is not respected.

Chapter 28

How Do You Know If You're Ready For Sex?

More than 4 in 10 boys and 6 in 10 girls who have had intercourse wish they had waited longer.

Here's a quiz to take about your relationship.

1. Is it committed, mutually kind, and understanding?

2. Do you trust and admire each other?

3. Have you experimented and found pleasure in non-penetrative behaviors?

4. Have you talked about sexual behaviors before they occur?

5. Is your motivation for this sexual relationship pleasure and intimacy?

6. Is the setting for the sexual relationship safe and comfortable?

Here's a quiz to take about you.

1. Are you physically mature?

2. Are you patient and understanding?

About This Chapter: Text in this chapter is from "How Do I Know If I'm Ready for Sex?" and "Feeling Good Means Feeling Safe," reprinted with permission of SIECUS, the Sexuality Information and Education Council of the United States (SIECUS), 130 W. 42nd Street, Suite 350, New York, NY 10036-7802. Phone 212-819-9770, Fax: 212-819-9776, E-Mail: siecus@siecus.org, Website: www.siecus.org. © 2002.

3. Are you knowledgeable about sexuality and sexual response?

4. Are you empathetic and able to be vulnerable?

5. Are you committed to preventing unintended pregnancies and STDs?

6. Are you able to handle responsibility for positive consequences?

7. Are you able to handle responsibility for potential negative consequences?

8. Are you honestly approving of the behavior?

✔ Quick Tip

Is Abstinence Right For You?

Some people feel sexual desire but choose not to be sexual with anyone else. That's just fine. The choice not to be sexual with anyone else is called sexual abstinence. It is a good choice and something you may choose at different times throughout your whole life. This can happen whenever you don't feel ready to be sexual with someone else, even when you do have a partner you have been sexual with in the past. Abstinence is one possible choice.

You can give and receive pleasure without sexual intercourse or genital sex. You may choose to express your sexual feelings by flirting, dancing, making out, and/or massaging your partner. Abstinence from sexual relations has benefits for teenagers. It is the best way to prevent pregnancy and to prevent becoming infected with HIV and other STDs. Being in a sexual relationship doesn't make you an adult. In fact, over a period of time there are many adults who choose abstinence now and then. Remember, for many young persons the choice to be abstinent is the best choice.

Source: " Abstinence—What's Right For Me," reprinted with permission of SIECUS, the Sexuality Information and Education Council of the United States, 130 W. 42nd Street, New York, NY 10036-7802. Phone 212-819-9770, Fax: 212-819-9776, E-Mail: siecus@siecus.org, Website: www.siecus.org. © 2002.

♣ It's A Fact!!
Sexual Involvement

For some people, touching another person in a sexual way, or expressing their sexual interest in someone, may be what they want and choose to do. There are many ways of touching another person's body that feel good. But there are ways that you do not want to be touched and ways that you may not want to touch someone else. If you decide to be sexual with another person, decide what your limits are. Share those limits with your partner before you actually begin being sexual with him or her. It may be hard to talk about it. Remember, you have the right to stop sexual activity at any time if you feel you have reached your limits. If you can talk about sexuality it will help you to learn how to make choices about expressing your own sexuality that are right for you.

Source: "Sexual Involvement," reprinted with permission of SIECUS, the Sexuality Information and Education Council of the United States, 130 W. 42nd Street, New York, NY 10036-7802. Phone 212-819-9770, Fax: 212-819-9776, E-Mail: siecus @siecus.org, Website: www.siecus. org. © 2002.

Unless you answered yes to all of these questions, you are not ready to be having intercourse.

Here are some more questions to ask yourself about having intercourse.

1. Is your relationship consensual? Have you talked about how far to go? Do you both agree?

2. Are you sure you aren't using each other?

3. Is it honest? If you have intercourse, do you know what it will mean?

4. Will it be mutually pleasurable? Have you enjoyed other sexual behaviors with your partner? Are they as committed to your pleasure as they are to their own?

5. Have you taken steps to protect yourself against pregnancy and/or disease? Have you obtained condoms and contraception (if penile/vaginal intercourse is planned)?

One way to remember these is by the mnemonic:

Can (consent)

U (not using)

Have (honest)

My (mutually pleasurable)

Pleasure (protected)

If you answered yes to all of these, and your values support teens having a sexual relationship, learn more about safer sex. If not, consider abstinence.

Feeling Good Means Feeling Safe

Both partners have a right to feel safe in a physical or sexual relationship. One way that a couple needs to feel safe is with each other. If you are thinking about taking part in a sexual relationship with someone, ask yourself:

- "Do I respect this person?"

- "Does this person respect me and my sexual comfort zone?"

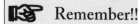 **Remember!!**
Your Sexual Rights

Always keep these rights in mind.

You have...

- The right to accurate information about sexuality and HIV/AIDS.

- The right to stop being physical or sexual with a partner at any point.

- The right to say no to an unwanted touch of any kind.

- The right to make decisions about sexuality, in your own time.

- The right to express your sexuality safely, without risk of pregnancy, or STDs including HIV/AIDS.

- The right not to be pressured into being physical or sexual

- The right not to express your sexuality unless you want to.

Source: "Teens' Sexual Rights!," reprinted with permission of SIECUS, the Sexuality Information and Education Council of the United States, 130 W. 42nd Street, New York, NY 10036-7802. Phone 212-819-9770, Fax: 212-819-9776, E-Mail: siecus @siecus.org, Website: www. siecus. org. © 2002.

- "Is there trust between us?"

- "Do we talk to each other and listen too?"

- "Is this person there for me if I need help?"

- "Do we share things other than sex?"

- "Can I talk about birth control and/or disease prevention with this person?"

If the answer to any of these questions is no, chances are that this is not a good person to have or continue to have a sexual experience with. Talking about sexuality with this person may be difficult. Ask yourself if you really want to be sexually involved with someone who you cannot talk to, who doesn't listen to how you feel, or who doesn't respect your sexual comfort zone. Take the time to stop, think, act and respond. If you are now having sex with someone and you don't want to keep having sex with that person, you can make the choice to stop having sex. It's your choice to make.

Chapter 29

What To Know About Date Rape

Date Rape

Date rape is a topic that few people are truly comfortable discussing. Below are some things you should remember about date and acquaintance rape—whether you are male or female.

Sexual Stereotyping And How Men And Women Talk To Each Other

Although things are changing, society still frequently encourages men to be competitive and aggressive and teaches women to be passive and avoid confrontation.

Men often misunderstand a woman's words and actions—the "She said no, but she meant yes" excuse.

Some people still believe that it's okay for a man to demand sex if he buys a woman dinner or gifts, and that it's not wrong for a man to rape a woman who previously had sex with him or other men.

About This Chapter: Text in this chapter is from "Date Rape," © 1995 National Crime Prevention Council. Reprinted with permission. Available online at http://www.ncpc.org/10yth3.htm. Despite the older date of this document, the information about date rape will provide helpful advice to the reader. Text is also included from "Avoiding Date Rape Drugs," from The National Women's Health Information Center, 2000. Available online at http://www.4woman.gov/faq/rohypnol.htm.

What A Girl Can Do To Prevent Date Rape

- Talk openly about sex, and keep talking as you get deeper into a relationship.

- Be careful not to let alcohol or other drugs decrease your ability to take care of yourself and make sensible decisions.

- Trust your gut feelings. If a place or the way he acts makes you nervous or uneasy, get out.

> ♣ **It's A Fact!!**
> Date rape is about power, control, and anger—not romance and passion.

- Check out a first date or a blind date with friends. Insist on going to a public place like a movie, sporting event, or restaurant. Carry money for a phone call and taxi, or take your own car.

- Don't leave a party, concert, game, or other social occasion with someone you just met or don't know well.

- Take a look at the men around you and be wary of anyone who puts you down, or tries to control how you dress or your choice of friends.

What a Guy Can Do To Prevent Date Rape

- Ask yourself how sexual stereotypes affect your attitudes and actions toward women.

- Accept a woman's decision when she says "no." Don't see it as a challenge.

- Avoid clouding your judgment and understanding of what another person wants by using alcohol and other drugs.

- Realize that forcing a woman to have sex against her will is rape, a violent crime with serious consequences.

- Never be drawn into a gang rape—at parties, fraternities, bars, or after sporting events.

- Seek counseling or a support group to help you deal with feelings of violence and aggression against women.

What To Do If Date Rape Happens to You

Get help. Phone the police, a friend, a rape crisis center, a relative. Don't isolate yourself, don't feel guilty, and don't try to ignore it. It is a crime that should be reported. Rape by someone you know is a violation of your body and your trust.

- Get medical attention as soon as possible. Do not shower, wash, douche, or change your clothes. Valuable evidence could be destroyed.

- Get counseling to help deal with the emotional trauma caused by rape.

What If It Happens to Someone You Know

- Believe her.

- Offer comfort and support. Go with her to the hospital, police station, or counseling center.

- Let her know she's not to blame.

Take a Stand Against Date Rape

- Ask your student government or a parent group to sponsor a workshop on date rape and sexual stereotyping for middle and high school students. Work with a hotline or crisis center to persuade rape survivors to join the panel.

- Volunteer at a rape crisis center or hotline.

- Monitor the media for programs or videos that reinforce sexual stereotypes. Write or call to protest. On the other side, publicly commend the media when they highlight the realities of date rape.

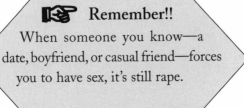

☞ Remember!!
When someone you know—a date, boyfriend, or casual friend—forces you to have sex, it's still rape.

- Ask college or professional athletes or other role models to talk to high school students about sexual stereotyping and responsible behavior.

- Ask your church or civic group to organize a speaker and panel discussion on this topic.

Avoiding "Date Rape" Drugs

What is the "date rape" drug?

The "date rape" drug is the common name for Rohypnol, generically called flunitrazepam. Rohypnol is manufactured by Hoffman-La Roche and prescribed as a sleeping pill in countries outside of the United States. It is used as a short-term treatment for insomnia, as a sedative hyp-

> **♣ It's A Fact!!**
> Date rape is a serious crime. It's a betrayal of trust and can leave long-lasting emotional injuries.

notic and a pre-anesthetic. It has physiological effects similar to Valium (diazepam), but is approximately ten times more potent. It is used also as an illicit drug, often in combination with other drugs, such as heroin, cocaine, and alcohol. Common names for Rohypnol include the following: rophies, roofies, R2, roofenol, Roche, roachies, la rocha, rope, rib, circles, Mexican valium, roach-2, roopies, and ropies. A similar drug is known as clonazepam (Klonopin in the U.S. and Rivotril in Mexico.)

What does Rohypnol look like?

Rohypnol tablets are white, scored on one side, with the word "ROCHE" and an encircled one or two (depending on the dosage) on the other. They are sold in pre-sealed bubble packs of one or two mg doses. Rohypnol can often be dissolved in a drink, and undetectable.

Is Rohypnol legal?

No, Rohypnol is not manufactured or sold legally in the United States. However, it is produced and sold legally by prescription in Europe and Latin America. It is smuggled into the United States by mail or delivery services.

Who uses Rohypnol and how?

Rohypnol use has been reported
on every inhabited continent. It is
often used in conjunction with
other drugs. It is usually ingested
orally, but can be snorted. Teen use of
Rohypnol is increasing. The most common pat-
tern of use is by teenagers and young adults as an alcohol extender in an
attempt to create a dramatic high most often in combination with beer, or as
a drug to incapacitate a victim before a sexual assault.

♣ It's A Fact!!
Rapists aren't always strangers.

Why has there been an increase in teen use of Rohypnol?

First, Rohypnol is a low-cost drug, sold at less than $5.00 per tablet.
Second, common misconceptions may explain the drug's popularity with
young people: 1) many erroneously believe that the drug is unadulterated
because it comes in pre-sealed bubble packs—and therefore tamper-proof
and safe; 2) many mistakenly think its use cannot be detected by urinalysis
testing.

What happens when you take Rohypnol? What are the side effects?

Rohypnol intoxication is generally associated with impaired judgment
and impaired motor skills and can make a victim unable to resist a sexual
attack. The combination of alcohol and Rohypnol is also particularly hazardous because together, their effects on memory and judgment are greater
than the effects resulting from either taken alone. Effects begin within thirty
minutes, peak within two hours, and can persist for up to eight hours. It is
commonly reported that persons who become intoxicated on a combination
of alcohol and flunitrazepam have blackouts lasting eight to twenty-four
hours following ingestion. Disinhibition (losing your social inhibitions) is
another widely reported effect of Rohypnol, when taken alone or in combination with alcohol. Adverse effects of Rohypnol use include, decreased blood
pressure, memory impairment, drowsiness, visual disturbances, dizziness, confusion, gastrointestinal disturbances and urinary retention.

Is Rohypnol addictive?

Yes. Rohypnol can cause physical dependence. Withdrawal symptoms include headache, muscle pain, confusion, hallucinations and convulsions. Seizures may occur up to a week after cessation of use.

Why is Rohypnol called the "date rape drug?"

Rohypnol has been associated with date rape, and has also been called the "Forget Pill," "Trip-and-Fall," and "Mind-Erasers." In combination with alcohol, it can induce a blackout with memory loss and a decrease in resistance. Girls and women around the country have reported being raped after being involuntarily sedated with Rohypnol, which was often slipped into their drink by an attacker. The drug has no taste or odor so the victims don't realize what is happening. About ten minutes after ingesting the drug, the woman may feel dizzy and disoriented, simultaneously too hot and too cold, or nauseated. She may experience difficulty speaking and moving, and then pass out. Such victims have no memories of what happened while under the drug's influence.

Are there other "date rape" type drugs?

Since about 1990, GHB (gamma-hydroxybutyrate) has been abused in the U.S. for euphoric, sedative, and anabolic (bodybuilding) effects. As with Rohypnol, GHB has been associated with sexual assault in cites throughout the country. Common names include, "liquid ecstasy," "somatomax," "scoop," or "grievous bodily harm."

How can I avoid becoming a victim of rape under the influence of Rohypnol or GHB?

Here are a few suggestions for staying aware and alert:

- Be wary about accepting drinks from anyone you don't know well or long enough to trust. If you are accepting a drink, make sure it's from an unopened container and that you open it yourself.

- Don't put your drink down and leave it unattended, even to go to the restroom.

- Notify other females you know about the effects of this dangerous drug.

- If you think that you have been a victim, notify the authorities immediately.

👉 **Remember!!**

Girls and women around the country have reported being raped after being involuntarily sedated with Rohypnol, which was often slipped into their drink by an attacker. The drug has no taste or odor so the victims don't realize what is happening.

Chapter 30

The Sex Education Debate

Opportunity To Educate Teens About Sexual Issues Is Often Overlooked

Most high school students undergoing routine physical examinations do not talk to their health care practitioner about preventing sexually transmitted diseases (Stds) or pregnancy, according to a Centers for Disease Control (CDC) study released at a National STD Prevention Conference. The findings suggest that a greater effort is needed to encourage health care providers to talk with teenage patients about STD and pregnancy prevention.

The study found that among high school students who had received a routine check-up during the previous year, only 42.8 percent of females and 26.4 percent of males had discussed STD or pregnancy prevention with their health care provider. The study, authored by CDC researcher Gale Burstein and colleagues, was based on data from CDC's 1999 Youth Risk Behavior Survey, a nationally representative survey of 15,349 high school students.

About This Chapter: Text in this chapter is from "Most Teens Not Provided STD or Pregnancy Prevention Counseling During Check-Ups," a press release from the Centers for Disease Control and Prevention (CDC), 2000. Available online at http://www.cdc.gov/nchstp/dstd/Press_Releases/Teens2000.htm. Individual citations are provided for separate articles offering opposing views on abstinence-based education.

"Many health care providers are missing important opportunities to provide STD and pregnancy prevention counseling to youth," said Helene Gayle, M.D., M.P.H., director of CDC's National Center for HIV, STD, and TB Prevention (NCHSTP). "Many teens are sexually active and STDs remain a serious threat to their health. Comprehensive health education in schools, communities and homes needs to be supplemented with communication between doctors and their teen patients about STD and pregnancy prevention."

The CDC study identified demographic and behavioral characteristics that were associated with discussions about STDs and pregnancy prevention during routine check-ups. Not surprisingly, both male and female high school students were more likely to have these discussions if they were sexually experienced, and female students ages 17 or older were more likely to have the discussions than were female students ages 14 or younger.

Teenagers remain at high risk for STD infection. By the twelfth grade, 65 percent of high school students have had sexual intercourse, and one in five has had four or more sexual partners. Teens account for a significant proportion of the 15 million STD infections in the United States each year. Forty percent of chlamydia cases are reported among young people age 15 to 19, females in that age group also have the highest rates of gonorrhea. Many STDs can cause serious health problems—pelvic inflammatory disease, infertility, ectopic pregnancy and increase risk for HIV transmission—if they are not detected and treated.

♣ It's A Fact!!

Among high school students who had received a routine check-up during the previous year, only 42.8 percent of females and 26.4 percent of males had discussed STD or pregnancy prevention with their health care provider. (Source: CDC)

In Support Of Abstinence-Based Education

Source: "Sex-Ed Bill Says To Abstain Or Use Condoms," by M.D. Harmon, *Portland Herald Press,* March 25, 2002, p. 7A; © 2002 Portland Press Herald/Maine Sunday Telegram; reprinted with permission. Presentation of this opinion does not imply endorsement.

♣ **It's A Fact!!**

Abstinence provides 100 percent protection from pregnancy and sexually transmitted diseases (some of which cannot be cured, and some of which produce either sterility or even death).

Source: *Portland Press Herald.*

There's always been this kind of strange dichotomy about some sex educators. They're the ones who say they're only giving teens the best information when they tell them about the benefits of abstaining from sex on the one hand, and the benefits of using condoms or other (doubtfully) protective devices on the other.

The simple fact is that abstinence provides 100 percent protection from pregnancy and sexually transmitted diseases (some of which cannot be cured, and some of which produce either sterility or even death).

Yet those who want a balanced approach to sexuality education—balanced, apparently, between health and harm—are only playing the averages with their young charges' lives.

Those who recommend abstinence can know that no one who follows their advice will ever come to harm. Teens who are given the mixed message, however, often take a gamble with their futures.

In truth, there's no "safe sex," only "safer sex." Even that is a fundamentally dishonest term. With a study by the Alan Guttmacher Institute showing a one-in-seven failure rate for condom use by teens, "safer sex" is almost exactly as hazardous as Russian roulette, pointing a six-shooter loaded with one bullet at your head and pulling the trigger.

Condoms fail to protect against pregnancy as much as 22.5 percent of the time in the first 12 months of use by a teenage girl. Against some diseases, such as chlamydia and human papillomavirus, they provide hardly any protection at all. The risk of HIV transmission is also always present.

Perhaps that's why a national survey reported that the percentage of high school sexuality educators saying that abstinence is the most important message they can give their students rose from 24.8 percent in 1988 to 41.4 percent in 1999.

This is important for Mainers, because there's a bill pending in Augusta—L.D. 1603—that would establish condom-pushing as the gold standard for public school sexuality education in Maine.

The bill is awaiting an amendment that strengthens its abstinence wording (but condom training remains a central part of the curriculum).

It once had a fiscal note of $750,000, which now is suspended due to state funding shortfalls. So why are its backers still pushing it, especially since they acknowledge that local control means that any community wanting to teach abstinence-only sex education will be able to do so?

Well, it remains an open question whether such school districts will be able to get state assistance under this law, and the state has refused to accept millions in federal funds for abstinence-only education.

The bill's proponents are adamant that abstinence education "doesn't work," citing recent studies. However, a 1997 article in the *Journal of the American Medical Association* reported that, from a large national sample of

♣ **It's A Fact!!**

By the twelfth grade, 65 percent of high school students have had sexual intercourse, and one in five has had four or more sexual partners. (Source: CDC)

teens, those who had abstinence education and taken virginity pledges "were at a significantly lower risk of early age of sexual debut."

Dr. Joe McIlhaney, president of the Medical Institute for Sexual Health in Austin, Texas, has noted that the studies cited most often about the inadequacies of abstinence education omitted some results that contradicted that conclusion.

He added, "The uncomfortable part is what these (new) studies called successful. I don't think that most parents would accept as successful anything less than a program that assures their child won't get pregnant, won't get a disease and won't have sex."

Early and frequent sexual activity, after all, is not only associated with high rates of pregnancy and disease, but with low academic achievement and unsuccessful relationships later in life. Maybe there's a reason most human cultures and faiths have discouraged promiscuity throughout recorded history.

There's something else about L.D. 1603. If it is ever funded, the money can be funneled out to "local family planning programs." With that in mind, let's consider a germane point made by Dr. James Dobson, head of Focus on the Family, a faith-based group that provides resources on family issues to millions of people.

Describing his experiences on a federal panel exploring teenage pregnancy, he relates how almost all the other members vociferously opposed abstinence-only education:

> "I can't describe how emotional they were. . . . Millions of jobs and entire industries are supported by teen sexual irresponsibility. The abortion business alone generates up to $1 billion annually. Why would physicians and nurses working in abortion clinics, and medical suppliers, and school-based sex-education counselors prefer that adolescents abstain until marriage? If that idea ever caught on, who would need the services of Planned Parenthood and their ilk?"

Especially, why do we need them setting the standards for sexuality education for our children?

Abstinence-Only Education Is Inadequate

Source: Reproduced with permission of the Alan Guttmacher Institute from: Boonstra, H. *Legislators Craft Alternative Vision of Sex Education to Counter Abstinence-Only Drive.* The Guttmacher Report on Public Policy. 2002, 5(2): 1-3. Presentation of this opinion does not imply endorsement.

Last summer, then Surgeon General David Satcher drew the ire of White House officials with the release of his long awaited Call to Action to Promote Sexual Health and Responsible Sexual Behavior. Citing research findings on the effectiveness of various program interventions, the Satcher report stresses the importance of sex education that balances encouragement of abstinence for young people with assuring "awareness of optimal protection from sexually transmitted diseases and unintended pregnancy, for those who are sexually active...." Satcher's conclusion is echoed in *Healthy People 2010*, the Department of Health and Human Services' set of official national goals for improved public health, which emphasizes the need to reduce teenage pregnancy and sexually transmitted disease (STD) rates in part through comprehensive sex education programs.

> ✦ **It's A Fact!!**
> Fewer than one in five adults say that sex education programs should teach only about abstinence.
>
> Source: Alan Guttmacher Institute.

Endorsing sex education that includes information about condoms and contraceptive use to avoid STDs and unintended pregnancy along with positive messages about the value of delaying sexual activity is hardly a radical idea. Indeed, it is the position of the nation's leading medical, public health and educational organizations. Moreover, the overwhelming majority of Americans support this type of sex education. In a 1998 poll conducted by the Kaiser Family Foundation and ABC Television, 81% of adults said that sex education programs should teach both abstinence and pregnancy and STD prevention; only 18% thought programs should teach only abstinence.

Nonetheless, the exclusive promotion of abstinence is the sex education policy that prevails at the federal level. Currently, three separate programs support the most restrictive abstinence-only approach—an approach that requires condemnation of sex outside of marriage for people of all ages and allows no teaching about contraceptive methods beyond failure rates. For the current fiscal year, federal spending earmarked for this type of abstinence education totals $102 million. And the Bush administration has announced that it wants more, a $33 million increase for FY 2003 ("Abstinence Promotion and Teen Family Planning: The Misguided Drive for Equal Funding," *TGR*, February 2002, page 1).

Advocates of a more comprehensive, or abstinence-plus, approach to sex education have long noted that the effectiveness of the abstinence-only approach has not been demonstrated. But as a practical matter, there has been no alternative policy proposal for these advocates to rally around. Legislation introduced in the House of Representatives in December 2001, however, sets out an alternative vision for how U.S. policy might best meet the needs of young people.

The Need For Action

In the United States, as in other developed Western countries, the majority of adolescents become sexually active during their teenage years. Roughly two-thirds (63%) of U.S. teens have had sexual intercourse by their 18th birthday. But while this level of sexual activity is hardly unique among developed countries, teens in the United States do have uniquely higher rates of unplanned pregnancy. Despite significant reductions in the U.S. teen pregnancy rate over the last decade or so, nearly 900,000 teenagers still become pregnant each year and almost four in five (78%) of these pregnancies are unintended.

Research conducted by The Alan Guttmacher Institute between 1998 and 2001 indicates that U.S. teens are more likely to become pregnant because they are less likely to use any contraceptive method than young people in other developed countries and are also less likely to use methods that in actual use have the highest effectiveness rates, such as the pill ("Teen Pregnancy: Trends and Lessons Learned," *TGR*, February 2002, page 7). In 1995, one in four American adolescents did not use any method at first intercourse, and one in five were not currently using any method.

Teen STD rates in the United States are also high. Every year, roughly four million teens acquire an STD. Young people aged 15-19 account for one-third of all gonorrhea and chlamydia cases in the United States. On average, two young people in the United States are infected with HIV every hour of every day. Racial and ethnic minorities have been disproportionately infected with STDs, especially HIV/AIDS. For example, although blacks represent less than 16% of the adolescent population, they account for nearly half of all reported adolescent AIDS cases.

Preventing pregnancy and STDs among teenagers, therefore, is a major public health priority—and the role that sex education can play in achieving this goal is a question of major importance. Research has demonstrated that program interventions that urge teens to postpone having intercourse but also discuss contraception can be effective in helping teens delay sexual activity and increase contraceptive use when they do become sexually active. At the same time, most abstinence-only programs and strategies have not been proven effective in delaying teens' sexual initiation or in reducing the frequency of intercourse and number of sex partners. Indeed, recent evidence suggests that these programs and strategies—including virginity pledges, which have been shown to help some teenage girls postpone intercourse for up to 18 months—may actually increase young people's risk of pregnancy and disease by deterring the use of contraceptives, including condoms, when they become sexually active.

Heeding The Evidence

Based on this research and the realities of teen sexual activity in the United States, a broad constituency of child development, education, health care, and youth-serving agencies is committed to assuring that more comprehensive sex education is provided to young Americans. To date, well over 100 organizations—including many of the most prominent medical, public health and educational associations in the United States—have signed on to a statement to demonstrate their support. Calling abstinence "a key component of sexuality education," the statement contends that, "Society should encourage adolescents to delay sexual behaviors until they are ready physically, cognitively, spiritually, socially and emotionally for mature sexual relationships and their consequences." At the same time, the statement asserts, "Society must also recognize that a majority of adolescents have become involved in sexual relationships during their teenage years. Scientific research indicates that comprehensive approaches to sexuality education can help young people postpone intercourse and use contraception and STD prevention."

Several recent studies and surveys suggest that sex education that includes information about both abstinence and contraception also has strong support among teachers and parents, as well as among teens themselves ("Sex Education: Politicians, Parents, Teachers and Teens," *TGR*, February 2001, page 9). A study published in *Family Planning Perspectives* in 2000 reports that more than nine in 10 public school teachers believe that students should be taught about contraception. According to interviews conducted for the Kaiser Family Foundation in 2000, parents overwhelmingly want schools to do more to prepare their children for real life. More than eight in 10 believe sex education courses should discuss the use of birth control, including condoms. Three-quarters say abortion and sexual orientation should be discussed in a balanced way that presents different views in society. Kaiser-sponsored research also indicates that teens want more information about sexual and reproductive health issues than they are currently receiving in school.

♣ It's A Fact!!

- More than nine in 10 public school teachers believe that students should be taught about contraception.

- More than eight in 10 parents believe sex education courses should discuss the use of birth control, including condoms.

- Teens want more information about sexual and reproductive health issues than they are currently receiving in school.

Source: Alan Guttmacher Institute.

♣ It's A Fact!!

Selected Medical, Public Health And Educational Organizations Supporting Comprehensive Sexuality Education

American Academy of Child and Adolescent Psychiatry

American Academy of Pediatrics

American Association for Health Education

American Association of Family and Consumer Sciences

American Association of School Administrators

American College of Nurse-Midwives

American College of Obstetricians and Gynecologists

American Counseling Association

American Medical Association

American Medical Women's Association

American Nurses Association

American Psychiatric Association

American Psychological Association

American Public Health Association

American School Health Association

Association of State and Territorial Health Officials

Federation of Behavioral, Psychological and Cognitive Sciences

National Alliance of State and Territorial AIDS Directors

National Association of County and City Health Officials

National Association of School Psychologists

National Center for Health Education

National Council on Family Relations

National Education Association

National Medical Association

National Mental Health Association

National Organization on Adolescent Pregnancy, Parenting and Prevention

National School Boards Association

Society for Adolescent Medicine

Source: Alan Guttmacher Institute.

Putting It Together

The Family Life Education Act, according to its original cosponsors, Reps. Barbara Lee (D-CA) and James Greenwood (R-PA), sets out a vision of U.S. sex education policy that is research-based and that has the support of medical, public health and educational organizations, as well as the American people. The bill would authorize $100 million annually for five years to support state programs that operate under a nine point definition of "family life education programs" that stands in sharp contrast to the eight point definition of an "eligible abstinence education program" that now governs federal support in this area.

Funding under the Family Life Education Act also could be used to carry out "educational and motivational activities" that would teach young people about human physical and emotional development, promote male involvement in decision-making and help young people develop self-esteem and healthy attitudes about body image, gender roles, racial and ethnic diversity, sexual orientation and other issues. The legislation provides for both national and state level evaluations of the programs' effectiveness in helping young people delay the initiation of sexual intercourse, preventing teen pregnancy and STDs, and increasing contraceptive knowledge and use among teens who are sexually active.

Into The Fray

Not only has the president proposed a major increase in funding for abstinence-only education for the upcoming fiscal year, but social conservatives have made abstinence-only education a major priority as Congress prepares to reconsider the 1996 welfare law, which houses the eight point definition that governs all three federal abstinence education programs.

Advocates of more comprehensive sex education hope that the arrival of the Family Life Education Act on the scene will help them stave off efforts to extend and expand the reach of federal abstinence-only policy. By setting out a vision of responsible sex education for the future, they hope it will highlight for policymakers that the current policy is highly restrictive, censors information about contraception and is out of step with what research has shown to be effective and what most Americans say should be taught.

"Denying our sons and daughters the information they need to protect their health and their lives is not only naive and misguided," said Rep. Lee in a recent press statement, "[it is] irresponsible and extremely dangerous....We can't risk our children's future by not fully educating them about their options."

Sexuality Education, As Defined By The Family Life Education

Act According to the Family Life Education Act, a program of family life education is one that:

1. is age-appropriate and medically accurate;

2. does not teach or promote religion;

3. teaches that abstinence is the only sure way to avoid pregnancy or sexually transmitted diseases;

4. stresses the value of abstinence while not ignoring those young people who have had or are having sexual intercourse;

5. provides information about the health benefits and side effects of all contraceptives and barrier methods as a means to prevent pregnancy;

6. provides information about the health benefits and side effects of all contraceptives and barrier methods as a means to reduce the risk of contracting sexually transmitted diseases, including HIV/AIDS;

7. encourages family communication about sexuality between parent and child;

8. teaches young people the skills to make responsible decisions about sexuality, including how to avoid unwanted verbal, physical, and sexual advances and how not to make unwanted verbal, physical, and sexual advances; and

9. teaches young people how alcohol and drug use can affect responsible decision making.

Source: Alan Guttmacher Institute.

Because the Family Life Education Act would require that funded programs provide information about contraception as well as encourage abstinence, its sponsors and supporters hope it will help policymakers voice their opposition to the strictest form of abstinence-only education while still

Abstinence Education, As Defined By Current Federal Law

According to current law, an abstinence education program eligible for federal funding is one that:

A. has as its exclusive purpose, teaching the social, physiological, and health gains to be realized by abstaining from sexual activity;

B. teaches abstinence from sexual activity outside marriage as the expected standard for all school age children;

C. teaches that abstinence from sexual activity is the only certain way to avoid out-of-wedlock pregnancy, sexually transmitted diseases, and other associated health problems;

D. teaches that a mutually faithful monogamous relationship in context of marriage is the expected standard of human sexual activity;

E. teaches that sexual activity outside of the context of marriage is likely to have harmful psychological and physical effects;

F. teaches that bearing children out-of-wedlock is likely to have harmful consequences for the child, the child's parents, and society;

G. teaches young people how to reject sexual advances and how alcohol and drug use increases vulnerability to sexual advances; and

H. teaches the importance of attaining self sufficiency before engaging in sexual activity.

Source: Alan Guttmacher Institute.

remaining supportive of abstinence messages. Over time, they hope it will help redirect the federal government's sexuality education spending toward more comprehensive models with demonstrated effectiveness in helping young people both delay having sex and protect themselves when they eventually do become sexually active.

Part 5

Preventing Pregnancy

Chapter 31

Some Facts And Stats On Pregnancy

Following are some questions and answers about teen pregnancy in the United States.

How many teen girls in the U.S. get pregnant each year?

Nearly one million teen girls get pregnant each year. Nearly four out of 10 young women get pregnant at least once before they turn 20. Each year the federal government alone spends about $40 billion to help families that began with a teenage birth.

But aren't the teen pregnancy and birth rates declining?

Yes, but they are still too high. The overall U.S. teenage pregnancy rate declined 19 percent from its all time high in 1991 to 1997 (the most recent year available), from 117 pregnancies per 1,000 women aged 15–19 to 94.3 per 1,000. The national teen birth rate declined 5 percent between 1998 and 2000, reaching a rate of 48.5 births per 1,000 women ages 15–19—the lowest rate ever recorded. Since 1991, the teen birth rate has declined 22 percent.

About This Chapter: Text in this chapter is from "The Facts Of Life: A Guide For Teens And Their Families," © 2002 National Campaign to Prevent Teen Pregnancy. Reprinted with Permission. For more information visit their website at http://www.teenpregnancy.org.

Does the U.S. have a higher teen pregnancy rate than other countries?

Yes, by a long shot. Although rates here are declining, the U.S. has the highest rates of teen pregnancy, birth, and abortion in the industrialized world. In fact, the U.S. teen pregnancy and birth rates are nearly double Canada's, at least four times those of France and Germany, and more than eight times those of Japan.

Isn't everyone having sex?

No. Fewer than one-half of high school students have had sex.

So, does that mean more kids think it's "cool" to be a virgin?

Teens are showing signs of being more conservative sexually. Close to six in ten teens (58 percent) surveyed recently said sexual activity for high school-age teens is not acceptable, even if precautions are taken against pregnancy and sexually transmitted diseases. In fact, the vast majority of teens (87 percent) surveyed said they do not think it is embarrassing for teens to admit they are virgins.

♣ It's A Fact!!

- Nearly one million U.S. teen girls get pregnant each year.

- Nearly 40% of young women get pregnant at least once before they turn 20.

- The U.S. government spends about $40 billion annually to help families that began with a teenage birth.

- U.S. teen pregnancy and birth rates are nearly double Canada's, at least four times those of France and Germany, and more than eight times those of Japan.

- 63 percent of teens who have had sexual intercourse said they wish they had waited.

- Children of teen mothers are 50 percent more likely to repeat a grade.

- Daughters of teen mothers are 22 percent more likely to become teen mothers themselves.

- Sons of teen mothers are 13 percent more likely to end up in prison.

- Only 20 percent of fathers marry the teen mothers of their first children.

Do teens have a general opinion about whether their peers should be sexually active?

In a recent poll, nearly eight of ten teens surveyed (78 percent) agreed that teens should not be sexually active. However, the majority of teens (54 percent) said teens who are sexually active should have access to birth control.

Are younger teen girls more sexually active than they used to be?

While teen sexual activity is down among most teens, it has risen among girls younger than 15. In 1995 (the most recent year for which data is available) almost one-fifth (19 percent) of teen girls reported they had sex before age 15. And, the younger teen girls are when they first have sex, the more likely they are to report that sex was unwanted or non-voluntary.

Are teen guys more sexually active than they were in the past?

The percentage of unmarried teen guys aged 17–19 that reported having sex dropped from 75.5 percent in 1988 to 68.2 percent in 1995.

Do teens who have had sex wish they had waited?

Most do. In a recent poll, 63 percent of teens who have had sexual intercourse said they wish they had waited. More than one-half of teen boys (55 percent) and nearly three out of four teen girls (72 percent) surveyed said they wish they had waited longer to have sex. Sixty-four percent of teens also said the advice they'd give a younger sibling or friend would be: "Don't have sex until you're at least out of high school, but, if you do, be sure to protect yourself against pregnancy and STDs."

Can you get pregnant if you use birth control?

Yes. Even if used perfectly, all methods of birth control have a failure rate, ranging from 0.05 percent for Norplant to 9 percent for the sponge and calendar rhythm. The only way to make 100-percent sure that you won't get pregnant or get someone pregnant is to not have sex. The next best thing is to use birth control correctly every time you have sex. Many sexually active teens don't use protection at all or use it inconsistently or incorrectly.

Are sexually active teens using birth control?

More teens are now using contraception the first time they have sex, but are less likely than in previous years to use contraception the most recent time they've had sex. Moreover, thirty-one percent of girls were completely unprotected the last time they had sex, and one-third of sexually active teens who do use contraception use it inconsistently.

Why don't teens use birth control every time?

In a recent poll, teen boys (49.3 percent) and teen girls (54.2 percent) agree that pressure from their partners is one of the main reasons teens fail to use birth control. Alcohol and drugs can also play a role. Many young women say that they used alcohol—or were even drunk—when they first had sex. And many of these same young women say that they were so drunk that they were unable to use birth control (especially condoms) properly at the time. In one study of unplanned pregnancies in 14–21 year olds, one-third of the girls who had gotten pregnant had been drinking when they had sex; 91% of them reported that the sex was unplanned.

You can't get pregnant the first time, right?

Wrong. Teen girls can get pregnant the first time they have sex, and every time after that. A couple that doesn't use birth control has an 85 percent chance of pregnancy within one year.

Do most teens who choose to raise the child get married when they find out they're pregnant?

In 1960, only 15 percent of teen births were to unmarried teens. In 2000, 79 percent of teen births were to unmarried teens.

Aren't there a lot of teen girls who want to get pregnant?

The majority of pregnancies to 15- to 19-year-olds—78 percent—are not planned.

Do the teen girls who get pregnant keep their babies?

Just over one-half of all pregnancies to teens aged 19 or younger end in births. Thirty percent of teen pregnancies end in abortion and 14 percent end in miscarriage. Of those teens that give birth, most keep their children. According to a 1995 survey, only 1 percent of all single women choose adoption.

What happens to teen mothers?

Less than one-third of teen mothers complete high school.

Many teen mothers go on to have more children—about one-fourth of teen mothers have a second child within 24 months of the first birth.

A 1990 study shows that almost one-third of all teen mothers and one-half of unmarried teen mothers go on welfare within the first year of the birth of their first child. Within five years after the birth of their first child, almost one-half of all teen mothers and over three-quarters of unmarried teen mothers began receiving welfare.

What happens to the children of teen moms?

Children of teen mothers are more likely to be born prematurely and at low birth weight, which raises the chances of blindness, deafness, mental retardation, cerebral palsy, and other disabilities.

Children of teen mothers are 50 percent more likely to repeat a grade. They also perform much worse on standardized tests and ultimately they are less likely to complete high school than children of mothers who waited to have a baby.

The daughters of teen mothers are 22 percent more likely to become teen mothers themselves. The sons of teen mothers are 13 percent more likely to end up in prison.

Remember!!

Teen girls can get pregnant the first time they have sex, and every time after that. A couple that doesn't use birth control has an 85 percent chance of pregnancy within one year.

Who are the fathers, and where are they now?

Nearly 40 percent of the fathers of children born to teen mothers are age 20 or older. Only 20 percent of the fathers marry the teen mothers of their first children. On average, the remaining 80 percent pay less than $800 annually for child support.

Where can I find out about teen pregnancy rates in my state?

Check out this link: www.teenpregnancy.org/america/states

You'll find all kinds of interesting information about your state, including teen pregnancy and birth rates, changes in pregnancy and birth rates over the past several years, and racial and ethnic breakdowns of the numbers.

Chapter 32

Contraceptives 101

Deciding to have sexual intercourse is a big decision and one thing that comes along with it is deciding which method of contraception or birth control to use. Not using some form of protection exposes you to the possibility of becoming (or getting someone) pregnant and getting an STD (sexually transmitted diseases). It is very important to talk with your partner about birth control before you have sexual intercourse and to get the facts to help you decide which methods are best for you and your partner.

Following are some general facts about the different types of birth control available.

Abstinence

Abstinence means waiting to have sexual intercourse. Some people remain abstinent until marriage.

Effectiveness

When practiced all the time, abstinence is the only 100 percent effective method of preventing pregnancy and STDs. This makes it the best overall choice for teens.

About This Chapter: "Contraceptives 101," is reprinted with permission from the Campaign For Our Children, Inc. (CFOC). © 2000. For additional information contact CFOC at 120 West Fayette Street, Baltimore, MD 21201, 410-576-9015, or visit their website at www.cfoc.org.

Abstaining from sexual intercourse is easier than you think. The following tips will help:

- Talk openly with your partner about your decision to wait. Talking to a parent or other adult can also be helpful in answering your questions and concerns about making the right decisions. Remember adults were once teenagers too.

- Practice using effective refusal skills:

  Use the word NO—there is no good substitute.

  Use strong nonverbal messages—your body language should also say "No!"

  Repeat the message as much as needed; do not give in.

  Suggest alternative activities.

  When appropriate—reject the activity not the person.

Goal Setting

Set realistic long and short-term goals. Stick to your goals. Avoid getting involved in risky things that could interfere with your goals.

Cost

There is no cost.

Advantages

- Offers 100% protection against HIV and other STDs.

♣ It's A Fact!!

- Not everybody is having sex. About 75% of 15 year olds have not had sex and even many older teens that are 17 and 18 are practicing abstinence.

- It is okay to decide to practice abstinence even if you have had sex in the past.

- Women and men often stop practicing abstinence without being prepared to protect themselves from pregnancy and HIV/STDs. It is important to talk to your partner about relationship expectations. Talk before it's too late.

- Practicing abstinence every now and then does not offer the same amount of protection against pregnancy and HIV/STDs as practicing abstinence each and every time.

- It may be hard to remain abstinent, but be confident—you can do it.

- 100% effective way to avoid pregnancy.
- No medical or hormonal side effects.
- Doesn't cost anything.
- Many religious groups support the choice of abstinence among unmarried people.

Disadvantages

- One partner may decide he/she no longer wants to remain abstinent while the other partner wants to continue practicing abstinence.

Condoms

The male condom is made out of a thin piece of latex or natural rubber which is placed over the erect penis in order to prevent sperm from entering the vagina. Condoms also protect both males and females from some STDs. However, sheep skin condoms do not prevent STDs. Because all condoms can slip off during sex, they are not as effective at preventing disease.

Effectiveness

The condom is 86% to 97% effective at preventing pregnancy depending on if it is used correctly. The reason condoms break is usually because a person used it wrong rather than something being wrong with the condom.

✔ **Quick Tip**

How To Use A Condom

1. A condom is placed on the erect penis before any genital contact.

2. For detailed instructions on how to use the condom correctly look on the condom box or wrapper.

3. Never re-use a condom.

4. Never use oil-based lubricants. Lubricants such as Vaseline, hand lotion, or massage oil weaken latex and make condoms break.

How To Get Condoms

Condoms are available in drugstores, family planning clinics, vending machines in restrooms, school-based health centers, and some supermarkets.

Cost

• Ranges from 25 cents each to $2.50 each.

• A pack of 12 condoms range from $5 to $15.

• Condoms are sometimes given away for free at clinics.

Advantages

• Only form of birth control other than abstinence that offers protection against some STDs and HIV.

• Very easy to get.

• Reliable back-up or second method of birth control. A lot of people use the condom with birth control pills. People who use both methods are not only using two effective methods to prevent pregnancy in case one method fails, but they are also getting protection from STDs. The pill does not offer any protection from STDs, but the condom does.

Disadvantages

• Some males or females may be allergic to latex rubber and feel irritation.

♣ It's A Fact!!

• Choose latex condoms. Make sure that the condom is not lubricated with nonoxynol-9. Recent research shows that nonoxynol-9 can increase your risk of STDs because it irritates the lining of the vagina.

• Contraceptive creams, jellies, suppositories, and foam containing anti-sperm agents (other than nonoxynol-9) are the best types of lubricant to use with condoms because they provide additional protection from STDs. Do NOT use oil-based lubricants.

• Do not unroll condoms before putting them on.

• Do not reuse condoms or expose condoms to heat.

• Do not store condoms in wallets. They can get punctured easily in wallets without you even knowing it.

• Always check the expiration date before using a condom. If it is expired, throw it away.

- Condoms do not offer protection from all STDs like herpes and genital warts—which is caused by HPV (Human Papilloma Virus). Both of these STDs can spread or infect areas that the condom does not cover which means a person can still get an STD even when a condom is being used.

The Pill (Oral Contraceptives)

The most common type of birth control pill is the combination pill which has two synthetic or fake hormones in it called, estrogen and progestin which are similar to the hormones the ovaries normally produce. Mini-pills are a type of pill which only contains progestin. When the pill is taken daily and properly, it prevents ovulation or stops the ovaries from releasing an egg.

Effectiveness

When taken according to instructions the pill is 99.9% effective. However, when people do not use the pills correctly they are only 95% to 98% effective. The most common reason for not using the pill correctly are skipping pills and using antibiotics while on the pill without a second method of birth control.

✔ Quick Tip

How To Use The Pill

1. Visit your doctor, family planning clinic, HMO, or health center to be prescribed oral contraceptives and take as directed.

2. Pills must be taken daily. Pregnancy CAN happen anytime after you STOP taking the pill.

3. Take the pill the same time every day.

4. The pill is not effective during the first month of use. A backup method of birth control is needed during this time period.

5. Ask your doctor or other health care provider any questions or concerns you have.

Where To Get Pills

Visit a family planning clinic, HMO, or private doctor for a prescription. Pills may be purchased at a clinic or drugstore.

Cost

A monthly package costs between $15 and $35. The cost is usually less at a clinic. Generic brands can also be purchased which can lower the cost. Be sure you first get a pelvic examination which ranges from about $35-$125, depending on insurance. Pelvic exams are usually cheaper at clinics.

Advantages

• Menstrual periods become more regular.

• Fewer menstrual cramps and a lighter flow during your menstrual period.

• Less iron deficiency anemia, pelvic inflammatory disease (PID), and ectopic (tubal) pregnancies.

• Protection against ovarian and endometrial cancers and non-cancerous breast tumors and ovarian cysts.

♣ It's A Fact!!

Pregnancy can happen if a person does not use the pill correctly. A second form of birth control should be used if:

• pills are missed

• pills are started too late in the cycle.

Also, if you have been prescribed antibiotics MAKE SURE you use a second form of birth control. Antibiotics counteract with the pill and make them less effective or cause them to not work.

Call your clinician/doctor immediately if you have:

• sudden shortness of breath, pain in the abdomen, chest or arm, or blurred, double or loss of vision in one eye

• severe headache

• yellowing of the skin or eyes

• severe depression

• unusual swelling or pain in the legs.

You shouldn't use the pill if you have ever had:

• unexplained vaginal bleeding

• blood clots in the veins

• cancer of the breast or uterus

• a skin cancer called malignant melanoma.

• Women over 35 who smoke more than 15 cigarettes a day should NOT be on the pill.

- Convenient and easy to use.
- Now there are pills available with lower doses of hormones that have fewer side effects.

Disadvantages

- Offers no protection against STDs and HIV.
- May cause side effects ranging from nausea to spotting between periods.
- Must remember to take it everyday.

Depo-Provera (Injectable Progestin)

Depo-Provera is a synthetic or fake hormone which must be injected into a woman's body every 3 months (or 12 weeks) by a doctor or clinician. The hormone is shot into the muscles of the buttock or arm. A thorough physical examination and medical history is required before a person receives the shot. Depo-Provera prevents pregnancy in one of three ways: by causing the ovaries to stop releasing eggs; by thickening the cervical mucus which stops sperm from joining the egg; and by preventing the fertilized egg from implanting into the uterus.

Effectiveness

Better than 99% effective at preventing pregnancy.

How To Use Depo-Provera

A person on Depo-Provera needs to get a shot given by a doctor every three months.

Where To Get Depo-Provera

Depo-Provera must be given by a private doctor, HMO, or family planning clinic since it cannot be purchased in stores.

Cost

- Cost of an examination ranges from $35-$125.
- Cost of each injection ranges from $22-$30.

- Costs are cheaper at clinics.

Advantages

- Does not need to be taken daily or used right before sexual intercourse.

- Prevents pregnancy for 12 weeks.

Disadvantages

- Offers no protection against STDs and HIV.

- Some women suffer from side effects such as hair loss, change in appetite, longer menstrual flow or spotting.

Norplant (Implantable Hormone System)

Norplant is implanted under the skin in the upper arm. It prevents pregnancy by releasing small amounts of progestin, a hormone, into a woman's body. Similar to Depo-Provera, the hormone interferes with ovulation and causes the cervical mucus to thicken.

Effectiveness

Norplant is 99.5 percent effective against preventing pregnancy.

Facts About Getting Norplant

1. First get a physical exam and medical history from your clinician or doctor.

♣ It's A Fact!!

Woman should not use Depo-Provera if they:

- are pregnant

- have unexplained vaginal bleeding

- have ever had cancer of the breast

- have recently had blood clots in the legs, lungs, or eyes

- have a serious liver disease or any kind of growths of the liver

- are allergic to Depo-Provera

- are taking medication for Cushing's syndrome.

Tell your clinician immediately if you have:

- vaginal bleeding that lasts longer and is much heavier than your normal period

- severe headaches

- major depression

- sudden severe abdominal pain.

✤ It's A Fact!!

• Norplant can be removed anytime before the five year removal time period.

• Women should not use Norplant if they: are pregnant; have unexplained vaginal bleeding; are breast feeding in the first six weeks after delivery; have blood clots or inflammation of the veins; have serious liver disease; have ever had breast cancer.

Tell your clinician immediately if:

• you have vaginal bleeding that lasts longer and is heavier than your normal period

• your period is late after a long period of regular cycles

• you have severe abdominal pain

• there is pain, pus, or bleeding at the area where the implant was inserted

• one of the implants seems to be coming out.

2. A clinician will numb a small area in your upper arm and will make one small cut. Six capsules that look like match sticks will be attached under the skin of the arm.

3. The procedure takes about 10 minutes and protection against pregnancy begins within 24 hours after the procedure.

4. A follow-up with the doctor is needed during the first 3 months after the implant.

5. Norplant is removed after five years—at this time it stops working. Getting Norplant removed is similar to getting it inserted. It takes about 15-20 minutes. When the old Norplant is removed, a new one can be inserted at this time.

Where To Get Norplant

Like Depo-Provera, you can get Norplant from a private doctor, HMO, or family planning clinic.

Cost

• Between $500 and $750 for the medical exam, implants, and getting it inserted. This equals a little over $100 a year over a five-year period.

• Removal may cost $100 to $200.

Advantages

- Birth control that lasts up to five years.
- Can be used while breast feeding (six weeks after delivery).
- Does not have to be taken daily.

Disadvantages

- Offers no protection against STDs and HIV.
- Beginning costs are high.
- Some women suffer from side effects.

The Female Condom

The female condom is made out of lubricated polyurethane that fits into the vagina and prevents sperm and other bodily fluids from entering the vagina. There are flexible rings at both ends of the condom and it is inserted like a diaphragm is inserted.

Effectiveness

Because the female condom is more difficult to use and some people may not follow the instructions properly, it is about 79 to 95 percent effective at preventing pregnancy.

How To Use A Female Condom

1. It is recommended to use spermicide before the female condom is inserted.

2. The inner ring fits behind the pubic bone and the outer ring remains outside of the body—instructions on how to use it are on the package. Follow directions carefully.

3. After intercourse, the condom is removed by first squeezing and twisting the outer ring to keep semen inside the condom, then by gently pulling the condom out of the vagina. Once it has been removed, throw it away—do not flush.

Where To Get Female Condoms

Female condoms can be purchased without a prescription at drugstores, clinics, and at some supermarkets.

Cost

About $2.50 each.

Advantages

- Allows females to take responsibility for STD protection.

- Allows females to take responsibility for pregnancy prevention.

- When used correctly, it offers better protection against genital warts and genital herpes.

- It can be inserted before sex.

- It's made of polyurethane which has been proven to offer better protection than latex against viruses such as HIV.

♣ It's A Fact!!

- Stop intercourse if the penis slips between the condom and the walls of the vagina or if the outer ring is pushed into the vagina.

- Do not reuse the condoms.

Disadvantages

- Before you use the female condom, you must completely understand the directions and follow them exactly.

- The inner and outer rings may cause some women discomfort.

- Generally, the female condoms cost more than male condoms.

The Diaphragm And The Cervical Cap

Both the diaphragm and the cervical cap are barrier methods of birth control that fit securely over the cervix—the lowest part of the uterus—to prevent sperm from entering the uterus. The uterus is where the egg is implanted and a baby grows. Both methods of birth control are used with a spermicidal cream or jelly that kills sperm.

Effectiveness

The diaphragm is between 80 and 94 percent effective at preventing preg nancy. The cervical cap is between 80 and 91 percent effective at preventi pregnancy among women who have not had a child. The cervical cap is on 60 to 74 percent effective for women who have had children.

♣ **It's A Fact!!**

- You should not douche while using a diaphragm or cervical cap. As a matter of fact, doctors never recommend douching.

- Women who have had a full-term pregnancy, an abortion or mis- carriage beyond the first three months of pregnancy, or pelvic sur- gery, should check to see if the diaphragm or cervical cap are still the right size.

- The diaphragm should also be checked after a weight gain or loss of 10 or more pounds.

- Check for weak spots or pin holes by holding the diaphragm or cervical cap up to the light.

- Perfumed powder and talc and petroleum jelly can cause damage to both methods.

- Tell your doctor/clinician if:

     you or your partner have any discomfort while the method is in place

     you have problems keeping it in place

     you have irritation or itching in the genital area

     you have frequent bladder infections or unusual discharge from the vagina.

- Never borrow or use someone else's diaphragm or cervical cap.

How To Use The Diaphragm And The Cervical Cap

1. Both methods should always be fitted by a physician or other trained health care provider to get the right size.

2. Place about one tablespoon of spermicide inside the dome of the diaphragm or cervical cap. Your doctor will tell you the proper way to insert and remove the diaphragm/cervical cap.

3. Both methods may be inserted into the vagina up to 2 hours before intercourse and should be left in place for 8 hours after intercourse.

4. The diaphragm and cervical cap should be washed with warm soap and water, rinsed and dried after each use.

Where To Get A Diaphragm Or Cervical Cap

To get the diaphragm or the cervical cap you need a prescription from a doctor, HMO, or family planning clinic. With the prescription, you may purchase them at a drugstore or clinic.

Cost

• Fitting visit may cost between $50 to $125.
• Cervical caps and diaphragms cost between $13 to $25.
• Spermicidal jelly or cream costs about $4 to $8 a kit.

Advantages

• The cervical cap may be left in the vagina for up to 48 hours and still work against preventing pregnancy.
• The diaphragm used with a spermicidal cream or jelly containing nonoxynol-9 may offer some protection against STDs and HIV.

Disadvantages

• An uncomfortable diaphragm may cause pain and cramping especially if it is too big.
• Women need to be very familiar with their reproductive organs and anatomy in order to use the cervical cap correctly.

- Even though side effects are rare with these methods, some women will develop bladder infections from using the diaphragm.

The IUD (Intrauterine Device)

The IUD is a small device made of plastic that contains copper or a natural hormone. It prevents pregnancy by making sperm not able to move, by speeding the movement of the egg through the Fallopian tube, and by stopping the egg from implanting itself. The IUD can be left in place for eight years and is recommended for women who do not want any more children, who have had at least one child and who are in a monogamous relationship (a sexual relationship with only one person). The reason it is not recommended for other women is because the IUD increases a woman's chance of infection and tubal scarring which can lead to infertility or not being able to have children. Only a doctor or other skilled health care provider can insert or remove the IUD.

Effectiveness

The IUD is about 97.4 to 99.2 percent effective at preventing pregnancy.

How To Use The IUD

1. The IUD should be inserted by a physician during the first few days of menstruation.

2. A string is attached to the IUD. After each menstrual period, the string should be checked to ensure that the IUD is in place.

3. After the first six weeks of use, a doctor needs to check to make sure it is in the proper place.

4. Depending on the type of IUD, the amount of time it can stay in a woman's body varies. Progestasert IUDs must be changed every year and ParaGard IUDs can be left in place for up to 10 years.

Where To Get IUDs

To get an IUD visit a private doctor, HMO, or family planning clinic.

♣ It's A Fact!!

- The IUD method of birth control is recommended for women with only ONE sex partner and/or women who have had a baby because the IUD can cause infections which lead to infertility.

- The IUD may cause infection of the fallopian tubes which can cause a woman to not be able to have children. This is why the IUD is not recommended for women who have not yet had any children or women who may want more children in the future. This method is not recommended for teenagers.

- You should not use the IUD if you have:

  unexplained abnormal vaginal bleeding

  a recent history of pelvic infection

  a history of tubal pregnancies

  had an abnormal Pap test recently

  any disease that decreases your ability to fight infections such as leukemia or HIV.

- Tell your physician immediately if you:

  are not able to feel the string attached to the IUD

  have a missed, late, or light period

  have severe cramping or pain that won't stop in the lower abdomen

  have unexplained fever and/or chills

  have pain or bleeding during sex

  have a larger amount than usual or a bad-smelling vaginal discharge.

Cost

$250 to $450—this cost includes the exam, getting it inserted, and a follow-up visit.

Advantages

- The IUD does not change the hormone levels in the body.
- The IUD decreases blood loss during periods and reduces menstrual cramps.
- The IUD works as birth control for up to 10 years.

Disadvantages

- Some women experience side effects ranging from more menstrual cramps to pelvic infections.
- Offers no protection against STDs and HIV.

Foams, Creams, Jellies, Films And Suppositories

These methods are liquids or solids that melt after they are inserted and spread around inside the vagina. They prevent pregnancy by blocking the entrance of the uterus. These methods contain spermicide which kills sperm.

Effectiveness

How well these methods prevent pregnancy range from 74 to 95 percent effective. Effectiveness depends on a person's ability to follow directions. Most often these methods are only 78 percent effective because people may not use them correctly. Foams, creams, jellies, films and suppositories are more effective if used with condoms—more than 99 percent effective at preventing pregnancy when both methods are used.

How To Use Foams, Creams, Jellies, Films And Suppositories

- Follow the instructions on the package carefully.
- Instructions are a little different for each method.
- Usually a person needs to wait 10 minutes between the time the method is inserted to the time they have sex.

- These methods do not work for more than an hour after they have been inserted.

Where To Get Foams, Creams, Jellies, Films And Suppositories

Each of these methods may be purchased without a prescription at drug-stores, some supermarkets, health centers and family planning clinics.

Cost

A kit of foam and gel are about $8-$18. Refills cost $4 to $8. You get between 20 to 40 in each pack.

Advantages

- A person can get these methods without a prescription from a doctor.

Disadvantages

- These methods do not give a person much or any protection against STDs and HIV. Methods that have spermi-cide with nonoxynol-9 in them may only offer some protection.

- One or both partners may be allergic to the spermicides. If allergic, these methods can cause some irritation to the vagina or penis.

> ### ♣ It's A Fact!!
> - Effectiveness depends mostly on being able to follow instructions exactly and very carefully.
>
> - Using a condom with one of these methods, reduces your chance of pregnancy and STDs by a lot.

Fertility Awareness Methods

This method of birth control helps a woman predict when ovulation will happen. Ovulation is when an egg is released from the ovaries and ready for fertilization from a sperm. Women using this method can predict when pregnancy is most likely to happen. They can find out the safe and unsafe days to have sex. There are three different types of fertility awareness methods: basal body temperature method (BBT), cervical mucus method, calendar or rhythm method.

Effectiveness

The more irregular a female's menstrual cycle, the less effective each method is. Teens are more likely to have irregular periods because they have just started their child-bearing years.

BBT is 65 to 85 percent effective at preventing pregnancy. How well it works depends on how regular a woman's menstrual cycle is and how carefully instructions are followed.

Cervical Mucus Method is 78 to 80 percent effective at preventing pregnancy when done correctly.

Calendar method is 85 to 65 percent effective at preventing pregnancy when done correctly.

How To Use Fertility Awareness Methods

BBT

1. Consult with a doctor or trained health care provider to get detailed instructions.

2. Take your temperature every morning before getting out of bed. Every day record the data on a chart.

3. Your temperature rises between 0.4 and 0.8 degrees Fahrenheit on the day of ovulation and remains at this level until your next period.

4. The first three full days after ovulation a woman is fertile. During this time women have the greatest chance of becoming pregnant; therefore, sex should be avoided or a form of birth control should be used.

5. Before a woman can accurately tell when ovulation will happen, it takes 3 to 4 months in a row of recording body temperature.

NOTE: Sperm can live up to 5 days inside a woman's body in the reproductive system. A person needs to remember this and make sure sperm is not inside the reproductive system during the fertile times of the month.

Cervical Mucus Method

1. Consult with a doctor or trained health care provider to get detailed instructions.

2. Observe the changes in your cervical mucus and record the changes daily on a chart. During a woman's menstrual cycle, the cervical mucus varies from dry to white and cloudy to clear and stringy.

3. The consistency of your cervical mucus tells you when you are most fertile or most likely to become pregnant. A few days before ovulation the mucus will become clear and slippery.

Calendar Method

1. Keep track of your menstrual cycles each month by marking on a calendar the days of your period.

2. Consult with a trained health care provider to get detailed instructions.

Where To Learn About BBT, The Mucus Method, And The Calendar Method

Family planning clinics, church centers and health departments can give you more information about these methods.

Cost

Charts for recording information are provided by family planning clinics. They usually cost very little or nothing.

Temperature kits can be purchased at drugstores for $5 to $10.

Advantages

- Most religious groups find these methods of birth control acceptable and not against any of their beliefs.

- There are no hormonal side effects and little cost involved.

- BBT helps women understand and learn about their bodies and their fertility.

- BBT is very helpful for women who want to become pregnant.

Disadvantages

- Offers no protection against STDs and HIV.

- Sickness and not enough sleep can cause false temperature readings when relying on the BBT method.

- The cervical mucus method will not work as well if a woman has a vaginal infection or if a woman is using any products or medications for the vaginal area.

- The calendar method and BBT are not recommended for teens and for women with irregular periods.

- Some women do not produce enough mucus to track changes throughout the cycle.

♣ **It's A Fact!!**

- Women with irregular periods or irregular body temperature patterns should NOT use these methods.

- It is very important to be exact when using these methods.

- To prevent pregnancy with these methods, women must not have sex or must use a form of birth control during times of the month that pregnancy is possible.

Surgical Sterilization

Sterilization is a form of birth control that requires surgery. This method is meant to be permanent. Tubal sterilization is the surgery for women to become sterile or to not be able to have children. A vasectomy is the surgery for men to become sterile. Surgical sterilization for both men and women is a procedure done in an operating room where the transport tubes—for women, the fallopian tubes; for men, the vas deferens—are either tied shut or cut so that the sperm or eggs can't get through.

Effectiveness

Sterilization is 98 to 99.4 percent effective at preventing pregnancy. How sterilization is used:

1. Both men and women considering sterilization should first get a physical exam and complete a health history. A person needs to get all the facts before deciding to have this operation.

2. For both men and women who have gone through sterilization, a back up method of birth control should be used after the surgery. Women need to use a second method of birth control until their first menstrual cycle and men need to use a second method of birth control for the next 20 ejaculations.

Where To Get The Procedure Done

- A vasectomy may be performed as an out-patient in a hospital or in a medical office under local (the person is awake) anesthesia.

- Tubal sterilization can also be done as an out-patient procedure and must be done by a physician in a hospital or clinic. This procedure can be performed under local or general (the person is asleep) anesthesia and is often done following another gynecologic procedure, like delivering a baby.

Cost

A vasectomy costs between $240 and $1,000.

Tubal sterilization is more expensive because the costs include a physician, surgical fees, hospital costs, and anesthesia fees. Costs range from $1,000 to $2,500.

♣ It's A Fact!!

- Pregnancy is rare after sterilization, but it may happen. If you have late or missed periods, severe lower abdominal pain, and/or nausea and breast tenderness contact your physician immediately.

- Sterilization is best for individuals who are sure they do not want any more children.

- A person may become pregnant after having a tubal sterilization if the tubes rejoin or if an error happened during the surgery.

- Males may not be sterile immediately after the operation and should use a second method of birth control during the first 20 ejaculations.

Advantages

- Permanent protection against pregnancy.
- One-time expense only.
- The procedure is effective and safe.

Disadvantages

- No protection against STDs and HIV.
- Mild side effects may occur after both operations.
- A person may decide in the future they want to have children.
- A person may experience pain for some time after the procedure.

Withdrawal (Coitus Interruptus)

Withdrawal is the removal of the penis from the vagina before ejaculation occurs. Even though some people practice withdrawal, it is not a form of birth control. If you practice withdrawal because you think it prevents pregnancy, think again. This method is not very effective and should not be practiced. One reason it is not very effective is because of pre-ejaculatory fluid, which is a fluid that the penis secretes during sex. Even though this fluid happens before ejaculation, or cum, it does contain sperm.

Effectiveness

This method is between 75 and 96 percent effective at preventing pregnancy, if done correctly.

How To Use Withdrawal

Ejaculation must happen outside of the vagina and away from the outside parts of the female's genitalia.

♣ It's A Fact!!
When a guy gets excited sexually a small amount of fluid known as pre-ejaculatory fluid comes out of the tip of the penis. Because the pre-ejaculatory fluid may contain sperm, a woman could get pregnant even if ejaculation did not happen inside the vagina.

Cost

There is no cost.

Advantages

The method uses no chemicals or devices.

Disadvantages

- Offers no protection against HIV and other STDs.

- Withdrawal requires a great amount of self control, and trust.

- During sex, it is difficult for men to know exactly when they will or have ejaculated. Ejaculation can happen without either partner knowing it.

Sources

Meeks, L., Heit, P., & Burt, J. (1993). *Education for Sexuality and HIV/AIDS.* Meeks Heit Publishing Company, Inc.

Ortho Pharmaceutical Corporation. "Contraception: The Choice Is Yours— A Guide to Choosing a Method That's Right for You." November 1991. PO3-101.

Planned Parenthood Federation of America, Inc. "Facts about Birth Control." March 1994.

San Francisco AIDS Foundation. "Condoms for Couples." 1996.

Chapter 33

The Truth About Latex Condoms

Sexually involved individuals owe it to themselves to get accurate, unbiased information about condoms and the part they play in preventing unwanted pregnancies and sexually transmitted diseases.

This chapter includes information on both their reliability and their effective use.

Effectiveness

- Condoms are only effective when used consistently and correctly.[1]

- Using a condom during intercourse is more than 10,000 times safer than not using a condom.[2]

- Condoms are 98 percent effective in preventing pregnancy when used correctly[3]—and up to 99.9 percent effective in reducing the risk of STD transmission when combined with spermicide.[4]

- The first-year pregnancy failure rate among typical condom users averages about 12 percent and includes pregnancies resulting from errors in condom use.[5]

About This Chapter: Text in this chapter is from "The Facts Of Life: A Guide For Teens And Their Families," reprinted with permission of SIECUS, the Sexuality Information and Education Council of the United States (SIECUS), 130 W. 42nd Street, Suite 350, New York, NY 10036-7802. Phone: 212-819-9770, Fax: 212-819-9776, E-Mail: siecus@siecus.org, Website: www.siecus.org. © 2002.

- Studies of hundreds of couples show that consistent condom use is possible when sexual partners have the skills and motivation.[6]

Regulations And Tests

- In the United States, manufacturers follow the voluntary performance standards for condoms established by the American Society for Testing and Materials and recommended by the Food and Drug Administration (FDA).[7]

- Before packaging, every condom is tested electronically for defects. In addition, the FDA tests samples from every batch using water leak and air burst tests.[8]

- The average batch of condoms tests better than 99.7 percent defect free.[9]

- During the water leak test, if there is a leak in more than four per 1,000 condoms, the entire lot is discarded.[10]

- Laboratory studies show that sperm and disease-causing organisms (including HIV) cannot pass through intact latex condoms.[11]

HIV Transmission

- Condom use substantially reduces the risk of HIV transmission.[12]

- A study published in *The New England Journal of Medicine* observed heterosexual couples where one was HIV-positive and the other was HIV-negative (sero-discordant couples), for an average of 20 months. Findings included:[13]

  - No seroconversion occurred among the 124 couples who used condoms consistently and correctly for vaginal or anal intercourse.[14]

  - 10 percent of the HIV-negative partners (12 of 121) couples became infected when condoms were used inconsistently for vaginal or anal intercourse.[15]

  - Of the 121 couples who used condoms inconsistently, 61 used condoms for at least half of their sexual contacts ad 60 rarely or never used condoms. The rate of seroconversion was 10.3 percent for the couples using condoms inconsistently and 15 percent for couples not using condoms.[16]

- A study published in *The Journal of Acquired Immune Deficiency Syndromes* observed sero-discordant heterosexual couples and showed that only three out of 171 who consistently and correctly used condoms became HIV infected; eight out of 55 who used condoms inconsistently became HIV infected; and eight out of 79 who never used condoms became HIV infected.[17]

Consistent And Correct Condom Use*

Individuals who use condoms to prevent unwanted pregnancies and STDs must understand the meaning of consistent and correct condom use.

Consistent Use: Use a condom with every act of sexual intercourse, from start to finish, including penile-vaginal intercourse, oral and anal intercourse.

Correct Use: Store condoms in a cool place out of direct sunlight (not in wallets or glove compartments). Latex will become brittle from changes in temperature, rough handling or age. Don't use damaged, discolored, brittle or sticky condoms.

- Check the expiration date.

- Carefully open the condom package—teeth or fingernails can tear the condom.

- Use a new condom every time a person has sexual intercourse.

- Put on the condom after the penis is erect and before it touches any part of a partner's body. If a penis is uncircumcised, the person must pull back the foreskin before putting on the condom.

- Put on the condom by pinching the reservoir tip and unrolling it all the way down the shaft of the penis from head to base. If the condom does not have a reservoir tip, pinch it to leave a half-inch space at the head of the penis for semen to collect after ejaculation.

- Withdraw the penis immediately if the condom breaks during sexual intercourse and put on a new condom before resuming intercourse.

When a condom breaks, use spermicidal foam or jelly and speak to a health-care provider about emergency contraception.

• Use only water-based lubrication. Do not use oil-based lubricants such as cooking/vegetable oil, baby oil, hand lotion or petroleum jelly— these will cause the condom to deteriorate and break.

• Withdraw the penis immediately after ejaculation, while the penis is still erect, grasp the rim of the condom between the fingers and slowly withdraw the penis (with the condom still on) so that no semen is spilled.

*Items under the heading "Consistent and Correct Use" are from the U.S. Centers for Disease Control and Prevention (CDC), "Questions and Answers About Male Latex Condoms to Prevent Sexual Transmission of HIV," CDC Update (Centers for Disease Control: Atlanta, GA: April 1997).

Resources

1. U.S. Centers for Disease Control (CDC), "Questions and Answers about Male Latex Condoms to Prevent Sexual Transmission of HIV," CDC Update (CDC: Atlanta, GA: April 1997).

2. R. F. Carey, et al, "Effectiveness of Latex Condoms As a Barrier to Human Immunodeficiency Virus-Sized Particles under the Conditions of Simulated Use," *Sexually Transmitted Diseases*, 19, no. 4 (July/Aug. 1992), p.230.

3. J. Trussell, et al, "Contraceptive Failure in the United States: An Update," *Studies in Family Planning*, 21, no. 1 (Jan./Feb. 1990), p. 52.

4. P. Kestelman and J. Trussell, "Efficacy of the Simultaneous Use of Condoms and Spermicides," *Family Planning Perspectives*, 23, no. 5 (Sept./Oct. 1991), p. 227.

5. R. A. Hatcher, et al, *Contraceptive Technology*, Sixteenth Revised Edition (New York: Irvington Publishers, Inc., 1994), pp. 154-55.

6. CDC (April 1997).

7. R. A. Hatcher, et al (1994), pp. 159-60; CDC (April 1997).

8. R. A. Hatcher, et al (1994), p. 160; CDC (April 1997).

9. CDC (April 1997).

10. Consumers Union of the United States, Inc. "How Reliable Are Condoms?" *Consumer Reports* (May 1995), p. 3.

11. CDC, "Facts about Condoms and Their Use in Preventing HIV and Other STDs," *Condoms and STD/HIV Prevention* (July 1993), p.2.

12. I. De Vincenzi, "A Longitudinal Study of Human Immunodeficiency Virus Transmission by Heterosexual Partners," *The New England Journal of Medicine*, 331, no. 6 (Aug. 11, 1994), p. 341-6.

13. I. De Vincenzi (Aug. 11, 1994), p. 341.

14. I. De Vincenzi (Aug. 11, 1994), p. 343.

15. Ibid.

16. I. De Vincenzi (Aug. 11, 1994), p. 342-4.

17. A. Saracco, et al, "Man-to-Woman Sexual Transmission of HIV: Longitudinal Study of 343 Steady Partners of Infected Men," *Journal of Acquired Immune Deficiency Syndromes*, 6, no. 5 (1993), p. 499.

Chapter 34

Emergency Contraception: "The Morning-After Pill"

What Is It?

An emergency dose of certain birth control pills that prevents the sperm from meeting the egg or prevents the egg from attaching to the wall of the uterus (also called "the morning-after pill")

How Does It Work?

The pills contain hormones that can prevent pregnancy when taken in larger-than-normal doses. The first dose of pills can be taken within 72 hours of unprotected intercourse. The next dose of pills is usually taken 12 hours after the first set or however prescribed by the doctor. Each dose is made up of two, four, or five pills, depending on the type of pill.

What Is The Failure Rate?**

Perfect-use failure rate 25%.

About This Chapter: This information was provided by TeensHealth, one of the largest resources online for medically reviewed health information written for parents, kids, and teens. For more articles like this one, visit www.TeensHealth.org, or www.KidsHealth.org. © 2001 The Nemours Center for Children's Health Media, a division of The Nemours Foundation.

☞ **Remember!!**

Emergency contraception is not recommended as a regular birth control
method. Instead, it is used for emergencies only.
If you are having sex and the condom breaks or slips
off, if your diaphragm or cervical cap slips out of place,
or you forget your birth control pills 2 days in a row,
you may want to consider using emergency
contraception. It is also available to teens
who are forced to have unprotected
sex against their will.

Protection Against STDs?

No. A condom must be used to protect against STDs.

Possible Side Effects?

Nausea, vomiting, breast tenderness, and headache.

Who Uses It?

Emergency contraception is not recommended as a regular birth control
method. Instead, it is used for emergencies only. If you are having sex and
the condom breaks or slips off, if your diaphragm or cervical cap slips out of
place, or you forget your birth control pills 2 days in a row, you may want to
consider using emergency contraception. It is also available to teens who are
forced to have unprotected sex against their will.

How Do You Get It?

Emergency contraception must be prescribed by a doctor. It is also available at many health clinics. You must call as soon as possible after having
unprotected sex because it is most effective during the first 72 hours. Call
(888) NOT-2-LATE.

How Much Does It Cost?

Depending on the type of pills that are prescribed, the emergency contraception pill costs between $8 and $35. It may be covered by your parents' health insurance.

**NOTE: there are two percentages provided to describe the failure rates for each birth control method:

- *Perfect-use failure rate:* the percentage of people using the method correctly who will become pregnant anyway after 1 year of using that method. (For example, if the "perfect-use failure rate" is 2%, then that means 2 out of 100 people who are used that method [and always used it perfectly] will become pregnant after using it for a year.)

- *Typical-use failure rate:* the percentage that's closer to reality because most people don't use birth control perfectly each time. This is then the percentage of people who will become pregnant after a year of using that particular form of birth control.

☞ **Remember!!**
Abstinence (the decision to not have sex) is the only method with a 0% failure rate.

Part 6

Avoiding Sexually Transmitted Diseases

Chapter 35

An Introduction To Sexually Transmitted Diseases

Sexually transmitted diseases (STDs), once called venereal diseases, are among the most common infectious diseases in the United States today. More than 20 STDs have now been identified, and they affect more than 13 million men and women in this country each year. The annual comprehensive cost of STDs in the United States is estimated to be well in excess of $10 billion.

Understanding the basic facts about STDs—the ways in which they are spread, their common symptoms, and how they can be treated—is the first step toward prevention. The National Institute of Allergy and Infectious Diseases (NIAID), a part of the National Institutes of Health, has prepared a series of fact sheets about STDs to provide this important information. Research investigators supported by NIAID are looking for better methods of diagnosis and more effective treatments, as well as for vaccines and topical microbicides to prevent STDs. It is important to understand at least five key points about all STDs in this country today:

1. STDs affect men and women of all backgrounds and economic levels. They are most prevalent among teenagers and young adults. Nearly two-thirds of all STDs occur in people younger than 25 years of age.

About This Chapter: Text in this chapter is from a fact sheet produced by the National Institutes of Allergy and Infectious Diseases (NIAID), July 1999. Available online at http://www.niaid.nih.gov/factsheets/stdinfo.htm.

2. The incidence of STDs is rising, in part because in the last few decade
    young people have become sexually active earlier yet are marrying late
    In addition, divorce is more common. The net result is that sexual
    active people today are more likely to have multiple sex partners durir
    their lives and are potentially at risk for developing STDs.

3. Most of the time, STDs cause no symptoms, particularly in wome.
    When and if symptoms develop, they may be confused with those (
    other diseases not transmitted through sexual contact. Even when a
    STD causes no symptoms, however, a person who is infected may l
    able to pass the disease on to a sex partner. That is why many docto
    recommend periodic testing or screening for people who have more tha
    one sex partner.

4. Health problems caused by STDs tend to be more severe and more fre
    quent for women than for men, in part because the frequency of asymp
    tomatic infection means that many women do not seek care until seriou
    problems have developed.

    •   Some STDs can spread into the uterus (womb) and fallopian tubes
        to cause pelvic inflammatory disease (PID), which in turn is a
        major cause of both infertility and ectopic (tubal) pregnancy. The
        latter can be fatal.

    •   STDs in women also may be associated with cervical cancer. One
        STD, human papillomavirus infection (HPV), causes genital warts
        and cervical and other genital cancers.

    •   STDs can be passed from a mother to her baby before, during, or
        immediately after birth; some of these infections of the newborn
        can be cured easily, but others may cause a baby to be permanently
        disabled or even die.

5. When diagnosed and treated early, many STDs can be treated effec
    tively. Some infections have become resistant to the drugs used to trea
    them and now require newer types of antibiotics. Experts believe tha
    having STDs other than AIDS increases one's risk for becoming in
    fected with the AIDS virus.

HIV Infection And AIDS

AIDS (acquired immunodeficiency syndrome) was first reported in the United States in 1981. It is caused by the human immunodeficiency virus (HIV), a virus that destroys the body's ability to fight off infection. An estimated 900,000 people in the United States are currently infected with HIV. People who have AIDS are very susceptible to many life-threatening diseases, called opportunistic infections, and to certain forms of cancer. Transmission of the virus primarily occurs during sexual activity and by sharing needles used to inject intravenous drugs. If you have any questions about HIV infection or AIDS, you can call the AIDS Hotline confidential toll-free number: 1-800-342-AIDS.

✔ Quick Tip

If you have any questions about HIV infection or AIDS, call the AIDS Hotline: 1-800-342-AIDS.

Chlamydial Infection

This infection is now the most common of all bacterial STDs, with an estimated 4 to 8 million new cases occurring each year. In both men and women, chlamydial infection may cause an abnormal genital discharge and burning with urination. In women, untreated chlamydial infection may lead to pelvic inflammatory disease, one of the most common causes of ectopic pregnancy and infertility in women. Many people with chlamydial infection, however, have few or no symptoms of infection. Once diagnosed with chlamydial infection, a person can be treated with an antibiotic.

Genital Herpes

Genital herpes affects an estimated 60 million Americans. Approximately 500,000 new cases of this incurable viral infection develop annually. Herpes infections are caused by herpes simplex virus (HSV). The major symptoms of herpes infection are painful blisters or open sores in the genital area. These may be preceded by a tingling or burning sensation in the legs, buttocks, or genital region. The herpes sores usually disappear within two to three weeks, but the virus remains in the body for life and the lesions may recur from time to time. Severe or frequently recurrent genital herpes is treated with one of several antiviral drugs that are available by prescription. These drugs help control the symptoms but do not eliminate the herpes virus from the body. Suppressive antiviral therapy can be used to prevent

♣ It's A Fact!!
Genital herpes is caused by the herpes simplex virus (HSV). It infects about a half a million people every year, and there is no cure. Pregnant women with HSV can pass the virus to their babies. Untreated HSV in newborns can lead to serious consequences.

occurrences and perhaps transmission. Women who acquire genital herpes during pregnancy can transmit the virus to their babies. Untreated HSV infection in newborns can result in mental retardation and death.

Genital Warts

Genital warts (also called venereal warts or condylomata acuminata) are caused by human papillomavirus, a virus related to the virus that causes common skin warts. Genital warts usually first appear as small, hard painless bumps in the vaginal area, on the penis, or around the anus. If untreated, they may grow and develop a fleshy, cauliflower-like appearance. Genital warts infect an estimated 1 million Americans each year. Genital warts can be injected with a type of interferon. If the warts are very large, they can be removed by surgery.

Gonorrhea

Approximately 400,000 cases of gonorrhea are reported to the U.S. Centers for Disease Control and Prevention (CDC) each year in this country. The most common symptoms of gonorrhea are a discharge from the vagina or penis and painful or difficult urination. The most common and serious complications occur in women and, as with chlamydial infection, these complications include PID, ectopic pregnancy, and infertility. Historically, penicillin has been used to treat gonorrhea, but in the last decade, four types of antibiotic resistance have emerged. New antibiotics or combinations of drugs must be used to treat these resistant strains.

Syphilis

The incidence of syphilis has increased and decreased dramatically in recent years, with more than 11,000 cases reported in 1996. The first symptoms of syphilis may go undetected because they are very mild and disappear spontaneously. The initial symptom is a chancre; it is usually a painless open sore that usually appears on the penis or around or in the vagina. It can also occur near the mouth, anus, or on the hands. If untreated, syphilis may go on to more advanced stages, including a transient rash and, eventually, serious involvement of the heart and central nervous system. The full course of the disease can take years. Penicillin remains the most effective drug to treat people with syphilis.

Others

Other diseases that may be sexually transmitted include trichomoniasis, bacterial vaginosis, cytomegalovirus infections, scabies, and pubic lice.

STDs in pregnant women are associated with a number of adverse outcomes, including spontaneous abortion and infection in the newborn. Low birth weight and prematurity appear to be associated with STDs, including chlamydial infection and trichomoniasis. Congenital or perinatal infection (infection that occurs around the time of birth) occurs in 30 to 70 percent of infants born to infected mothers, and complications may include pneumonia, eye infections, and permanent neurologic damage.

What Can You Do To Prevent STDs?

The best way to prevent STDs is to avoid sexual contact with others. If you decide to be sexually active, there are things that you can do to reduce your risk of developing an STD.

- Have a mutually monogamous sexual relationship with an uninfected partner.

- Correctly and consistently use a male condom.

- Use clean needles if injecting intravenous drugs.

- Prevent and control other STDs to decrease susceptibility to HIV infection and to reduce your infectiousness if you are HIV-infected.

- Delay having sexual relations as long as possible. The younger people are when having sex for the first time, the more susceptible they become to developing an STD. The risk of acquiring an STD also increases with the number of partners over a lifetime.

Anyone who is sexually active should:

- Have regular checkups for STDs even in the absence of symptoms, and especially if having sex with a new partner. These tests can be done during a routine visit to the doctor's office.

- Learn the common symptoms of STDs. Seek medical help immediately if any suspicious symptoms develop, even if they are mild.

- Avoid having sex during menstruation. HIV-infected women are probably more infectious, and HIV-uninfected women are probably more susceptible to becoming infected during that time.

♣ **It's A Fact!!**
Sexually transmitted diseases (STDs), once called venereal diseases, are among the most common infectious diseases in the United States today. More than 20 STDs have now been identified, and they affect more than 13 million men and women in this country each year. The annual comprehensive cost of STDs in the United States is estimated to be well in excess of $10 billion.

- Avoid anal intercourse, but if practiced, use a male condom.

- Avoid douching because it removes some of the normal protective bacteria in the vagina and increases the risk of getting some STDs.

Anyone diagnosed as having an STD should:

- Be treated to reduce the risk of transmitting an STD to an infant.

- Discuss with a doctor the possible risk of transmission in breast milk and whether commercial formula should be substituted.

- Notify all recent sex partners and urge them to get a checkup.

- Follow the doctor's orders and complete the full course of medication prescribed. A follow-up test to ensure that the infection has been cured is often an important step in treatment.
- Avoid all sexual activity while being treated for an STD.

Sometimes people are too embarrassed or frightened to ask for help or information. Most STDs are readily treated, and the earlier a person seeks treatment and warns sex partners about the disease, the less likely the disease will do irreparable physical damage, be spread to others or, in the case of a woman, be passed on to a newborn baby.

Private doctors, local health departments, and STD and family planning clinics have information about STDs. In addition, the American Social Health Association (ASHA) provides free information and keeps lists of clinics and private doctors who provide treatment for people with STDs. ASHA has a national toll-free telephone number, 1-800-227-8922. The phone number for the Herpes Hotline, also run by ASHA, is 919-361-8488. Callers can get information from the ASHA hotline without leaving their names.

Research

STDs cause physical and emotional suffering to millions and are costly to individuals and to society as a whole. NIAID conducts and supports many research projects designed to improve methods of prevention, and to find better ways to diagnose and treat these diseases. NIAID also supports several large university-based STD research centers.

Within the past few years, NIAID-supported research has resulted in new tests to diagnose some STDs faster and more accurately. New drug treatments for STDs are under investigation by NIAID researchers. This is especially important because some STDs are becoming resistant to the standard drugs. In addition, vaccines are being developed or tested for effectiveness in preventing several STDs, including AIDS, chlamydial infection, genital herpes, and gonorrhea.

It is up to each individual to learn more about STDs and then make choices about how to minimize the risk of acquiring these diseases and spreading them to others. Knowledge of STDs, as well as honesty and openness

with sex partners and with one's doctor, can be very important in reducir
the incidence and complications of sexually transmitted diseases.

Table 35.1. Sexually Transmitted Diseases And The Organisms
Responsible

Disease	Organism(s)
Acquired Immunodeficiency Syndrome (AIDS)	Human immunodeficiency virus
Bacterial vaginosis	*Bacteroides* *Gardnerella vaginalis* *Mobiluncus spp.* *Mycoplasma hominis* *Ureaplasma urealyticum*
Chancroid	*Haemophilus ducreyi*
Chlamydial infections	*Chlamydia trachomatis*
Cytomegalovirus infections	Cytomegalovirus
Genital herpes	Herpes simplex virus
Genital (venereal) warts	Human papillomavirus
Gonorrhea	*Neisseria gonorrhoeae*
Granuloma inguinale (donovanosis)	*Calymmatobacterium granulomatis*
Leukemia-Lymphoma/Myelopathy	HTLV-I and II
Lymphogranuloma venereum	*Chlamydia trachomatis*
Molluscum contagiosum	Molluscum contagiosum virus
Pubic lice	*Phthirus pubis*
Scabies	*Sarcoptes scabiei*
Syphilis	*Treponema pallidum*
Trichomoniasis	*Trichomonas vaginalis*
Vaginal yeast infections	*Candida albicans*

Chapter 36

Intimate Danger

Do you think practicing safe sex is simply a matter of using condoms? Did you know there are sexually transmitted diseases more widespread and easier to get than HIV? You're going to be stunned by the following story. It's about teens and young adults who think they know how to protect themselves. But as Perri Peltz learned, when it comes to sex, a lot of people don't know the rules have changed.

The following conversation is from the transcript of "Intimate Danger," which aired on the news program *20/20*, September 3, 1999.

Jennie Miller: I was a sophomore in college. And it was somebody that I didn't know very well. I had had an abnormal Pap a few months before I noticed the bumps.

Melissa Webber: We'd done the right things. We'd been in a monogamous relationship. It didn't seem like a possibility that I could have herpes.

Unidentified Woman: The first time I had sex with anybody, I got chlamydia. So one week I was a virgin, and two weeks later, I had an STD.

Perri Peltz, ABC News: All it takes is one time, and you can get a sexually transmitted disease. Even in this age of the AIDS virus and safe sex, STDs

like chlamydia and genital warts are rampant. One in five Americans ha
herpes. The fact is, your chance of getting an STD by the time you are 2
years old is an overwhelming one in three.

Dr. Penny Hitchcock, National Institutes of Health: I would call that an epi
demic.

Perri Peltz: Dr. Penny Hitchcock heads the sexually transmitted disease
branch at the National Institutes of Health and says the most stunning fac
is the age groups hardest hit by STDs—teens and young adults.

Dr. Penny Hitchcock: These kids are not promiscuous. They're practicing
serial monogamy. A partner a year, let's say. If you start having sex at 15, by
the time you are 24, in terms of partners of partners, you've been exposed to
over 500 people.

Perri Peltz: And exposed to all the possible diseases those people migh
have.

Jennie Miller: I found some bumps that, you know, hadn't been there the
week before.

Perri Peltz: Jennie Miller started having sex when she was 18 years old
Just over a year later, she learned she was infected with HPV, the human
papilloma virus. When the doctor told you that, Jennie, what did you think

Jennie Miller: There was a lot of shame. And the first thing that came
into my mind was, "I am never going to have sex again." But, you know
nobody—I'll never date again.

Perri Peltz: But that's the least of her worries. HPV is incurable and contagious. And in Jennie's case, she contracted two forms—one which cause
genital warts and the other which can cause a more serious problem—cervical cancer.

Dr. Penny Hitchcock: Two hundred fifty-thousand women a year globally have
died of cervical cancer due to HPV infection. That's five million women that.

Perri Peltz: Died?

Dr. Penny Hitchcock: Who are dead because of HPV infection.

Perri Peltz: Cervical cancer is curable if detected early. So regular pap smears are important. But STDs don't discriminate. They attack both women and men. Which is why it's surprising that most people think they are not at risk and know very little about the subject. How many of you know what HPV is?

1st Male College Student: I don't even know what that is.

2nd Male College Student: No. I never heard of HPV.

Perri Peltz: You never heard of it? These young men are college students in Minneapolis. What about some of the others? Herpes—who knows what the symptoms are? Ryan, do you know what the symptoms are?

Ryan: No clue.

Perri Peltz: Are you concerned about getting it?

Ryan: No.

Perri Peltz: Why?

Ryan: The people that I do stuff with I know are safe and—and I don't feel like I'm too much at risk.

Perri Peltz: But no one can really be sure. As unbelievable as it seems, people who know they are infected often don't tell their partners. Jennie, who works part-time at a women's health clinic, never told her ex-boyfriend.

Jennie Miller: I didn't tell him, no. I haven't told him.

Perri Peltz: So you're somebody who works in a clinic setting. You know better than anyone that not telling your partner that you have an STD is the exact way that these things are spread.

Jennie Miller: Yes.

Perri Peltz: And yet, you decided not to tell?

Jennie Miller: It's just that huge fear of rejection.

Perri Peltz: In your current relationship, you did tell your partner?

Jennie Miller: Yes.

Perri Peltz: How did you do that?

Jennie Miller: I told him that I had it. And I kind of, you know, watched his face. And he didn't freak out. So I thought that was a good sign.

Perri Peltz: Jennie says she and her boyfriend use condoms to reduce his risk of getting HPV. But don't assume condoms are foolproof. They cannot protect you against HPV or herpes. These infections, unlike other STDs, can be spread by simple skin contact, which need not involve sexual intercourse. It happened to Melissa Webber, a 20-year-old engineering student who got genital herpes from a common cold sore on her fiancé's mouth.

Melissa Webber: After an experience with oral sex, it was a week later, I started noticing red bumps, the fever. They were open sores. It felt like pouring lemon juice into an open paper cut. It was very painful.

Perri Peltz: And the way Melissa got it surprised them both.

Melissa Webber: It never entered my mind that this could have happened from oral sex. And that the same virus that causes a cold sore could have caused this horrible pain that I was having now.

Perri Peltz: Though medication can help control outbreaks, herpes is incurable, and it is highly contagious even when there are no visible sores. And having herpes or any other STD, for that matter, puts you at an increased risk of getting the AIDS virus. Sexually transmitted diseases can make their presence known by a variety of symptoms. HPV can produce itching and wart-like bumps. You can spot herpes sometimes by the painful blistering sores. And the bacterial STDs—chlamydia, gonorrhea and syphilis—can charge a discharge and a burning sensation. But this may surprise you. More often than not, these same STDs typically show no symptoms at all. So that means with no visible signs, you may not know if the person you are with is infected. Or for that matter, if you are infected yourself.

Even worse, STDs can have long-term consequences. Among them, chlamydia or gonorrhea, if undetected and left untreated, can leave you sterile and infertile. Just ask Kim Orlando.

Kim Orlando: I became violently ill. I had 105 fever, severe, severe abdominal cramps, throwing up.

Perri Peltz: A few years ago, Kim was diagnosed with PID—pelvic inflammatory disease—a severe infection of the upper reproductive tract. The cause? Undetected chlamydia. But that wasn't the worst news.

Kim Orlando: The conclusion was, yes, that I was infertile. My tubes had been damaged beyond repair.

Perri Peltz: Chlamydia, a simple bacterial STD that can be cured with antibiotics changed Kim's life forever. Kim is now married to a man she met several years later. They have two children, one adopted and one after many attempts of in vitro fertilization.

Kim Orlando: I was sexually active, and I needed to take care, and I didn't. And I was an educated person. Had I had the information, maybe this wouldn't have happened to me.

Melissa Webber: We have some safer sex information packets.

Dr. Penny Hitchcock: Education and having information is the first step to making good decisions. And prevention, I think, is really where our emphasis needs to be.

Perri Peltz: And that means condom use, which again only protects you from some types of STDs. The most important thing doctors say is if you are sexually active, you and your partner should get tested twice a year. For most STDs, it involves no more than a blood or urine sample, though there is currently no test for HPV. There is one thing that is certain.

Jennie Miller: It doesn't take sleeping with 10 people or 20 people. You can sleep with one person and get an STD.

Kim Orlando: One single act of sex can change your life dramatically.

Hugh Downs: Experts remind us that abstinence is the only absolute protection against sexually transmitted disease. Don't assume that you are safe just because you are in a monogamous relationship and using condoms. For more information on sexually transmitted disease, including information on how to reach the national STD hotline, log on to our website, www.abcnews.com.

Chapter 37

How Are HIV And STDs Spread?

STDs are spread easily by sexual touch with any part of the body which carries the infection, such as the penis, vagina, anus, and even the mouth. STDs include diseases such as gonorrhea, syphilis, HIV, Chlamydia, genital warts (HPV) and herpes. We now know that if you have an STD it is much easier to become infected with HIV. In 1990 alone, more than three million teenagers became infected with STDs.

Probably by now you know that HIV is the virus that causes AIDS. Because HIV is a very fragile virus, it is hard to become infected with HIV unless you put yourself at risk. The truth is you probably will not become infected with HIV if you understand how it is transmitted and if you always take actions to protect yourself.

Here is how most people become infected with HIV:

• By sharing needles and works to shoot drugs or steroids with someone who is infected with HIV.

About This Chapter: "How Are HIV & STDs Spread?" (available online at http://www.siecus.org/teen/teen0011.htm) and "Safer Sex," (available online at http://www.siecus.org/teen/teen0012.html), both reprinted with permission of SIECUS, the Sexuality Information and Education Council of the United States (SIECUS), 130 W. 42nd Street, Suite 350, New York, NY 10036-9770. Phone: 212-819-9770, Fax: 212-819-9776, E-Mail: siecus@siecus.org, Website: www.siecus.org. © 2002.

- Sharing needles for ear piercing or tattooing can also cause HIV infection.

- Taking part in any type of unprotected sexual intercourse—anal, oral or vaginal.

- Children who are born to HIV-positive women may also be infected with HIV.

Remember, an HIV-positive person may not look sick and probably feels healthy. That person may not even know he or she is HIV-positive. But, an HIV-positive person can infect a sexual partner, whether that partner is heterosexual, gay, lesbian, or bisexual.

☞ Remember!!

STDs and HIV are spread by sexual touch with parts of the body that carry the infection, including the penis, vagina, anus, and even the mouth. You can learn ways to show your affection and express your sexual interest or attraction, but that don't put you or your partner at risk for STDs, HIV, or getting pregnant.

Safer Sex

Many adults say that they only safe sex is no sex, meaning not taking part in sexual intercourse. Sexual abstinence is the only 100% effective way to protect ourselves from getting pregnancy or an STD.

If you do become involved in a sexual relationship, you need to protect yourself from getting HIV and other sexually transmitted diseases (STDs). You also need to find ways to protect yourself from an unplanned pregnancy or from getting your partner pregnant. There are a lot of sexual activities that people enjoy that will not put you at risk for becoming infected with HIV or other STDs. Some of them may surprise you because you may not think that they are sexual activities at all. Remember that sexuality is more than just having sex, or taking part in sexual intercourse, and there are many ways of expressing how you feel about someone. Of course, not everybody enjoys all sexual activities and that's okay. And, many teenagers choose not to have any kind of sex at all, or express their sexuality with another person, and that's okay too.

Here are some ways to show your affection and express your sexual interest or attraction that can make you feel good, but that don't put you or your partner at risk for STDs, HIV or getting pregnant:

- Dry Kissing. Kissing on the lips and mouth, ears, neck, etc.

- Flirting. Catching someone's attention and showing your sexual interest by a look, words or special actions.

- Holding Hands. Holding another person's hands.

- Hugging. Holding someone close to you and giving or getting hugs.

- Massage. Rubbing, pressing, gently touching or firmly stroking another's body, perhaps with special massage oils—this can also help with pain and muscle tension.

- Back Rubs or Foot Rubs. A way of touching with light hand strokes or pressure on another person's back or feet; can be soothing, playful and release muscle tension.

- Masturbation. Giving pleasure sexually to your own body; releasing sexual tension by rubbing or stroking sexual parts of your own body.

- Stories, Art, Movies, Music, and TV. These often have a message about sexuality and can help possible sexual partners express their affection and sexual interest when they are ready; use them as reasons to begin to talk about sex before you do anything sexual.

- French, Wet or Deep Kissing. Kissing with the tongue in the mouth; deep open mouth kissing has not been found to cause HIV infection; however if you have sores in your mouth it is better not to kiss this way.

- Mutual Masturbation. Touching the genitals of a sexual partner; sometimes both people do this to each other at the same time. If there are not cuts in the fingers skin, touching the sexual parts of another person can be pleasurable and release sexual tension; wear a clean latex glove for best protection from infection through cuts on fingers.

Here are some activities that have some risk of transmission of HIV or other STDs depending on how well you protect yourself:

- Sexual Intercourse with Protection. Vaginal and anal intercourse must be protected using lubricated condoms with nonoxynol-9. Another way to increase protection is to withdraw the penis before ejaculation. This is sometimes called pulling out. It should not be the only kind of protection that is used by a male. Pulling out should be done while using a condom as well. Oral sex on a woman must be protected with a barrier between the mouth and the vulva. You may cut a non-lubricated latex condom lengthwise up the side and open it up to make a flat surface then cover the vulva. All of these will help you protect yourself from becoming infected with HIV and other STDs.

There are other kinds of birth control that will protect females from pregnancy, but not from HIV and other STDs. These include Norplant, the pill, Depo-Provera, Intrauterine Devices (IUD's) and diaphragms.

Chapter 38

Condoms And STDs

This chapter is to help you understand why it's important to use condoms (rubbers, prophylactics) to help reduce the spread of sexually transmitted diseases. These diseases include AIDS, chlamydia, genital herpes, genial warts, gonorrhea, hepatitis B, and syphilis. You can get them through having sex—vaginal, anal, or oral.

The surest way to avoid these diseases is to not have sex altogether (abstinence). Another way is to limit sex to one partner who also limits his or her sex in the same way (monogamy). Condoms are not 100% safe, but if used properly, will reduce the risk of sexually transmitted diseases, including AIDS. Protecting yourself against the AIDS virus is of special concern because this disease is fatal and has no cure.

About two-thirds of the people with AIDS in the United States got the disease during sexual intercourse with an infected partner. Experts believe that many of these people could have avoided the disease by using condoms.

Condoms are used for both birth control and reducing the risk of disease. That's why some people think that other forms of birth control—such as the IUD, diaphragm, cervical cap or pill—will protect them against diseases,

About This Chapter: "Condoms and Sexually Transmitted Diseases," a brochure produced by the U.S. Food and Drug Administration (FDA). Reviewed 1999. Available online at http://www.fda.gov/oashi/aids/condom.html.

♣ It's A Fact!!

- Sexually transmitted diseases (STDs) affect 12 million men and women in the United States each year.

- Anyone can become infected through sexual intercourse with an infected person.

- Many of those infected are teenagers or young adults.

- Changing sexual partners adds to the risk of becoming infected.

- Sometimes, early in the infection, there may be no symptoms, or symptoms may be easily confused with other illnesses.

Sexually transmitted diseases can cause:

- Tubal pregnancies, sometimes fatal to the mother and always fatal to the unborn child

- Death or severe damage to a baby born to an infected woman

- Sterility (loss of ability to get pregnant)

- Cancer of the cervix in women

- Damage to other parts of the body, including the heart, kidneys, and brain

- Death to infected individuals

See a doctor if you have any of these symptoms of STDs:

- Discharge from the vagina, penis, and/or rectum

- Pain or burning during urination and/or intercourse

- Pain in the abdomen (women), testicles (men), and buttocks and legs (both)

- Blisters, open sores, warts, rash, and/or swelling in the genital area, sex organs, and/or mouth

- Flu-like symptoms, including fever, headache, aching muscles, and/or swollen glands

too. But that's not true. So if you use any other form of birth control, you still need a condom in addition to reduce the risk of getting sexually transmitted diseases.

A condom is especially important when an uninfected pregnant woman has sex, because it can also help protect her and her unborn child from a sexually transmitted disease. Note well: Condoms are not 100% safe, but if used properly, will reduce the risk of sexually transmitted diseases, including AIDS.

You can get more information about preventing sexually transmitted diseases by calling the National AIDS Hotline, the National Sexually Transmitted Diseases Hotline, or your state or local hotlines.

Who Should Use A Condom?

A person who takes part in risky sexual behavior should always use a condom. The highest risk comes from having intercourse—vaginal, anal, or oral—with a person who has a sexually transmitted disease. If you have sex with an infected person, you're taking a big chance. If you know your partner is infected, the best rule is to avoid intercourse (including oral sex). If you do decide to have sex with an infected partner, you should always be sure a condom is used from start to finish, every time.

And it's risky to have sex with someone who has shared needles with an infected person. It's also risky to have sex with someone who had sex with an infected person in the past. If your partner had intercourse with a person infected with HIV (the AIDS virus), he or she could pass it on to you. That can happen even if the intercourse was a long time ago and even if you partner seems perfectly healthy.

With sexually transmitted diseases, you often can't tell whether your partner has been infected. If you're not sure about yourself or your partner, you should choose to not have sex at all. But if you do have sex, be sure to use a condom that covers the entire penis to reduce your risk of being infected. This includes oral sex where the penis is in contact with the mouth. If you think you and your partner should be using condoms but your partner refuses, then you should say NO to sex with that person.

> ✔ **Quick Tip**
>
> To get the most protection from condoms:
> - Choose the right kind of condoms to prevent disease.
> - Store them properly.
> - Remember to use a new condom every time you have sex.
> - Use the condom the right way, from start to finish.

Will A Condom Guarantee I Won't Get A Sexually Transmitted Disease?

No. There's no absolute guarantee even when you use a condom. But most experts believe that the risk of getting AIDS and other sexually transmitted diseases can be greatly reduced if a condom is used properly. In other words, sex with condoms isn't totally safe sex, but it is less risky sex.

How Does A Condom Protect Against Sexually Transmitted Diseases?

A condom acts as a barrier or wall to keep blood, or semen, or vaginal fluids from passing from one person to the other during intercourse. These fluids can harbor germs such as HIV (the AIDS virus). If no condom is used, the germs can pass from the infected partner to the uninfected partner.

How Do I Choose The Right Kind Of Condoms To Prevent Disease?

Always read the label. Look for two things:

- The condoms should be made of latex (rubber). Tests have shown that latex condoms can prevent the passage of the AIDS, hepatitis and herpes viruses. But natural (lambskin) condoms may not do this. In the future, manufacturers may offer condoms of other materials and designs for disease prevention. As with all new products that make medical claims, such as "prevention of sexually transmitted disease," these new condoms would have to be reviewed by the Food and Drug Administration (FDA) before they are allowed to be sold.

- The package should say that the condoms are to prevent disease. If the package doesn't say anything about preventing disease, the condoms may not provide the protection you want, even though they may be the most expensive ones you can buy. Novelty condoms will not say anything about either disease prevention or pregnancy prevention on the package. They are intended only for sexual stimulation, not protection. Condoms which do not cover the entire penis are not labeled for disease prevention and should not be used for this purpose. For proper protection, a condom must unroll to cover the entire penis. This is another good reason to read the label carefully.

What Is The Government Doing About Condom Quality?

The FDA is working with condom manufacturers to help ensure that the latex condoms you buy are not damaged. Manufacturers spot check their condoms using a water-leak test. FDA inspectors do a similar test on sample condoms they take from warehouses. The condoms are filled with water and checked for leaks. An average of 996 of 1000 condoms must pass this test. (Don't try the water-leak test on condoms you plan to use, because this kind of testing weakens condoms.) Government testing cannot guarantee that condoms will always prevent the spread of sexually transmitted diseases. How well you are protected will also depend a great deal on which condoms you choose and how you store, handle and use them.

Are Condoms Strong Enough For Anal Intercourse?

The Surgeon General has said, "Condoms provide some protection, but anal intercourse is simply too dangerous to practice." Condoms may be more likely to break during anal intercourse than during other types of sex because of the greater amount of friction and other stresses involved. Even if the condom doesn't break, anal intercourse is very risky because it can cause tissue in the rectum to tear and bleed. These tears allow disease germs to pass more easily from one partner to the other.

Should Spermicides Be Used With Condoms?

In test tubes, a spermicide called nonoxynol-9 (a chemical used to kill the man's sperm for birth control) has been shown to kill the germs that cause sexually transmitted diseases. Some experts believe nonoxynol-9 may kill the AIDS virus during intercourse, too. So you might want to use a spermicide along with a latex condom as an added precaution in case the condom breaks during intercourse.

Condoms with spermicides have an expiration date. Pay attention to that date.

How Do I Buy Spermicides And How Should They Be Used?

Spermicides generally come in the form of jellies, creams or foams. You can buy them in pharmacies and some grocery stores. You can also buy condoms with a small amount of spermicide already applied. But some experts believe it's a good idea to add more spermicide to the amount that comes on the condom.

If you do add spermicide, place a small amount inside the condom at its tip. After the condom is on the penis, put more on the outside. Spermicides can also be put inside the woman's vagina. Follow the directions for use.

If you have oral sex, use a condom without a spermicide. Although swallowing small amounts of spermicide has not proven harmful in animal test, we don't know if this is always true for people. Spermicide products and condoms with spermicides have expiration dates. Don't buy or use a package that is outdated.

Should I Use A Lubricant With A Condom?

Some condoms are already lubricated with dry silicone, jellies, or creams. If you buy condoms not already lubricated, it's a good idea to apply some yourself. Lubricants may help prevent condoms from breaking during use and may prevent irritation, which might increase the chance of infection.

If you use a separate lubricant, be sure to use one that's water-based and made for this purpose. If you're not sure which to choose, ask your pharmacist. Never use a lubricant that contains oils, fats, or greases such as petroleum-based jelly, baby oil or lotion, hand or body lotions, cooking shortenings, or oily cosmetics like cold cream. They can seriously weaken latex, causing a condom to tear easily.

What Do The Dates Mean On The Package?

Some packages show "DATE MFG." This tells you when the condoms were made. It is not an expiration date. Other packages may show an expiration date. The condoms should not be purchased or used after that date.

Are Condoms From Vending Machines Any Good?

It depends. Vending machine condoms may be OK:

> ☞ **Remember!!**
> Condoms with spermicides have an expiration date.

- If you know you are getting a latex condom,
- If they are labeled for disease prevention,
- If you know the spermicide (if any) is not outdated, and
- If the machine is not exposed to extreme temperature and direct sunlight.

How Should Condoms Be Stored?

You should store condoms in a cool, dry place out of direct sunlight, perhaps in a drawer or closet. If you want to keep one with you, put it in a loose pocket, wallet, or purse for no more than a few hours at a time.

Extreme temperature—especially heat—can make latex brittle or gummy (like an old balloon). So don't keep these latex products in a hot place like a glove compartment

How Should Condoms Be Handled?

Gently. When opening the packet, don't use your teeth, scissors or sharp nails. Make sure you can see what you're doing.

What Defects Should I Look For?

If the condom material sticks to itself or is gummy, the condom is no good. Also check the condom tip for other damage that is obvious (brittleness, tears, and holes). Don't unroll the condom to check it because this could cause damage.

Never use a damaged condom.

How Should I Use A Condom?

Follow these guidelines

- Use a new condom for every act of intercourse.
- If the penis is uncircumcised, pull the foreskin back before putting the condom on.
- Put the condom on after the penis is erect (hard) and before any contact is made between the penis and any part of the partner's body.
- If using a spermicide, put some inside the condom tip.
- If the condom does not have a reservoir tip, pinch the tip enough to leave a half-inch space for semen to collect.
- While pinching the half-inch tip, place the condom against the penis and unroll it all the way to the base. Put more spermicide or lubricant on the outside.
- If you feel a condom break while you are having sex, stop immediately and pull out. Do not continue until you have put on a new condom and used more spermicide.
- After ejaculation and before the penis gets soft, grip the rim of the condom and carefully withdraw from your partner.
- To remove the condom from the penis, pull it off gently, being careful semen doesn't spill out.

- Wrap the used condom in a tissue and throw it in the trash where others won't handle it. Because condoms may cause problems in sewers, don't flush them down the toilet. Afterwards, wash your hands with soap and water.

- Finally, beware of drugs and alcohol. They can affect your judgment, so you may forget to use a condom. They may even affect your ability to use a condom properly.

Sexually Transmitted Diseases, Including AIDS, Can Be Prevented

Learn the facts so that you can protect yourself and others from getting infected. Condoms are not 100% safe, but if used properly, will reduce the risk of sexually transmitted diseases, including AIDS. If you have unprotected sex

---

Condom Shopping Guide   ✔ Quick Tip

It's most important to choose latex condoms that say "disease prevention" on the package. Other features are a matter of personal choice.

Use this handy shopping guide as a reminder of what to look for when buying condoms, lubricants and spermicides.

Be sure to choose:

- Latex
- Disease prevention claim on package label

Also consider:

- With spermicide
- Separate spermicide (gel, cream, foam)
- With lubricant
- Separate lubricant (Select only water-based lubricants made for this purpose.)

now, you can contract sexually transmitted diseases. Later, if you decide to have children, you might pass the disease on to them.

If you would like more information about condoms and how to prevent sexually transmitted diseases, talk with your doctor or call the National AIDS Hotline. It's open 24 hours a day. Trained operators will answer your questions and can send you more information.

Remember!!
Condoms are not 100% safe, but if used properly, will reduce the risk of sexually transmitted diseases, including AIDS. Protecting yourself against the AIDS virus is of special concern because this disease is fatal and has no cure.

Chapter 39

Chlamydia

What Is Chlamydial Infection?

Chlamydial (kla-MID-ee-uhl) infection is a curable sexually transmitted disease (STD), which is caused by a bacterium called *Chlamydia trachomatis*. You can get genital chlamydial infection during oral, vaginal, or anal sexual contact with an infected partner. It can cause serious problems in men and women as well as in newborn babies of infected mothers.

Chlamydial infection is one of the most widespread bacterial STDs in the United States. The U.S. Centers for Disease Control and Prevention (CDC) estimates that more than 4 million people are infected each year. Health economists estimate that chlamydial infections and the other problems they cause cost Americans more than $2 billion a year.

What Are The Symptoms Of This STD?

Because chlamydial infection does not make most people sick, you can have it and not know it. Those who do have symptoms may have an abnormal discharge (mucus or pus) from the vagina or penis or pain while urinating. These early symptoms may be very mild. Symptoms usually appear within

About This Chapter: "Chlamydial Infection," a fact sheet produced by the National Institute of Allergy and Infectious Diseases (NIAID), 2002. Available online at http://www.niaid.nih.gov/factsheets/stdclam.htm.

one to three weeks after being infected. Because the symptoms may be n or not exist at all, you might not seek care and get treated.

The infection may move inside the body if it is not treated. There, it cause pelvic inflammatory disease (PID) in women and epididymitis in m two very serious illnesses. *C. trachomatis* can cause inflamed rectum and flammation of the lining of the eye (pink eye). The bacteria also can in the throat from oral sexual contact with an infected partner.

How Does The Doctor Diagnose Chlamydial Infectio

Chlamydial infection is easily confused with gonorrhea because the sym toms of both diseases are similar and the diseases can occur together, thou rarely.

The most reliable ways to find out whether the infection is chlamy are through laboratory tests. Usually, a doctor or other health care wor will send a sample of pus from the vagina or penis to a laboratory t will look for the bacteria. The urine test does not require a pelvic exam swabbing of the penis. Results from the urine test are available within hours.

How Is Chlamydial Infection Treated?

If you are infected with *C. trachomatis*, your doctor or other health care worker will probably give you a prescription for an antibiotic such as azithromycin (taken for one day only) or doxycycline (taken for seven days) to treat people with chlamydial infection. Or, you might get a prescription for another antibiotic such as erythromycin or ofloxacin.

✔ Quick Tip

If you have chlamydial infection

- Take all of the prescribed medicine, even after symptoms disappear.

- If the symptoms do not disappear within one to two weeks after finishing the medicine, go to your doctor or clinic again.

- It is very important to tell your sex partners that you have chlamydial infection so that they can be tested and treated.

Doctors may treat pregnant women with azithromycin or erythromycin, or sometimes, with amoxicillin. Penicillin, which doctors often use to treat some other STDs, won't cure chlamydial infections.

What Can Happen If The Infection Is Not Treated?

In women, untreated chlamydial infections can lead to PID. In men, untreated chlamydial infections may lead to pain or swelling in the scrotal area, which is a sign of inflammation of a part of the male reproductive system located near the testicles known as the epididymis. Left untreated, these complications can prevent people from having children.

Each year up to 1 million women in the United States develop PID, a serious infection of the reproductive organs. As many as half of all cases of PID may be due to chlamydial infection, and many of these don't have symptoms. PID can cause scarring of the fallopian tubes, which can block the tubes and prevent fertilization from taking place. Researchers estimate that 100,000 women each year become infertile because of PID.

In other cases, scarring may interfere with the passage of the fertilized egg to the uterus during pregnancy. When this happens, the egg may attach itself to the fallopian tube. This is called ectopic or tubal pregnancy. This very serious condition results in a miscarriage and can cause death of the mother.

Can Chlamydial Infection Affect A Newborn Baby?

A baby who is exposed to *C. trachomatis* in the birth canal during delivery may develop an eye infection or pneumonia. Symptoms of conjunctivitis or pink eye, which include discharge and swollen eyelids, usually develop within the first 10 days of life.

Symptoms of pneumonia, including a cough that gets steadily worse and congestion, most often develop within three to six weeks of birth. Doctors can treat both conditions successfully with antibiotics. Because of these risks to the newborn, many doctors recommend that all pregnant women get tested for chlamydial infection.

How Can I Prevent Getting Chlamydial Infection?

You can reduce your chances of getting chlamydia or of giving it to y partner by using male latex condoms correctly every time you have se intercourse.

If you are infected but have no symptoms, you may pass the bacteria your sex partners without knowing it. Therefore, any doctors recommended that anyone who has more than one sex partner, especially women under years of age, be tested for chlamydial infection regularly, even if they d have symptoms.

What Research Is Going On?

Scientists are looking for better ways to diagnose, treat, and prev chlamydial infections. NIAID-supported scientists recently completed quencing the genome for *C. trachomatis*. The sequence represents an en clopedia of information about the organism. This accomplishment will g scientists important information as they try to develop a safe and effect vaccine. Developing topical microbicides (preparations that can be inser into the vagina to prevent infection) that are effective and easy for women use is also a major research focus.

 Remember!!

If left untreated, the complications of chlamydial infections can preven people from having children in the future.

Chapter 40

What To Know About Scabies

What Is Scabies?

Scabies is an infestation of the skin with the microscopic mite *Sarcoptes scabei*. Infestation is common, found worldwide, and affects people of all races and social classes. Scabies spreads rapidly under crowded conditions where there is frequent skin-to-skin contact between people, such as in hospitals, institutions, child-care facilities, and nursing homes.

What Are The Signs And Symptoms Of Scabies Infestation?

- Pimple-like irritations, burrows or rash of the skin, especially the webbing between the fingers; the skin folds on the wrist, elbow, or knee; the penis, the breast, or shoulder blades.

- Intense itching, especially at night and over most of the body.

How Did I Get Scabies?

By direct, prolonged, skin-to-skin contact with a person already infested with scabies. Contact must be prolonged (a quick handshake or hug will

About This Chapter: "Scabies," a fact sheet produced by the Centers for Disease Control and Prevention (CDC), 1999. Available online at http://www.cdc.gov/ncidod/dpd/parasites/scabies/factsht_scabies.htm.

usually not spread infestation). Infestation is easily spread to sexual partners and household members. Infestation may also occur by sharing clothing, towels, and bedding. It may also be transmitted sexually.

Who Is At Risk For Severe Infestation?

People with weakened immune systems and the elderly are at risk for a more severe form of scabies, called Norwegian or crusted scabies.

How Long Will Mites Live?

Once away from the human body, mites do not survive more than 48–72 hours. When living on a person, an adult female mite can live up to a month.

> ### ♣ It's A Fact!!
>
> The signs and symptoms of scabies are:
>
> - Pimple-like irritations, burrows or rash of the skin, especially the webbing between the fingers; the skin folds on the wrist, elbow, or knee; the penis, the breast, or shoulder blades.
>
> - Intense itching, especially at night and over most of the body.
>
> - Sores on the body caused by scratching. These sores can sometimes become infected with bacteria.

Did My Pet Spread Scabies To Me?

No. Pets become infested with a different kind of scabies mite. If your p is infested with scabies, (also called mange) and they have close contact wi you, the mite can get under your skin and cause itching and skin irritatic However, the mite dies in a couple of days and does not reproduce. T mites may cause you to itch for several days, but you do not need to treated with special medication to kill the mites. Until your pet is succe fully treated, mites can continue to burrow into your skin and cause you have symptoms.

How Soon After Infestation Will Symptoms Begin?

For a person who has never been infested with scabies, symptoms may take 4–6 weeks to begin. For a person who has had scabies, symptoms appear within several days. You do not become immune to an infestation.

How Is Scabies Infestation Diagnosed?

Diagnosis is most commonly made by looking at the burrows or rash. A skin scraping may be taken to look for mites, eggs, or mite fecal matter to confirm the diagnosis. If a skin scraping or biopsy is taken and returns negative, it is possible that you may still be infested. Typically, there are fewer than 10 mites on the entire body of an infested person; this makes it easy for an infestation to be missed.

Can Scabies Be Treated?

Yes. Several lotions are available to treat scabies. Always follow the directions provided by your physician or the directions on the package insert. Apply lotion to a clean body from the neck down to the toes and left overnight (8 hours). After 8 hours, take a bath or shower to wash off the lotion. Put on clean clothes. All clothes, bedding, and towels used by the infested person 2 days before treatment should be washed in hot water; dry in a hot dryer. A second treatment of the body with the same lotion may be necessary 7–10 days later. Pregnant women and children are often treated with milder scabies medications.

Who Should Be Treated For Scabies?

Anyone who is diagnosed with scabies, as well as his or her sexual partners and persons who have close, prolonged contact to the infested person should also be treated. If your health care provider has instructed family members to be treated, everyone should receive treatment at the same time to prevent re-infestation.

How Soon After Treatment Will I Feel Better?

Itching may continue for 2–3 weeks, and does not mean that you are still infested. Your health care provider may prescribe additional medication to

relieve itching if it is severe. No new burrows or rashes should appear 24-
hours after effective treatment.

🖝 Remember!!

Scabies is a skin infestation with a tiny
mite, *Sarcoptes scabiei*. Scabies has become
relatively common throughout the general population. It is highly contagious
and is commonly transmitted by contact
with skin, infested sheets, towels, or even
furniture. It may also be transmitted sexually.

Source: From "Other Important STDs,"
a fact sheet from the National Institute
of Allergy and Infectious Diseases
(NIAID), June 1998. Available online at
http://www.niaid.nih.gov/factsheets/
stdother.htm. Reviewed and updated in
January 2003, by Dr. David A. Cooke,
MD, Diplomate, American Board of Internal Medicine.

Chapter 41

The Facts On Genital Warts

What Is Human Papillomavirus?

Human papillomavirus (HPV) is one of the most common causes of sexually transmitted disease (STD) in the world. Health experts estimate that there are more cases of genital HPV infection than of any other STD in the United States. According to the American Social Health Association, approximately 5.5 million new cases of sexually transmitted HPV infections are reported every year. At least 20 million Americans are already infected.

Scientists have identified more than 100 types of HPV, most of which are harmless. About 30 types are spread through sexual contact. Some types of HPV that cause genital infections can also cause cervical cancer and other genital cancers.

Like many STDs, genital HPV infections often do not have visible signs and symptoms. One study sponsored by the National Institute of Allergy and Infectious Diseases (NIAID) reported that almost half of the women infected with HPV had no obvious symptoms. People who are infected but who have no symptoms may not know they can transmit HPV to others or that they can develop complications from the virus.

About This Chapter: "Human Papillomavirus and Genital Warts," a fact sheet produced by the National Institute of Allergy and Infectious Diseases (NIAID), 2001. Available online at http://www.niaid.nih.gov/factsheets/stdhpv.htm.

What Are Genital Warts?

Genital warts (condylomata acuminata or venereal warts) are the mos[t] easily recognized sign of genital HPV infection. Many people, however, hav[e] a genital HPV infection without genital warts.

Can HPV Cause Other Kinds Of Warts?

Some types of HPV cause common skin warts, such as those found o[n] the hands and soles of the feet. These types of HPV do not cause genital warts.

How Are Genital Warts Spread?

Genital warts are very contagious and are spread during oral, genital, or anal sex with an infected partner. About two-thirds of people who have sexual contact with a partner with genital warts will develop warts, usually within three months of contact.

♣ **It's A Fact!!**
About 30 types of HPV are spread through sexual contact, and some of these cause genital infections that can lead to cervical and other genital cancers.

In women, the warts occur on the outside and inside of the vagina, on the opening (cervix) to the womb (uterus), or around the anus. In men, genital warts are less commo[n] If present, they usually are seen on the tip of the penis. They also may b[e] found on the shaft of the penis, on the scrotum, or around the anus. Rarel[y] genital warts also can develop in the mouth or throat of a person who h[as] had oral sex with an infected person.

Genital warts often occur in clusters and can be very tiny or can sprea[d] into large masses in the genital or anal area.

How Are Genital Warts Diagnosed?

A doctor or other health care worker usually can diagnose genital war[ts] by seeing them on a patient. Women with genital warts also should be exam ined for possible HPV infection of the cervix.

The doctor may be able to identify some otherwise invisible warts in the genital tissue by applying vinegar (acetic acid) to areas of suspected infection. This solution causes infected areas to whiten, which makes them more visible, particularly if a procedure called colposcopy is performed. During colposcopy, the doctor uses a magnifying instrument to look at the vagina and cervix. In some cases, the doctor takes a small piece of tissue from the cervix and examines it under the microscope.

A Pap smear test also may indicate the possible presence of cervical HPV infection. In a Pap smear, a laboratory worker examines cells scraped from the cervix under a microscope to see if they are cancerous. If a woman's Pap smear is abnormal, she might have an HPV infection. If a woman has an abnormal Pap smear, she should have her doctor examine her further to look for and treat any cervical problems.

What Is The Treatment For Genital Warts?

Genital warts often disappear even without treatment. In other cases, they eventually may develop a fleshy, small raised growth that looks like cauliflower. There is no way to predict whether the warts will grow or disappear. Therefore, if you suspect you have genital warts, you should be examined and treated, if necessary.

✤ It's A Fact!!

The only way you can prevent getting an HPV infection is to avoid direct contact with the virus, which is transmitted by skin-to-skin contact. Athough treatments can get rid of the warts, none gets rid of the virus. Warts often come back again after treatment.

Depending on factors such as the size and location of the genital warts, a doctor will offer you one of several ways to treat them.

- Imiquimod, an immune response cream which you can apply to the affected area.

- A 20 percent podophyllin anti-mitotic solution, which you can apply to the affected area and later wash off.

- A 0.5 percent podofilox solution, applied to the affected area but shouldn't be washed off.

- A 5 percent 5-fluorouracil cream.

- Trichloroacetic acid (TCA).

If you are pregnant, you should not use podophyllin or podofilox because they are absorbed by the skin and may cause birth defects in your baby. In addition, you should not use 5-fluorouracil cream if you are expecting.

If you have small warts, the doctor can remove them by freezing (cryosurgery), burning (electrocautery), or laser treatment. Occasionally, the doctor will have to use surgery to remove large warts that have not responded to other treatment.

Some doctors use the antiviral drug alpha interferon, which they inject directly into the warts, to treat warts that have returned after removal by traditional means. The drug is expensive, however, and does not reduce the rate that the genital warts return.

Although treatments can get rid of the warts, none gets rid of the virus. Because the virus is still present in your body, warts often come back after treatment.

How Can HPV Infection Be Prevented?

The only way you can prevent getting an HPV infection is to avoid direct contact with the virus, which is transmitted by skin-to-skin contact. If you or your sexual partner have warts that are visible in the genital area, you should avoid any sexual contact until the warts are treated. Studies have not confirmed that male latex condoms prevent transmission of HPV itself, but results do suggest that condom use may reduce the risk of developing diseases linked to HPV, such as genital warts and cervical cancer.

Can HPV And Genital Warts Cause Complications?

Cancer

Some types of HPV can cause cervical cancer. Others, however, cause cervical cancer and also are associated with vulvar cancer, anal cancer, and cancer of the penis (a rare cancer).

Most HPV infections do not progress to cervical cancer. If a woman does have abnormal cervical cells, a Pap test will detect them. It is particularly important for women who have abnormal cervical cells to have regular pelvic exams and Pap tests so that they can be treated early, if necessary.

Pregnancy And Childbirth

Genital warts may cause a number of problems during pregnancy. Sometimes they get larger during pregnancy, making it difficult to urinate. If the warts are in the vagina, they can make the vagina less elastic and cause obstruction during delivery.

Rarely, infants born to women with genital warts develop warts in their throats (laryngeal papillomatosis). Although uncommon, it is a potentially life-threatening condition for the child, requiring frequent laser surgery to prevent obstruction of the breathing passages. Research on the use of interferon therapy in combination with laser surgery indicates that this drug may show promise in slowing the course of the disease.

What Research Is Going On?

Scientists are doing research on two types of HPV vaccines. One type would be used to prevent infection or disease (warts or pre-cancerous tissue changes). The other type would be used to treat cervical cancers. Researchers are testing both types of vaccines in people.

Chapter 42

Herpes: Highly Contagious

What Is Genital Herpes?

Genital herpes is a sexually transmitted disease (STD). This means that it is a disease that you get by having sex with someone who already has genital herpes. It is a viral infection caused by the herpes simplex virus. Once you are infected, the virus stays in your body for life. You can give herpes to another person if you have sex when your herpes virus is active.

What Are The Signs Of Genital Herpes?

The first signs of herpes show up two to ten days after having sex with an infected person. These signs can last from two to three weeks. The signs of genital herpes are:

1. Small red bumps on the penis, vagina, or wherever the infection began. These bumps may become blisters or painful open sores.

2. Itching or burning in the genital (sex organs) area.

3. Pain in the legs, bottom, or genital area.

4. Vaginal discharge.

About This Chapter: A fact sheet from the Office on Women's Health, Department of Health and Social Services (DHSS), 1999. Available online at http://www.4woman.gov/faq/Easyread/genital-etr.htm.

5. Feeling pressure or discomfort around your stomach.

6. Fever.

7. Headache.

8. Muscle aches.

9. Pain when urinating.

10. Swollen glands in the genital area.

I Just Got Over My First Outbreak Of Genital Herpe Will I Have Other Outbreaks?

Yes. Herpes can come back. It stays in the cells of your body, even after signs of the infection have gone away. When the virus comes back, you c infect people that you have sex with. Some people have herpes virus ou breaks only once or twice in their lives; other people have many outbreaks herpes each year. Doctors don't know what causes the virus to come bac Some women say the virus comes back when they are sick, under stress, c in the sun, or during their period.

How Is Genital Herpes Treated?

Genital herpes is treated with an oral medicine called Acyclovir. Acyclo can be taken the first time you get herpes and during later outbreaks of t virus. This medicine makes the herpes outbreaks last for less time and l intensity, but it does not cure genital herpes.

I Have Herpes. What Can I Do To Keep It From Spread ing To Other Parts Of My Body And To Other Peopl

Here are ways to keep genital herpes from spreading:

1. Do not have sex with anyone when you can see your herpes sores (wh your herpes infection is active). Use a condom if you have sex after t sores have healed.

2. Keep the infected area clean and dry.

3. Try to keep from touching the sores.

4. Wash your hands right away if you touch the sores.

Can Genital Herpes Cause Problems During Pregnancy?

Yes. A pregnant woman can pass the virus to her baby during delivery. Babies born with herpes may have brain damage, severe rashes, eye problems, or they may die. Doctors will do a C-section to deliver a baby if the mother has herpes near the birth canal. Also, Acyclovir can help babies born with herpes if they are treated right away.

How Can I Keep From Getting Genital Herpes?

Here are ways to keep from getting genital herpes.

1. Do not have sex (intercourse, oral, or anal).

2. If you have sex:

>   use a condom (also use a condom for oral and anal sex);

>   have sex with only one uninfected person—do not have multiple partners;

>   ask your sex partner(s) if he or she has genital herpes or other STDs, has had sex with someone who has an STD, or has sores, rashes, or discharge in the genital area; and

>   get regular check-ups for STDs if you have sex with more than one person. Get a check-up even if you don't have any signs of a STD. A check-up cannot prevent STDs, but it can help to detect them in their early stages so they can be treated.

☞ Remember!!

You can get genital herpes by having sex with someone who already has it. Once you are infected, the virus stays in your body for life.

Chapter 43

Know The Signs Of Syphilis

What Is Syphilis?

Syphilis is a sexually transmitted disease (STD). This means that it is a disease that you get by having sex with someone who already has syphilis. Syphilis is caused by bacteria, and can infect the mouth, genital area, or rectum. It also may get into your body through cuts or broken skin. If untreated, syphilis can infect other parts of your body.

What Are The Signs Of Syphilis?

The signs of syphilis change as the disease moves from the early to the late stages. The early sign of syphilis is a chancre on the body. A chancre is a sore that shows up ten days to three months after sex with an infected person. Chancres can be seen on the part of the body that was exposed to the syphilis such as the penis, vagina, cervix, tongue, or mouth. Some chancres are inside the body, where they cannot be seen.

How Is Syphilis Treated?

First, the doctor may need to do a physical exam and blood test to make sure your infection is syphilis and to find out what stage of the disease you

About This Chapter: A fact sheet produced by the Office on Women's Health, Department of Health and Social Services (DHSS), 2000. Available online at http://www.4woman.gov/faq/Easyread/syphilis-etr.htm.

have. Syphilis is treated with penicillin or other antibiotics (medicines that kill bacteria). Antibiotics can cure the disease, but they cannot fix damage to your body that has already been done by the syphilis. People who have sex with someone infected with syphilis should be tested and treated, even if they don't have signs of the disease.

You can get syphilis more than one time. Taking antibiotics does not protect you from getting syphilis again.

What Happens If Syphilis Isn't Treated?

If syphilis isn't treated, it can cause serious heart, nervous system, and mental problems;

♣ It's A Fact!!

Signs of syphilis include

- Chancres (shanker) or sores.
- Skin rash.
- Mild fever.
- Feeling very tired.
- Headache.
- Sore throat.
- Hair loss.
- Swollen lymph glands throughout the body.

✔ Quick Tip

Here's how you can take care of yourself and others:

1. Take all your medicine as instructed by the doctor.

2. Keep the infected area clean and dry.

3. Try to keep from touching the chancres.

4. Wash your hands right away if you touch the chancres.

5. Tell your sex partner(s) about your infection so that they can be tested and treated right away.

6. Do not have sex when you can see chancres on your body, or if you are getting treatment for syphilis.

7. Use a condom when you have sex after being treated for syphilis.

blindness; and death. Untreated syphilis can invade the nervous system causing headaches, stiff neck, fever, seizures, numbness, weakness, and trouble seeing.

You should get regular check-ups for syphilis and other STDs if you are sexually active, even if you don't have any symptoms.

Can Syphilis Cause Problems During Pregnancy?

Yes. Pregnant women can pass syphilis to their babies during labor. Syphilis can cause skin sores, rashes, fever, jaundice, anemia, physical problems, weak crying sounds, and swollen liver and spleen in babies. Testing and treating syphilis early in a pregnant woman is the best way to keep her baby from getting syphilis.

How Can I Keep From Getting Syphilis?

Here are ways to keep from getting syphilis:

Remember!!

You can get syphilis more than one time. Taking antibiotics does not protect you from getting syphilis again.

1. Do not have sex (intercourse, oral, or anal).

2. If you have sex:

    use a condom (also use a condom for oral and anal sex);

    ask your sex partner(s) if he or she has syphilis or other STDs, has had sex with someone who has a STD, or has sores, rashes, or discharge in the genital area; and

    get regular check-ups for syphilis and other STDs if you are sexually active, especially with more than one person. Get regular check-ups even if you don't have signs of an STD.

Chapter 44

Understanding Hepatitis

If you're thinking about getting a tattoo or piercing, you might want to consider what the Centers for Disease Control and Prevention (CDC) have to say about that first.

Scientists at the CDC state that tattooing or piercing any part of your body with a non-sterile needle can put you at risk for contracting viral hepatitis B or C, an infectious liver disease that is even more contagious than HIV (the virus that causes AIDS).

Like HIV, hepatitis B or C is spread through person-to-person contact with infected blood or other body fluids, and although people will recover from viral hepatitis, there is no cure.

Understanding The Liver And Hepatitis

Teens who understand the importance of a properly functioning liver will understand why they need to keep it healthy and why the vaccination is so important.

About This Chapter: This information was provided by TeensHealth, one of the largest resources online for medically reviewed health information written for parents, kids, and teens. For more articles like this one, visit www.TeensHealth.org, or www.KidsHealth.org. © 2001 The Nemours Center for Children's Health Media, a division of The Nemours Foundation.

"As the powerhouse of the body, the liver helps process nutrients a metabolizes medication. If it is not working properly, it will feel tender, a you won't feel well," says Dr. Catherine Lamprecht, an infectious disea: specialist. The liver also helps clear the body of toxic waste products.

Because the hepatitis virus is a mutating virus, it changes over time a can be difficult for the body to fight. In some cases hepatitis B or C c destroy the liver. The patient then will need a transplant, which is not alwa affordable or available. Dr. Lamprecht points out that this is not a comm concern of teens, but it is something they must be aware of if they particip: in any high-risk behaviors, like coming into contact with unsterilized need for any reason or having unprotected sex.

Signs And Symptoms

Hepatitis infection causes inflammation of the liver, which means that the liver is swollen and damaged and is losing its ability to function. People with hepatitis often get flu-like symptoms, which can leave them feeling weak, tired, or nauseated. This is why it is referred to as "the silent disease" and is often undiagnosed or confused with another illness. A blood test is usually needed to determine if you have hepatitis.

If you notice a yellowing of your skin or eyes, known as jaundice, you may have hepatitis and should see a doctor immediately, says Dr. Lamprecht.

> ### ♣ It's A Fact!!
>
> The symptoms of hepatitis include:
>
> - fever
> - vomiting
> - abdominal pain (on the upper right side)
> - light-colored bowel movements
> - dark urine

Dr. Lamprecht says other symptoms might include a fever, vomitin; abdominal pain (on the upper right side), light-colored bowel movement and dark urine. You may notice these symptoms anywhere from 15 days t 25 weeks after you've gotten the disease, depending on the type of hepatit: you have, she explains.

Types Of Hepatitis

There are five types of hepatitis. The three most common are hepatitis A (HAV), hepatitis B (HBV), and hepatitis C (HCV). Currently, vaccines exist only for hepatitis A and hepatitis B.

Hepatitis A

An estimated 180,000 hepatitis A infections occur in the United States each year. Hepatitis A is most commonly contracted by mouth through food or water that has been contaminated by fecal matter. It is considered to be the least destructive of the hepatitis viruses because, unlike the other types, it rarely leads to permanent liver damage. Within a few weeks, the symptoms will have gone away on their own and the hepatitis A virus will no longer be in your system.

Hepatitis B

Hepatitis B is a more serious infection and may lead to cirrhosis (permanent scarring of the liver) or liver cancer, both of which cause severe illness and even death. Although there is no cure, there are medications available to help stop the spread of the disease, but they are expensive and may not be available to families without health insurance. In addition, the side effects of the treatment can be just as bad as the disease itself.

Hepatitis B infects more than 100,000 people in the United States each year, with 70% of new cases occurring in people between the ages of 15 to 39—and 75% of these people are teens.

Teen deaths caused by full-blown hepatitis "are rare, accounting for less than 1% of the reported cases," says Dr. Rob Lyerla, a researcher at the CDC.

"First and foremost," Dr. Lyerla says, "hepatitis B is a sexually transmitted disease, and a doctor wouldn't know if that is how the patient contracted the disease if she didn't tell him. Then again, with adolescents, they either really may not know how they contracted the disease, or it might be that they don't want to say."

It is important to be honest with your doctor, says Dr. Lamprecht.

In most cases, a teen who gets hepatitis B will recover from the disease and develop a natural immunity, which means that a teen who has had hepatitis B will probably not get it again. "The 10% who can't shake the disease will have it forever," says Albert Gallardo of the Hepatitis Foundation.

Hepatitis C

Like hepatitis B, hepatitis C can lead to cirrhosis or liver cancer. Hepatitis C is the most serious type of hepatitis virus and is now the leading cause of liver failure requiring transplantation among adults. It leads to nearly 10,000 deaths each year.

An estimated 3.9 million Americans are infected with this virus, most often because of blood products or blood transfusions before 1990, drug use or unprotected sexual activities. More than 80% of those people will remain infected for the rest of their lives, and 20% of those will go on to develop cirrhosis and liver failure.

There is currently no vaccine to prevent hepatitis C, and the medications available to treat it are effective in less than 30% of the cases.

Protecting Yourself

Doctors recommend vaccination as the best way to protect yourself against hepatitis A or hepatitis B. Because hepatitis A is usually not a serious illness, doctors generally recommend this vaccination only for those at high risk for catching the disease, usually people who are traveling to certain parts of the world where sanitation isn't very good.

If you haven't been vaccinated against hepatitis A or B or are at risk for contracting hepatitis C, then you should be aware that the only other way to avoid getting hepatitis is by avoiding risky activities, such as:

- Having unprotected sexual intercourse—not only does unprotected sex put you at risk for many sexually transmitted diseases and pregnancy, but hepatitis B or C is also a significant risk.

- Intravenous drug use—hepatitis is only one of the life-threatening infections you can get from this dangerous activity if you share contaminated needles.

- Sharing straws when snorting cocaine—in addition to the dangers of using cocaine even once and the risk of addiction, you can pass along the hepatitis virus.

- Not washing hands before handling food or after using the bathroom—washing your hands thoroughly is one of the simplest, most important ways to prevent the spread of any infection, including hepatitis.

- Using nonsterile needles for piercing or tattooing—nonsterile needles used for piercings and tattoos put you at risk for hepatitis B or C.

- Sharing a toothbrush or razor—although sharing may be considered an act of friendship, it's better to use your own because hepatitis can be transmitted through sores on the mouth or cuts on the skin.

♣ **It's A Fact!!**
The three most common are hepatitis A (HAV), hepatitis B (HBV), and hepatitis C (HCV). Currently, vaccines exist only for hepatitis A and hepatitis B.

- Eating raw shellfish (such as clams or oysters)—you put yourself at risk for hepatitis A if you eat raw shellfish.

Hepatitis B or C can also be passed from a mother to baby at birth and possibly through blood transfusions, but no one can get hepatitis from sneezes, coughs, or holding hands. Hepatitis infection is serious, but following these simple guidelines can help protect you from this disease.

Chapter 45

Gonorrhea: Curable, But Serious

What Is Gonorrhea?

Gonorrhea is a sexually transmitted disease (STD). This means that it is a disease that you get by having sex with someone who already has gonorrhea. The disease is caused by bacteria. Gonorrhea may infect the cervix (mouth of the womb), urethra, mouth, or rectum. It can be treated and cured by antibiotics. However, taking antibiotics will not protect you from getting gonorrhea again.

How Is Gonorrhea Treated?

Antibiotic medicines (medicines that kill bacteria) are used to treat gonorrhea. Some antibiotics no longer work to cure gonorrhea, so doctors are using new antibiotics to treat this disease. People who have sex with someone infected with gonorrhea should be tested and treated for the disease even if they don't have any signs.

What Happens If Gonorrhea Isn't Treated?

If gonorrhea is not treated, the bacteria can move into the bloodstream and infect your reproductive organs, joints, heart valves, and brain. The most common problem from untreated gonorrhea is pelvic inflammatory disease

About This Chapter: A fact sheet produced by the Office on Women's Health, Department of Health and Social Services (DHSS), 1999. Available online at http://www.4woman.gov/faq/Easyread/gono-etr.htm.

(PID). PID is an infection of a woman's uterus, ovaries, and/or fallopian tubes that can cause infertility (not being able to get pregnant) and ectopic pregnancy (pregnancy in the fallopian tubes instead of the uterus). About one million women get PID each year in the United States.

You should get regular check-ups for gonorrhea and other STDs if you have sex with more than one person. Get a check-up even if you don't have signs of an STD.

Can Gonorrhea Cause Problems During Pregnancy?

♣ **It's A Fact!!**

Most women with gonorrhea have no signs of the disease. Some women may have the following signs:

1. Pain or burning during urination
2. Vaginal discharge.
3. Stomach and pelvic pain.
4. Bleeding between periods.
5. Throwing up.
6. Fever.
7. Discharge from the rectum.
8. Itching around the rectum.
9. Painful bowel movements.

Yes. A pregnant woman can pass gonorrhea to her baby during delive Most doctors say that babies must be treated with silver nitrate or oth medicine to keep them from getting gonorrhea in the eyes, which can cau blindness. Doctors say that all pregnant women should be tested for gono rhea. Pregnant women who have gonorrhea need to talk to their doctor abo what medicines are safe to take during pregnancy.

How Can I Keep From Getting Gonorrhea?

Here are ways to keep from getting gonorrhea:

1. Do not have sex (intercourse, oral, or anal).
2. If you have sex:

    use a condom (also use a condom for oral and anal sex);

    have sex with only one uninfected person—do not have multiple partners;

ask your sex partner(s) if he or she has gonorrhea or other STDs, has had sex with someone who has an STD, or has sores, rashes, or discharge in the genital area.

How Can I Take Care Of Others And Myself If I Have Gonorrhea?

Here's how you can take care of yourself and others:

1. Take all your medicine.

2. Tell your sex partner(s) about your infection so that they can be tested and treated right away.

3. Do not have sex when you are getting treatment for gonorrhea.

4. Use a condom when you have sex after being treated for gonorrhea.

Chapter 46

Nongonococcal Urethritis

What Is NGU?

NGU (NonGonococcal Urethritis) is an infection of the urethra caused by pathogens (germs) other than gonorrhea. Several kinds of pathogens can cause NGU, including:

- *Chlamydia trachomatis*

- *Ureaplasma urealyticum*

- *Trichomonas vaginalis* (rare)

- Herpes simplex virus (rare)

- Adenovirus

- *Haemophilus vaginalis*

- *Mycoplasma genitalium*

NGU is most often caused by chlamydia, a common infection in men and women. The diagnosis of NGU is more commonly made in men than women, primarily due to anatomical differences.

About This Chapter: From "Information to Live By: Nongonococcal Urethritis (NGU)," © 2001 The American Social Health Association (ASHA). Reprinted with permission. Available online at http://www.ahastd.org/stdfaqs/ngu.html. For more information visit the ASHA website at http://www.ashastd.org.

How Can I Get NGU?

Sexual

Most germs that cause NGU can be passed during sex (vaginal, anal or or that involves direct mucous membrane contact with an infected person.

These germs can be passed even if the penis or tongue does not go all t way into the vagina, mouth or rectum, and even if body fluids are not e changed.

Nonsexual

These causes of NGU may include:

- Urinary tract infections.

- An inflamed prostate gland due to bacteria (bacterial prostatitis).

- A narrowing or closing of the tube in the penis (urethral stricture).

- A tightening of the foreskin so that it cannot be pulled back from the head of the penis (phimosa).

- The result of a process such as inserting a tube into the penis (catheterization).

Perinatal

During birth, infants maybe exposed to the germs causing NGU in passage through the birth canal. This may cause the baby to have infections in the:

- eyes (conjunctivitis)

- ears

- lungs (pneumonia)

✎ **Weird Words**

Asymptomatic: Having no symptoms.

Bacterial Prostatitis: An inflamed prostate gland due to bacteria.

Catheterization: Inserting a tube into the penis or urethra.

Epididymitis: Inflammation of the epididymis—the elongated, cordlike structure along the posterior border of the testes.

Pathogens: germs

Urethral Stricture: A narrowing or closing of the tube in the penis.

Urethritis: Inflammation of the urethra.

What Are The Signs Or Symptoms Of NGU?

Men (Urethral Infection)

- Discharge from the penis
- Burning or pain when urinating (peeing)
- Itching, irritation, or tenderness
- Underwear stain

Women (Vaginal/Urethral Infection)

The germs that cause NGU in men might cause other infections in women. These might include vaginitis or mucopurulent cervicitis (MPC). Women may also be asymptomatic (have no symptoms). Symptoms of NGU in women can include:

- Discharge from the vagina
- Burning or pain when urinating (peeing)
- Abdominal pain or abnormal vaginal bleeding may be an indication that the infection has progressed to pelvic inflammatory disease (PID)

Anal Or Oral Infections

Anal infection may result in:

- Rectal itching
- Discharge or pain on defecation

Oral infection may occur. Most (90 percent) are asymptomatic, but some people might have a sore throat.

What Can I Do To Reduce My Risk Of Getting NGU?

- Abstinence from sex is the best form of prevention.
- Using latex condoms from start to finish every time you have oral, vaginal or anal sex.
- Having sex with only one uninfected partner whom only has sex with you (mutual monogamy).

- Water-based spermicides can be used along with latex condoms for additional protection during vaginal intercourse. Use of spermicide is not recommended nor found to be effective for oral or anal intercourse.

- Have regular check-ups if you are sexually active.

- If you have an STD, don't have sex (oral, vaginal, anal) until all partners have been treated.

- Prompt, qualified and appropriate medical intervention, treatment and follow-up are important steps in breaking the disease cycle.

- Know your partner(s). Careful consideration and open communication between partners may protect all partners involved from infection.

> ♣ **It's A Fact!!**
>
> An NGU diagnosis is made when a man has urethritis (inflammation of the urethra), but gonorrhea is ruled out because he has a negative gonorrhea culture and/or gram stain.
>
> Other tests include:
>
> **For Men:**
> - Chlamydia culture
> - Urinalysis (sometimes, but rarely)
>
> **Women:**
> - Chlamydia culture
> - Gonorrhea culture to rule out gonorrhea

What Is The Treatment For NGU?

The main treatments for NGU are azithromycin and doxycycline. Alternatives are erythromycin ofloxacin. Recommended treatment for recurrent/persistent urethritis is metronidazole with erythromycin.

A woman who is pregnant, or thinks she might be, should tell her doctor. This will ensure that a medicine will be used that will not harm the baby.

Follow-Up

- Take all medications—even if you start to feel better before you finish the bottle.

- Treat all partners.

Why Worry About NGU?

♣ It's A Fact!!

Left untreated, the germs that cause NGU—especially chlamydia—can lead to:

Men

- Epididymitis (inflammation of the epididymis, the elongated, cordlike structure along the posterior border of the testes) which can lead to infertility if left untreated.
- Reiter's syndrome (arthritis)
- Conjunctivitis
- Skin lesions
- Discharge

Women

- Pelvic Inflammatory Disease (PID) which can result in ectopic (tubal) pregnancy.
- Recurrent PID may lead to infertility.
- Chronic pelvic pain
- Urethritis
- Vaginitis
- Mucopurulent cervicitis (MPC)
- Spontaneous abortion (miscarriage)

Men or Women

- Infections caused by anal sex might lead to severe proctitis (inflamed rectum).

Infants

- Exposure to the germs causing NGU during passage through the birth canal may result in infants having. Conjunctivitis (If left untreated, this may lead to blindness.), or pneumonia.

- Inform all partners.

- Abstain from sex until all partners are treated.

- Return for evaluation by a health care provider if symptoms persist or if symptoms recur after taking all the prescribed medicine.

Do I Need To Talk To My Partner About NGU?

Yes. If you have been told that you have NGU, talk to your partner(s), and let them know so they can be tested and treated. The most common cause of NGU is chlamydia, and it is easy to pass from an infected partner to one who is not infected.

A man who is diagnosed with NGU should tell his female sex partner and ask her to get tested. He can prevent lasting damage to her body by telling her right away.

All sex partners of someone diagnosed with NGU should be treated because:

- They may have an infection and not know it.

- It keeps them from passing the infection back to you or to others.

- It prevents them from suffering possible complications.

Should I Talk To My Health Care Provider About NGU?

If you are sexually active with more than one person and do not use latex condoms, then you should talk to your health care provider about being tested for STDs and NGU. Not all STDs cause symptoms, and you may have one and not know it.

Chapter 47

Other Important STDs

As medical science has become more precise in diagnosing infectious diseases, the list of known sexually transmitted diseases (STDs) has grown. The National Institute of Allergy and Infectious Diseases (NIAID) has published separate fact sheets on some of the major STDs: chlamydial infection; gonorrhea; pelvic inflammatory disease (PID); trichomoniasis and other vaginal infections; syphilis; genital herpes; genital warts; and AIDS. Some of the other diseases that can be transmitted sexually such as, chancroid, cytomegalovirus infection, molluscum contagiosum, pubic "crab" lice, scabies, and HTLV-I and II, are less well-known in the United States than other STDs, they are still important—some are especially significant for pregnant women. Many of these infections are of serious concern for people in other parts of the world, particularly in developing countries.

Chancroid

Chancroid ("shan-kroid") is an important bacterial infection caused by *Haemophilus ducreyi*, which is spread by sexual contact. Periodic outbreaks of chancroid have occurred in the United States, the last one being in the late

About This Chapter: Text in this chapter if from fact sheet from the National Institute of Allergy and Infectious Diseases (NIAID), June 1998. Available online at http://www.niaid.nih.gov/factsheets/stdother.htm. Reviewed and updated in January 2003, by Dr. David A. Cooke, MD, Diplomate, American Board of Internal Medicine.

1980s. These outbreaks are usually seen in minority populations in the inner cities, especially in the southern and eastern portion of the country. Globally, this disease is common in sub-Saharan Africa among men who have frequent contact with prostitutes.

The infection begins with the appearance of painful open sores on the genitals, sometimes accompanied by swollen, tender lymph nodes in the groin. These symptoms occur within a week after exposure. Symptoms in women are often less noticeable and may be limited to painful urination or defecation, painful intercourse, rectal bleeding, or vaginal discharge. Chancroid lesions may be difficult to distinguish from ulcers caused by genital herpes or syphilis. A physician must therefore diagnose the infection by excluding other diseases with similar symptoms. People with chancroid can be treated effectively with one of several antibiotics. Chancroid is one of the genital ulcer diseases that may be associated with an increased risk of transmission of the human immunodeficiency virus (HIV), the cause of AIDS.

Cytomegalovirus Infections

Cytomegalovirus (CMV) is a very common virus that infects approximately one-half of all young adults in

♣ It's A Fact!!

Lesser-known sexually transmitted diseases and their symptoms include:

- Chancroid infection begins with the appearance of painful open sores on the genitals, sometimes accompanied by swollen, tender lymph nodes in the groin. Symptoms in women are often less noticeable.

- CMV usually produces no symptoms of infection in healthy adults.

- Molluscum contagiosum infection often produces no noticeable symptoms, although sometimes painless lesions itch or become irritated.

- The primary symptom of pubic lice infestation is itching in the pubic area.

- Scabies causes intense itching, and small red bumps or lines may appear.

the United States. It rarely causes serious consequences except in people with suppressed or impaired immune systems or in infants, whose immune systems are still developing. The virus, a member of the herpesvirus family, is found in saliva, urine, and other bodily fluids. Because it is often found in semen as well as in cervical secretions, the virus can be spread by sexual contact; it also can be easily spread by other forms of physical contact such as kissing. Day-care center staff for children under the age of 3 are at increased risk of CMV infection and should carefully wash their hands after changing diapers. Like other herpesvirus infections, CMV is incurable; people are infected with it for life. Although the virus usually remains in an inactive state, it can reactivate from time to time.

Symptoms. In healthy adults, CMV usually produces no symptoms of infection. Occasionally, however, mild symptoms of swollen lymph glands, fever, and fatigue may occur. These symptoms may be similar to those of infectious mononucleosis.

Diagnosis. The ELISA (enzyme-linked immunosorbent assay) test is commonly used to detect levels of antibodies (disease-fighting proteins of the immune system) in the blood. A number of other blood tests can suggest a diagnosis of CMV infection, but no blood test can reliably diagnose it. Although CMV can be isolated from urine or other body fluids, it may be excreted months or years after an infection; therefore, isolation of the virus from these fluids is not a reliable method of diagnosing recent infection.

Complications. Babies can be infected with CMV in the uterus if their mothers become infected with the virus or develop a recurrence of a previous infection during pregnancy. Although most babies infected with CMV before birth do not develop any symptoms, CMV is the leading cause of congenital infection in the United States. An estimated 6,000 babies each year develop life-threatening complications of congenital CMV infection at birth or suffer serious consequences later in life, including mental retardation, blindness, deafness, or epilepsy. Investigators supported by NIAID are currently studying how the virus interferes with normal fetal development and at which stages the fetus is most susceptible to infection. Congenital CMV is the most common cause of progressive deafness in children.

When CMV is acquired after birth, or if it reactivates, it can be life threatening for persons with suppressed immune systems, such as those receiving chemotherapy or persons who have received immunosuppressan drugs for organ transplantation. Persons with HIV infection or AIDS may develop severe CMV infections, including CMV retinitis, an eye disease that can lead to blindness.

Treatment. NIAID scientists are testing new antiviral drugs that migh be effective against CMV infections. The antiviral drugs foscarnet and ganciclovir have been approved for treating people with AIDS-associated CMV retinitis.

Prevention. There is no intervention to prevent CMV. Use of the male condom may reduce risk although virus in the saliva would be transmitted by kissing or oral intercourse. Some experts believe that primary or first-time exposure during pregnancy is a major cause of CMV infection in newborns. Infants infected before or just after birth are likely to be shedding CMV in saliva and urine, which can infect others. Hand washing and proper handling of diapers may reduce risk. Scientists are working to develop a vaccine and other methods to provide immunity to CMV and offer protection against severe disease.

✤ It's A Fact!!

- Cytomegalovirus (CMV) is a very common virus that infects approximately one-half of all young adults in the United States.

- CMV is incurable; people are infected with it for life. Although the virus usually remains in an inactive state, it can reactivate from time to time.

Molluscum Contagiosum

This common viral infection most often affects young children, who pass it to each other through saliva. In adults, however, the virus is transmitted sexually, resulting in lesions on the genitals, lower abdomen, buttocks, or inner thighs. Most people with the infection do not have noticeable symptoms, although sometimes the lesions, which are painless wart-like bumps, may itch or become irritated. The lesions often heal without treatment, although physicians may sometimes scrape them off or treat them with chemical irritants.

Pubic Lice

Pubic lice (*pediculosis pubis* or crab lice) are very tiny insects that infest the pubic hair and survive by feeding on human blood. These parasites are most often spread by sexual contact; in a few cases, they may be picked up through contact with infested bedding or clothing. An estimated 3 million people with new cases of the infestation are treated each year in the United States.

Symptoms. The primary symptom of infestation is itching in the pubic area. Scratching may spread the lice to other parts of the body; thus, every effort should be made to avoid touching the infected area, although this may be difficult.

Diagnosis. Pubic lice are diagnosed easily because they are visible to the naked eye. They are pinhead size, oval in shape, and grayish, but appear reddish-brown when full of blood from their host. Nits, the tiny white eggs, also are visible and usually are observed clinging to the base of pubic hair.

Treatment. Lotions and shampoos that will kill pubic lice are available both over the counter and by prescription. Creams or lotions containing lindane, a powerful pesticide, are most frequently prescribed for the treatment of pubic lice. Pregnant women may be advised not to use this drug, and a physician's recommendations for use in infants and small children should be followed carefully. Itching may persist even after the lice have been eradicated. This is because the skin has been irritated and requires time to heal. A soothing lotion such as calamine may offer temporary relief.

Prevention. All persons with whom an infested individual has come into close contact, including family and close friends as well as sex partners, should be treated to ensure that the lice have been eliminated. In addition, all clothing and bedding should be dry-cleaned or washed in very hot water (125° F), dried at a high setting, and ironed to rid them of any lice. Pubic lice die within 24 hours of being separated from the body. Because the eggs may live up to six days, it is important to apply the treatment for the full time recommended.

Scabies

Scabies is a skin infestation with a tiny mite, *Sarcoptes scabiei*. Scabies has become relatively common throughout the general population. It is highly contagious and is commonly transmitted by contact with skin, infested sheets, towels, or even furniture. It may also be transmitted sexually.

Symptoms. Scabies causes intense itching, which often becomes worse at night. Small red bumps or lines appear on the body at sites where the female scabies mite has burrowed into the skin to lay her eggs. The areas most commonly affected include the hands (especially between the fingers), wrists, elbows, lower abdomen, and genitals. The skin reaction may not develop until a month or more after infestation. During this time, a person may pass the disease unknowingly to a sex partner or to another person with whom he or she has close contact.

Diagnosis. Scabies may be confused with other skin irritations such as poison ivy or eczema. To make an accurate diagnosis, a doctor takes a scraping of the irritated area and examines it under a microscope, to reveal the presence of the mite.

Treatment. As with pubic lice, lindane is an effective treatment for scabies. Pregnant women should consult a doctor before using this product. Permethrin cream may also be effective. Nonprescription remedies such as sulfur ointment also are available. Sulfur is fairly effective but may be objectionable because of its odor and messiness. Itching can persist even after the infestation has been eliminated because of lingering skin irritation. A hydrocortisone cream or ointment or a soothing lotion may provide relief from itching.

Prevention. Family members and sex partners of a person with scabies are advised to undergo treatment. Twenty-four hours after drug therapy, a person with scabies infestation is no longer contagious to others, even though the skin irritation may persist for some time. As with pubic lice, special care must be taken to rid clothing and bedding of any mites.

Human T-Cell Lymphotropic Virus

The human T-cell lymphotropic viruses (retroviruses), HTLV-I and HTLV-II, are uncommon in the general U.S. population. They appear to be most prevalent among IV drug users and persons who have multiple sex partners, genital ulcers, or a history of syphilis. The virus can be transmitted by blood or intimate sexual contact, and can be passed from mother to child during pregnancy and through breast milk.

Most infected persons remain healthy carriers of the virus. In rare cases, however, HTLV-I can cause adult T-cell leukemia/lymphoma (ATL), a rare and aggressive cancer of the blood. Infected persons also may develop myelopathy, a neurologic disorder that affects the muscles in the legs. In addition, researchers think that HTLV-I plays a role in the development of B-cell chronic lymphocytic leukemia. HTLV-II can cause another rare cancer called hairy-cell leukemia. Because the chances of curing ATL rely on early detection, scientists are studying protein in the blood of HTLV-I-infected persons that may help predict who will develop the disease.

Blood donations are screened routinely for HTLV-I. Because lab tests cannot easily distinguish between HTLV-I and HTLV-II, experts believe many cases of HTLV-II are eliminated from the blood supply as well.

Research

STD research that is supported and conducted by NIAID will help in the search for new ways to diagnose, treat, and prevent these infections. This is important not only for the well-being of our adult population but also for the health of future generations.

Chapter 48

HIV And AIDS: Are You At Risk?

How HIV Is Transmitted

HIV is spread by sexual contact with an infected person, by sharing needles and/or syringes (primarily for drug injection) with someone who is infected, or, less commonly (and now very rarely in countries where blood is screened for HIV antibodies), through transfusions of infected blood or blood clotting factors. Babies born to HIV-infected women may become infected before or during birth or through breast-feeding after birth.

In the health care setting, workers have been infected with HIV after being stuck with needles containing HIV-infected blood or, less frequently, after infected blood gets into a worker's open cut or a mucous membrane (for example, the eyes or inside of the nose). There has been only one instance of patients being infected by a health care worker in the United States; this involved HIV transmission from one infected dentist to six patients. Investigations have been completed involving more than 22,000 patients of 63 HIV-infected physicians, surgeons, and dentists, and no other cases of this type of transmission have been identified in the United States.

About This Chapter: Excerpted from "HIV and Its Transmission," 2001 Centers for Disease Control and Prevention (CDC), available online at http://www.cdc.gov/hiv/pubs/facts/transmission.htm.

Some people fear that HIV might be transmitted in other ways; howeve no scientific evidence to support any of these fears has been found. If HI were being transmitted through other routes (such as through air, water, c insects), the pattern of reported AIDS cases would be much different from what has been observed. For example, if mosquitoes could transmit HI infection, many more young children and preadolescents would have bee diagnosed with AIDS.

All reported cases suggesting new or potentially unknown routes of trans mission are thoroughly investigated by state and local health departmen with the assistance, guidance, and laboratory support from CDC. No add tional routes of transmission have been recorded, despite a national sentin system designed to detect just such an occurrence.

✔ Quick Tip

To Prevent Exposure To HIV

- Gloves should be worn during contact with blood or other body fluids that could possibly contain visible blood, such as urine, feces, or vomit.

- Cuts, sores, or breaks on both the care giver's and patient's exposed skin should be covered with bandages.

- Hands and other parts of the body should be washed immediately after contact with blood or other body fluids, and surfaces soiled with blood should be disinfected appropriately.

- Practices that increase the likelihood of blood contact, such as sharing of razors and toothbrushes, should be avoided.

- Needles and other sharp instruments should be used only when medically necessary and handled according to recommendations for health-care settings. (Do not put caps back on needles by hand or remove needles from syringes. Dispose of needles in puncture-proof containers).

The following paragraphs specifically address some of the common misperceptions about HIV transmission.

HIV In The Environment

Scientists and medical authorities agree that HIV does not survive well in the environment, making the possibility of environmental transmission remote. HIV is found in varying concentrations or amounts in blood, semen, vaginal fluid, breast milk, saliva, and tears. To obtain data on the survival of HIV, laboratory studies have required the use of artificially high concentrations of laboratory-grown virus. Although these unnatural concentrations of HIV can be kept alive for days or even weeks under precisely controlled and limited laboratory conditions, CDC studies have shown that drying of even these high concentrations of HIV reduces the amount of infectious virus by 90 to 99 percent within several hours. Since the HIV concentrations used in laboratory studies are much higher than those actually found in blood or other specimens, drying of HIV-infected human blood or other body fluids reduces the theoretical risk of environmental transmission to that which has been observed—essentially zero. Incorrect interpretation of conclusions drawn from laboratory studies have unnecessarily alarmed some people.

Results from laboratory studies should not be used to assess specific personal risk of infection because (1) the amount of virus studied is not found in human specimens or elsewhere in nature, and (2) no one has been identified as infected with HIV due to contact with an environmental surface. Additionally, HIV is unable to reproduce outside its living host (unlike many bacteria or fungi, which may do so under suitable conditions), except under laboratory conditions, therefore, it does not spread or maintain infectiousness outside its host.

Households

Although HIV has been transmitted between family members in a household setting, this type of transmission is very rare. These transmissions are believed to have resulted from contact between skin or mucous membranes and infected blood. To prevent even such rare occurrences, precautions, as described in previously published guidelines, should be taken in all settings—including the home—to prevent exposures to the blood of persons who are HIV infected, at risk for HIV infection, or whose infection and risk status are unknown.

Businesses And Other Settings

There is no known risk of HIV transmission to co-workers, clients, or consumers from contact in industries such as food-service establishments. Food-service workers known to be infected with HIV need not be restricted

---

♣ It's A Fact!!

Risk Of HIV-Related Illness To Men Who Have Sex With Men

In the United States, HIV-related illness and death historically have had a tremendous impact on men who have sex with men (MSM). Even though the toll of the epidemic among injection drug users (IDUs) and heterosexuals has increased during the last decade, MSM continue to account for the largest number of people reported with AIDS each year. In 2000 alone, 13,562 AIDS cases were reported among MSM, compared with 8,531 among IDUs and 6,530 among men and women who acquired HIV heterosexually.

Overall, the number of MSM of all races and ethnicities who are living with AIDS has increased steadily, partly as a result of the 1993 expanded AIDS case definition and, more recently, of improved survival.

Abundant evidence shows a need to sustain prevention efforts for each generation of young gay and bisexual men. We cannot assume that the positive attitudinal and behavioral change seen among older men also applies to younger men. Recent data on HIV prevalence and risk behaviors suggest that young gay and bisexual men continue to place themselves at considerable risk for HIV infection and other sexually transmitted diseases (STDs).

Ongoing studies show that both HIV prevalence ratio (the proportion of people living with HIV in a population) and prevalence of risk behaviors remain high among some young MSM. In a sample of MSM 15-22 years old in seven urban areas, CDC researchers found that, overall, 7% already were in-from work unless they have other infections or illnesses (such as diarrhea or hepatitis A) for which any food-service worker, regardless of HIV infection status, should be restricted. CDC recommends that all food-service workers follow recommended standards and practices of good personal hygiene and food sanitation.

In 1985, CDC issued routine precautions that all personal-service workers (such as hairdressers, barbers, cosmetologists, and massage therapists)

fected with HIV. Higher percentages of African Americans (14%) and Hispanics (7%) were infected than were whites (3%).

In the 34 areas with confidential HIV reporting, data show that substantial numbers of MSM still are being infected, especially young men. In 2000, 59% of reported HIV infections among adolescent males aged 13-19 and 53% of cases among men aged 20-24 were attributed to male-to-male sexual contact.

Research among gay and bisexual men suggests that some individuals are now less concerned about becoming infected than in the past and may be inclined to take more risks. This is backed up by reported increases in gonorrhea among gay men in several large U.S. cities between 1993 and 1996. Despite medical advances, HIV infection remains a serious, usually fatal disease that requires complex, costly, and difficult treatment regimens that do not work for everyone. As better treatment options are developed, we must not lose sight of the fact that preventing HIV infection in the first place precludes the need for people to undergo these difficult and expensive therapies.

These data highlight the need to design more effective prevention efforts for gay and bisexual men of color. The involvement of community and opinion leaders in prevention efforts will be critical for overcoming cultural barriers to prevention, including homophobia. For example, there remains a tremendous stigma to acknowledging gay and bisexual activity in African American and Hispanic communities.

Source: "Prevention among Men Who Have Sex with Men," Centers for Disease Control and Prevention (CDC), 2002, available online at http://www.cdc.gov/hiv/pubs/facts/msm.htm.

should follow, even though there is no evidence of transmission from a personal-service worker to a client or vice versa. Instruments that are intended to penetrate the skin (such as tattooing and acupuncture needles, ear piercing devices) should be used once and disposed of or thoroughly cleaned and sterilized. Instruments not intended to penetrate the skin but which may become contaminated with blood (for example, razors) should be used for only one client and disposed of or thoroughly cleaned and disinfected after each use. Personal-service workers can use the same cleaning procedures that are recommended for health care institutions.

CDC knows of no instances of HIV transmission through tattooing or body piercing, although hepatitis B virus has been transmitted during some of these practices. One case of HIV transmission from acupuncture has been documented. Body piercing (other than ear piercing) is relatively new in the United States, and the medical complications for body piercing appear to be greater than for tattoos. Healing of piercings generally will take weeks, and sometimes even months, and the pierced tissue could conceivably be abraded (torn or cut) or inflamed even after healing. Therefore, a theoretical HIV transmission risk does exist if the unhealed or abraded tissues come into contact with an infected person's blood or other infectious body fluid. Additionally, HIV could be transmitted if instruments contaminated with blood are not sterilized or disinfected between clients.

Kissing

Casual contact through closed-mouth or social kissing is not a risk for transmission of HIV. Because of the potential for contact with blood during "French" or open-mouth kissing, CDC recommends against engaging in this activity with a person known to be infected. However, the risk of acquiring HIV during open-mouth kissing is believed to be very low. CDC has investigated only one case of HIV infection that may be attributed to contact with blood during open-mouth kissing.

Biting

In 1997, CDC published findings from a state health department investigation of an incident that suggested blood-to-blood transmission of HIV by a human bite. There have been other reports in the medical literature in which HIV appeared to have been transmitted by a bite. Severe trauma with extensive tissue tearing and damage and presence of blood were reported in each of these instances. Biting is not a common way of transmitting HIV. In fact, there are numerous reports of bites that did not result in HIV infection.

Saliva, Tears, And Sweat

HIV has been found in saliva and tears in very low quantities from some AIDS patients. It is important to understand that finding a small amount of HIV in a body fluid does not necessarily mean that HIV can be transmitted by that body fluid. HIV has not been recovered from the sweat of HIV-infected persons. Contact with saliva, tears, or sweat has never been shown to result in transmission of HIV.

Insects

From the onset of the HIV epidemic, there has been concern about transmission of the virus by biting and bloodsucking insects. However, studies conducted by researchers at CDC and elsewhere have shown no evidence of HIV transmission through insects—even in areas where there are many cases of AIDS and large populations of insects such as mosquitoes. Lack of such outbreaks, despite intense efforts to detect them, supports the conclusion that HIV is not transmitted by insects.

The results of experiments and observations of insect biting behavior indicate that when an insect bites a person, it does not inject its own or a previously bitten person's or animal's blood into the next person bitten. Rather, it injects saliva, which acts as a lubricant or anticoagulant so the insect can feed efficiently. Such diseases as yellow fever and malaria are transmitted through the saliva of specific species of mosquitoes. However, HIV lives for only a short time inside an insect and, unlike organisms that are transmitted via insect bites, HIV does not reproduce (and does not survive) in insects. Thus, even if the virus enters a mosquito or another sucking or biting insect, the insect does not become infected and cannot transmit HIV to the next human it feeds on or bites. HIV is not found in insect feces.

There is also no reason to fear that a biting or bloodsucking insect, such as a mosquito, could transmit HIV from one person to another through

♣ It's A Fact!!
Risk Of HIV-Related Illness To Women Who Have Sex With Women

Female-to-female transmission of HIV appears to be a rare occurrence. However, case reports of female-to-female transmission of HIV and the well-documented risk of female-to-male transmission of HIV indicate that vaginal secretions and menstrual blood are potentially infectious and that mucous membrane (e.g., oral, vaginal) exposure to these secretions have the potential to lead to HIV infection.

Through December 1998, 109,311 women were reported with AIDS. Of these, 2,220 were reported to have had sex with women; however, the vast majority had other risks (such as injection drug use, sex with high-risk men, or receipt of blood or blood products). Of the 347 (out of 2,220) women who were reported to have had sex only with women, 98% also had another risk—injection drug use in most cases.

Although female-to-female transmission of HIV apparently is rare, female sexual contact should be considered a possible means of transmission among WSW. These women need to know:

- that exposure of a mucous membrane, such as the mouth, (especially non-intact tissue) to vaginal secretions and menstrual blood is potentially infectious, particularly during early and late-stage HIV infection when the amount of virus in the blood is expected to be highest.

- that condoms should be used consistently and correctly each and every time for sexual contact with men or when using sex toys. Sex toys should not be shared. No barrier methods for use during oral sex have been evaluated as effective or approved by the FDA. However, women can use dental dams, cut-open condoms, or plastic wrap to help protect themselves from contact with body fluids during oral sex.

- their own and their partner's HIV status. This knowledge can help uninfected women begin and maintain behavioral changes that reduce their risk of becoming infected. For women who are found to be infected, it can assist in getting early treatment and avoiding infecting others.

Source: "Prevention among Women Who Have Sex with Women," 1999 Centers for Disease Control and Prevention (CDC), available online at http://www.cdc.gov/hiv/pubs/facts/wsw.htm.

HIV-infected blood left on its mouth parts. Two factors serve to explain why this is so—first, infected people do not have constant, high levels of HIV in their bloodstreams and, second, insect mouth parts do not retain large amounts of blood on their surfaces. Further, scientists who study insects have determined that biting insects normally do not travel from one person to the next immediately after ingesting blood. Rather, they fly to a resting place to digest this blood meal.

Effectiveness of Condoms

Condoms are classified as medical devices and are regulated by the Food and Drug Administration (FDA). Condom manufacturers in the United States test each latex condom for defects, including holes, before it is packaged. The proper and consistent use of latex or polyurethane (a type of plastic) condoms when engaging in sexual intercourse—vaginal, anal, or oral—can greatly reduce a person's risk of acquiring or transmitting sexually transmitted diseases, including HIV infection.

There are many different types and brands of condoms available—however, only latex or polyurethane condoms provide a highly effective mechanical barrier to HIV. In laboratories, viruses occasionally have been shown to pass through natural membrane (skin or lambskin) condoms, which may contain natural pores and are therefore not recommended for disease prevention (they are documented to be effective for contraception). Women may wish to consider using the female condom when a male condom cannot be used.

👉 **Remember!!**

HIV is spread:

• by sexual contact with an infected person

• by sharing needles and/or syringes (primarily for drug injection) with someone who is infected

• by transfusions of infected blood or blood clotting factors (this happens only very rarely in countries where blood is screened for the presence of the virus)

• during birth or through breast-feeding after birth when mothers are infected.

For condoms to provide maximum protection, they must be used consistently (every time) and correctly. Several studies of correct and consistent condom use clearly show that latex condom breakage rates in this country are less than 2 percent. Even when condoms do break, one study showed that more than half of such breaks occurred prior to ejaculation.

When condoms are used reliably, they have been shown to prevent pregnancy up to 98 percent of the time among couples using them as their only method of contraception. Similarly, numerous studies among sexually active people have demonstrated that a properly used latex condom provides a high degree of protection against a variety of sexually transmitted diseases, including HIV infection.

Chapter 49

You Can Get AIDS From Oral Sex

Many persons have inquired about the results of a study presented as a poster at the recent 7th National Conference on Retroviruses and Opportunistic Infections. The following questions and answers contain more specific information about the presented study results.

This study, one component of a primary and recent HIV infection study called the Options Project, is funded by the Centers for Disease Control and Prevention (CDC) at the University of California, San Francisco. The purpose of this particular study was to ascertain the extent of HIV transmitted by oral sex among men who have sex with men who were identified with HIV within 12 months of becoming infected.

Hasn't Oral Sex Already Been Identified As A Method Of Transmitting HIV?

Yes. However, this is the most definitive study to date. Earlier studies have been published.

About This Chapter: Text in this chapter is from "Primary HIV Infection Associated with Oral Transmission," a fact sheet produced by the Centers for Disease Control and Prevention (CDC), 2001. Available online at http://www.cdc.gov/hiv/pubsfacts/oralsexqa.htm.

What Is The Risk Of HIV Transmission From Oral Se

The likelihood of transmission of HIV from an infected person to uninfected person varies significantly depending on the type of exposure contact involved. The risk of becoming infected with HIV through unpr tected (without a condom) oral sex is lower than that of unprotected anal vaginal sex. However, even a lower risk activity can become an importa way people get infected if it is done often enough. The Options Proje found that 7.8% (8 of 102) of recently infected men who have sex with m in San Francisco were probably infected through oral sex. Most of these m believed that the risk was minimal or non-existent.

What Are The Exact Ways That HIV Was Transmitte In This Study?

Nearly half (3 of 8) of these cases reported oral problems, including occ sional bleeding gums. Almost all (7 of 8) of these men reported to have h: oral contact with pre-semen or semen.

How Do You Know If The Study Participants Were Tel ing The Truth About Their Sexual History?

Oral transmission of HIV is very difficult to single out as the only w: that HIV is transmitted because few people engage exclusively in oral sex. number of specific questions were asked by a trained evaluator. The partic

✔ Quick Tip

CDC operates a toll-free, confidential National STD/AIDS Hotline which can assist callers with these types of concerns. The English service (24 hours a day, 7 days a week) can be reached by calling 1-800-342-2437; Spanish is 1-800-344-7432 and TTY service for Deaf and Hard of Hearing is 1-800-243-7889.

pants' risk behaviors were assessed by using clinical interviews, counselor intervention, epidemiologic interview, partner interview when possible, and final disposition of transmission risk. Of the 8 cases, 4 reported protected anal intercourse, without the condom breaking, with persons who were either HIV infected or had an unknown serostatus. Men in this study who reported that they were uncertain if the condom was used properly were eliminated from this study.

Was This A Surprise Finding?

Yes and No. The percentage of recently infected men enrolled in this study who were probably infected through oral sex (8%) was higher than many researchers had thought likely or found in other studies. More media attention appeared to be placed on this particular study, probably because of the higher number of study participants. There appears to be evidence that higher risk activities (anal sex) among men who have sex with men is decreasing while lower risk activities (oral sex) among these men is increasing. Oral sex has always been considered a lower risk activity but is certainly not risk free.

What Can Be Done To Prevent HIV?

The study results emphasize that any type of sexual activity with an infected person is a risk of HIV transmission. Oral sex with someone who is infected with HIV is certainly not risk free. Prevention of HIV is more important than ever. Some persons have indicated that they are less concerned about HIV because of new treatments and are being less careful. This study presents a wake-up call to everyone that HIV is far from over and remains a serious, lifelong disease that is best to prevent. CDC's recommendations on how to prevent sexual transmission of HIV remain the same. Protection requires abstaining from sexual activity or taking precautions with all types of intercourse—either having sex with only one uninfected partner, using condoms for sexual intercourse and oral sex, and using lower risk activities such as mutual masturbation.

Resources

Berrey M, Shea T. Oral sex HIV transmission (letter). *J AIDS* 1997; 475.

Bratt GA, Berglund T, Glantzberg BL, Albert J, Sandstrom E. Two cases of oral to genital HIV-1 transmission. *Intl J STD & AIDS* 1997; 8:522-525.

Clifford L. HIV seroconversion and oral intercourse. *AJPH* 1991;81:698.

Edwards SK, White C. HIV seroconversion illness after orogenital contact with successful contact tracing. *International Journal of STD & AIDS*. 1995; 6:50-51.

Keet PM, Albrecht Van Lent IV, Sandfort TG, Coutinho RA, Van Griensven GJ. Orogenital sex and the transmission of HIV among homosexual men. *AIDS* 1992;6:223-226.

Lifson AR, O'Malley PM, Hessol NA, Buchbinder SP, Cannon L, Rutherford GW. HIV seroconversion in two homosexual mean after receptive oral intercourse with ejaculation. *AJPH* 1991;80:1509-1510.

Quarto C, Germinario C, Troiano T, Fontana A, Barbuti S. HIV transmission by fellatio (letter). *Europ J Epidemiol* 1990;9:339-340.

Robinson ED, Evans BG. Oral sex and HIV transmission. *AIDS* 1999;16(6):737-8.

Schacker T, Collier AC, Hughes J, Shea T, Corey L. Clinical and epidemiologic features of primary HIV infection. *Ann Intern Med* 1996;125:256-264.

Spitzer P, Weiner NJ. Transmission of HIV infection from a woman to a man by oral sex (letter). *N Engl J Med* 1989;320:251.

Part 7

If You Need More Information

Chapter 50

Internet Resources:
Teen Sexuality And Sexual Health

This chapter contains a list of websites that can help you find information related to sexuality, sexual health, and other related topics. Although some sites are intended for all audiences, many are written specifically for teens. A separate list of organizations that can help in times of crisis is also included.

Sexuality, Sexual Health, and Related Topics

Advocates for Youth
http://www.advocatesforyouth.org

American Academy of Family Physicians
Health for Teens
http://familydoctor.org/teens.html

Aware Foundation
http://www.awarefoundation.org

Campaign for Our Children, Inc.
http://www.cfoc.org

Centers for Disease Control and Prevention
Division of Sexually Transmitted Diseases
http://www.cdc.gov/nchstp/dstd/dstdp.html

Coolnurse
http://www.coolnurse.com

Focus Adolescent Services
Teen Sexual Behaviors
http://www.focusas.com/
SexualBehavior.html

4 Girls Health
http://www.4girls.gov

Girl Power
http://www.girlpower.gov

It's Great to Wait
http://www.greattowait.com

Go Ask Alice!
http://
www.goaskalice.columbia.edu

Healthfinder
http://www.healthfinder.gov/
justforyou

Iwannaknow
http://www.iwannaknow.org

Keep Kids Healthy
Adolescent Health Center
http://www.keepkidshealthy.com/
adolescent/adolescent.html

MEDLINEplus
Teen Sexual Health
http://www.nlm.nih.gov/
medlineplus/teensexualhealth.html

National Campaign to Prevent Teen Pregnancy
http://www.teenpregnancy.org

Not Me, Not Now
http://www.notmenotnow.org

OBGYN.net: Young Woman
http://www.obgyn.net/yw/yw.asp

Parents, Families and Friends of Lesbians and Gays
http://www.pflag.org

Pediatrician OnCall™: Teen Care
http://www.pediatriconcall.com/
forpatients/TeenCare/
teencarepat.asp

Planned Parenthood Federation of America
http://www.plannedparenthood.org

Puberty 101
http://www.puberty101.com

Sex Etc.
http://www.sxetc.org

Sexuality and U
Society of Obstetricians and
Gynaecologists of Canada
http://sexualityandu.ca/eng/teens

Sexuality Information and Education Council of the U.S.
http://www.siecus.org

Stop, Think, Be Safe!
http://www.stopthinkbesafe.org

Teen Health Centre
http://teenhealthcentre.com

Teen Health Website
http://www.chebucto.ns.ca/Health/TeenHealth

TeenCentral.Net
http://www.teencentral.net

TeenGrowth
http://www.teengrowth.com

TeenHealthFX
http://www.teenhealthfx.com

TeensHealth.org
http://www.teenshealth.org

Teenwire
http://www.teenwire.com

Virtual Children's Hospital: Teen Health
http://www.vh.org/navigation/vch/topics/pediatric_provider_teen_health.html

World Health Organization
Adolescent Sexual and Reproductive Health
http://www.who.int/reproductive-health/adolescent

Worth the Wait
http://www.worththewait.org

Youth Resource
http://www.youthresource.com

Other Organizations That Can Help in Times of Crisis

Al-Anon/Alateen
For information about alcoholism and alcohol abuse
http://www.al-anon.org/alateen.html

Childhelp USA
For information about child abuse
http://www.childhelpusa.org

Suicide Crisis Center
For a list of suicide prevention hotlines
http://www.suicidehotlines.com

National Institute on Drug Abuse
For information about addiction and drug use
http://www.nida.nih.gov

National Runaway Switch-board

Help for runaways and their families
http://www.nrscrisisline.org

National STD/HIV Hotline

Call 800-227-8922 or visit the website for more information
http://www.cdc.gov/nchstp/dstd/dstdp.html

Chapter 51

Family Service and Other Related Organizations

For more information about sexuality including sexually transmitted diseases, crisis pregnancies, and other sexual health issues, contact the following organizations:

Resources For Information About Sexual Health

Advocates for Youth
Suite 200 Vermont Avenue, N.W.
Washington, DC 20005
Tel: 202-347-5700
Fax: 202-347-2263
Internet: http://
www.advocatesforyouth.org
E-Mail:
info@advocatesforyouth.org

Alan Guttmacher Institute
120 Wall Street
21st Floor
New York, NY 10005
Tel: 212-248-1111
Fax: 212-248-1951
Internet: http://www.agi-usa.org
E-Mail: info@guttmacher.org

About This Chapter: The resources listed in this chapter were compiled from many different sources. Inclusion does not constitute endorsement. All resources were verified in January 2003.

American Academy of Family Physicians

11400 Tomahawk Creek Parkway
Leawood, KS 66211-2672
Toll Free: 800-274-2237
Tel: 913-906-6000
E-Mail: fp@aafp.org

American Academy of Pediatrics

141 Northwest Point Boulevard
Elk Grove Village, IL 60007-1098
Tel: 847-434-4000
Fax: 847-434-8000
Internet: http://www.aap.org

American Social Health Association

P.O. Box 13827
Research Triangle Park, NC 27709
Tel: 919-361-8400
Fax: 919-361-8425
Internet: http://www.ashastd.org
Teen-oriented Web site: http://www.iwannaknow.org

Campaign for Our Children, Inc.

120 West Fayette Street
Baltimore, MD 21201
Tel: 410-576-9015
Internet: http://www.cfoc.org

Center for Adolescent Health Promotion and Disease Prevention (CAHPDP)

Johns Hopkins University
2007 East Monument Street
Baltimore, MD 21205
Tel: 410-614-3952
Fax: 410-614-3956
Internet: http://www.jhsph.edu/hao/cah

Centers for Disease Control and Prevention

Office of Women's Health
1600 Clifton Road
Atlanta, GA 30033
Tel: 404-639-7230
Internet: http://www.cdc.gov
National STD Hotline: 800-227-8922
National AIDS Hotline for Teens: 800-234-TEEN
National AIDS Hotline: 800-342-AIDS

Center for Young Women's Health

300 Longwood Avenue
Boston, MA 02115
Tel: 617-355-2994
Fax: 617-232-3136
Internet: http://youngwomenshealth.org
E-Mail: cywh@tch.Harvard.edu

Children's Hospital National Medical Center

111 Michigan Ave., N.W.
Washington, DC 20010
Tel: 202-884-5000
Fax: 202-884-3711
Internet: http://www.cnmc.org

Club Varsity

800 S. Pacific Coast Highway #8-501
Redondo Beach, CA 90277
Tel: 562-429-0357
Fax: 310-891-6932
Internet: http://www.clubvarsity.org

Diakon Lutheran Social Ministries

798 Hausman Road
Allentown, PA 18104
Toll Free: 888-582-2230
Fax: 610-682-1055
Internet: http://www.lsn.org

Family Research Council

801 G Street NW
Washington, DC 20001
Tel: 202-393-2100
Internet: http://www.frc.org
State Directory of Family Help:
http://www.focusas.com/
Directory.html

Focus Adolescent Services

Toll Free: 877-362-8727
Tel: 410-341-4342
Internet: http://www.focusas.com
E-Mail: help@focusas.com

Gay and Lesbian Adolescent Social Services

650 North Robertson Street
Suite A
West Hollywood, CA 90069
Tel: 310-358-8727
Internet: http://www.glassla.org

Gay and Lesbian National Hotline

Toll Free: 888-THE-GLNH (843-4564)

Great to Wait

Internet: http://
www.greattowait.com
E-Mail: g2w@mail.greattowait.com

IGY National Hotline

1-800-347-TEEN

National Abstinence Clearinghouse

801 East 41st Street
Sioux Falls, SD 57105
Internet: http://www.abstinence.net

National Black Women's
Health Project
600 Pennsylvania Ave., SE
Suite 310
Washington, DC 20003
Tel: 202-548-4000
Fax: 203-543-9743
Internet: http://www.nbwhp.org
E-Mail: nbwhp@nbwhp.org

National Center for HIV,
STD, and TB Prevention
Division of Sexually Transmitted
Diseases
Centers for Disease Control and
Prevention
1600 Clifton Road
Atlanta, GA 30333
Toll Free: 800-227-8922 (STD/
HIV Hotline)
Toll Free: 888-232-3228 (Voice
Information System)
Fax: 888-232-3299
Internet: http://www.cdc.gov/
nchstp/dstd/dstdp.html

National Herpes Hotline
Tel: 919-361-8488

National HPV and Cervical
Cancer Hotline
Tel: 919-361-4848

National Institute of Allergy
and Infectious Diseases
Building 31, Room 7A-50
31 Center Drive, MSC 2520
Bethesda, MD 20892-2520
Tel: 301-496-0545
Internet: http://niaid.nih.gov

National Sexual Assault
Hotline
Toll Free: 800-656-HOPE (656-
4673)

Nemours Foundation/Teen
Health
1600 Rockland Road
Wilmington, DE 19803
Tel: 303-651-4046
Internet: http://kidshealth.org/
teen/index2.html
E-Mail: info@kidshealth.org

OutYouth Austin Helpline
Toll Free: 800-96-YOUTH

Planned Parenthood
Federation of America
810 Seventh Avenue
New York, NY 10019
Toll Free: 800-829-PPFA
Tell: 212-541-7800
Internet: http://
www.plannedparenthood.org

Sexuality Information and Education Council of the United States (SIECUS)

130 West 42nd Street
Suite 350
New York, NY 10036-7802
Tel: 212-819-9770
Fax: 212-819-9776
Internet: http://www.siecus.org
E-Mail: siecus@siecus.org

Trevor Helpline Crisis Intervention for LGBT (Lesbian, Gay, Bisexual, and Transgendered) Youth

Toll Free: 800-850-8078

U.S. Department of Health and Human Services (DHHS)

200 Independence Avenue, S.W.
Washington, DC 20201
Toll Free: 877-696-6775
Tel: 202-619-0257
Internet: http://www.hhs.gov

U.S. Food and Drug Administration

5600 Fishers Lane
Rockville, MD 20857
Toll Free: 888-463-6332
Internet: http://fda.gov

Resources For Information About Contraception and Abortion

Association of Reproductive Health Professionals (ARHP)

2401 Pennsylvania Avenue, N.W.
Suite 350
Washington, DC 20037-1718
Tel: 202-466-3825
Fax: 202-466-3826
Internet: http://www.arhp.org

Center for Reproductive Rights

120 Wall Street
New York, NY 10005
Tel: 917-637-3600
Fax: 917-637-3666
Internet: http://www.crlp.org
E-Mail: info@reprorights.org

CHOICE (Concern for Health Options: Information, Care and Education)
1233 Locust Street
Suite 301
Philadelphia, PA 19107
Hotline: 215-985-3300
Children's Health Line:
215-985-3301
Community AIDS Hotline:
215-985-AIDS
TTY: 215-985-3309
Fax: 215-985-2838
Internet: http://www.choice-phila.org

Emergency Contraception Hotline
Toll Free: 888-NOT-2-LATE

Emory Grady Teen Services Program
Adolescent Reproductive Health Center
80 Butler Street, S.E.
Box 26158
Atlanta, GA 30335-3801
Tel: 404-616-3513
Fax: 404-616-2457
Internet: http://
www.gradyhealthsystem.org

National Abortion Federatio Hotline
Toll Free: 800-772-9100
Internet: http://www.prochoice.or

National Organization for Women
P.O. Box 1848
Merrifield, VA 22116-8048
Tel: 202-628-8669
Fax: 202-785-8576
Internet: http://www.now.org

National Campaign to Prevent Teen Pregnancy
1776 Massachusetts Avenue, N.W
Suite 200
Washington, DC 20036
Tel: 202-478-8500
Internet: http://
www.teenpregnancy.org
E-Mail:
campaign@teenpregnancy.org

National Partnership for Women and Families
1875 Connecticut Ave., N.W.
Suite 650
Washington, DC 20009
Tel: 202-986-2600
Fax: 202-986-2539
Internet: http://
www.nationalpartnership.org
E-Mail:
info@nationalpartnership.org

Office of Adolescent Pregnancy Programs (OAPP)
Department of Health and Human Services
4350 East-West Highway
Suite 200 West
Bethesda, MD 20814
Tel: 301-594-4004
Fax: 301-594-5981
Internet: http://
opa.osopha.dhhs.gov/titlexx/
oapp.html

Planned Parenthood Health Center Locator
Toll Free: 800-230-PLAN
Internet: http://ec.princeton.edu

Social Health Education, Inc.
7162 Reading Road
Suite 705
Cincinnati, OH 45203
Tel: 513-924-1444
Internet: http://
www.socialhealtheducation.org
E-Mail: socialhealth@fuse.net

Teen Choices
American Institute for Teen AIDS Prevention
P.O. Box 136116
Fort Worth, TX 76136
Tel: 817-237-0230
Fax: 817-238-2048

Crisis Pregnancy, Family Services, And Adoption Resources

Adoption by Gentle Care
389 Library Park South
South Columbus, OH 43215
Toll Free: 800-824-9633
Tel: 614-469-0007
Fax: 614-621-2229
Internet: http://
www.adoptionbygentlecare.org

Adoption House, Inc.
3411 Silverside Road
The Webster Building
Suite 101
Wilmington, DE 19810
Toll Free: 877-236-7847
Fax: 302-477-0944
Fax: 302-477-0955
Internet: http://
www.adoptionhouse.org
E-Mail: adopt@adoptionhouse.org

Adoption Service Information Agency (ASIA)
8555 16th Street
Suite 200
Silver Spring, MD 20910
Tel: 301-587-7068
Fax: 301-587-3869
Internet: http://www.asia-adopt.org

Bethany Christian Services
901 Eastern Ave. N.E.
P.O. Box 294
Grand Rapids, MI 49501-0294
Toll Free: 800-BETHANY (8am-12pm EST, 7 days/week)
Phone: 616-224-7617
Internet: http://www.bethany.org
E-Mail: info@bethany.org

Birthright
P.O. Box 98363
Atlanta, GA 30359-2063
Toll Free: 800-550-4900
Internet: http://www.birthright.org

CASI Foundation For Children
816 Connecticut Ave., NW
Washington, DC 20006
Toll Free: 800-376-0558
Tel: 202-974-0970
Fax: 202-974-0975
Internet: http://www.adoptcasi.org
E-Mail: info@adoptcasi.org

Catholic Charities
1731 King Street
Alexandria, VA 22314
Toll Free: 800-CARE-002
Tel: 703-549-1390
Fax: 703-549-1656
Internet: http://www.catholiccharitiesusa.org

Children's Bureau of New Orleans
Plaza Tower
210 Baronne Street
Suite 722
New Orleans, LA 70112
Tel: 504-525-2366
Fax: 504-525-7525
Internet: http://www.childrens-bureau.com
E-Mail: pemas@childrens-bureau.com

CareNet
109 Carpenter Dr., Suite 100
Sterling, VA 20164
Toll Free: 800-395-HELP
Tel: 703-478-5661
Fax: 703-478-5668
Internet: http://www.care-net.org
E-Mail: info@care-net.org

Catholic Home Bureau
1011 First Avenue, 7th Floor
New York, NY 10022
Tel: 212-371-1000 ext. 2100
Fax: 212-755-4110
Internet: http://
www.catholichomebureau.org

Community Maternity Services
27 North Main Avenue
Albany, NY 12203
Tel: 518-482-8836
Fax: 518-482-5805
Internet: http://www.cccms.com
E-Mail: smal@ccms.com

Deaconess Home Pregnancy and Adoption
5300 N. Meridian
Suite 9
Oklahoma City, OK 73112
Tel: 405-949-4200
Fax: 405-945-9673

Family and Children's Services
1503 University Blvd.
Albuquerque, NM 87102
Tel: 505-243-2551
Fax: 505-243-0446
Internet: http://www.FACS.net
E-Mail: Facs_bg@wizrealm.com

Family and Youth Services Bureau
Administration for Children and
Families
Department of Health and Human
Services
330 C St., S.W.
Washington, DC 20201
Tel: 202-205-8702
Internet: http://www.acf.dhhs.gov/
programs/fysb/index.html

Family Service Canada/ Service a la famille-Canada
404-383 Parkdale Ave.
Ottawa, Ontario K1Y 4R4
Toll Free: 800-668-7808
Tel: 613-722-9006
Fax: 613-722-8610
Internet: http://
www.familyservicecanada.org
E-Mail:
info@familyservicecanada.org

Florence Crittenton Home and Services
901 North Harris
Helena, MT 59601
Tel: 406-442-6950
Fax: 406-442-6571
Internet: http://
www.florencecrittenton.org
E-Mail: mothers@initco.net

Girls and Boys Town

14100 Crawford St.
Boys Town, NE 68010
Toll Free: 800-448-3000
Fax: 498-1348
Internet: http://
girlsandboystown.org
E-Mail:
publicrelations@girlsandboystown.org

LDS Family Services

National Headquarters
10 East South Temple
Suite 1250
Salt Lake City, UT 84133-1106
Tel: 801-240-6500
Fax: 801-240-5508
E-Mail: fam-ut-
saltlake@ldschurch.org

Lifeline Children's Services, Inc.

2908 Pump House Road
Birmingham, AL 35243
Toll Free: 800-875-5595 (Preg-
nancy related inquiries)
Tel: 205-967-0811
Fax: 205-969-2137
Internet: http://
www.lifelineadoption.org
E-Mail:
lifeline@lifelineadoption.org

L.I.G.H.T. House

1409 East Meyer Boulevard
Kansas City, MO 64131
Tel: 816-361-2233
Fax: 816-361-8333
Internet: http://www.lighthouse-
inc.org

Mid-Atlantic Network of Youth and Family Services

135 Cumberland Road
Suite 201
Pittsburgh, PA 15237
Tel: 412-366-6562
Fax: 412-366-5407
Internet: http://www.manynet.org

National Crisis Pregnancy Helpline

Toll Free: 800-521-5530 (24 Hour

National Life Center

686 North Broad St
Woodbury, NJ 08096
Toll Free: 800-848-LOVE
Internet: http://
www.nationallifecenter.com

Nebraska Children's Home Society

3549 Fontenelle Boulevard
Omaha, NE 68104
Tel: 402-451-0787
Toll Free: 800-390-6754 (pregnancy hotline)
Fax: 402-451-0360
Internet: http://www.nchs.org
E-Mail: nchomaha@radiks.net

New Beginnings Adoption and Counseling Agency

1316 Wynnton Court
Suite A
Columbus, GA 31906
Toll Free: 800-482-0844
Tel: 706-571-3346
Fax: 706-571-3305
Internet: http://
www.newbeginningsadopt.qpg.com

New Beginnings Maternity Home

499 Walnut Street
Winfield, MO 63389
Tel: 314-566-8600
Fax: 314-668-6260

Nurturing Network

P.O. Box 1489
White Salmon, WA 98672
Toll Free: 800-TNN-4MOM (M-F, 9-5)
Tel: 509-493-4026
Fax: 509-493-4027
Internet: http://
www.nurturingnetwork.org
E-Mail: tnn@nurturingnetwork.org

Salvation Army

Social Services for Children
120 West 14th Street
New York, NY 10011
Tel: 212-337-7200
Fax: 212-337-7478
Internet: http://
www.salvationarmy.org

Several Sources Foundation

P.O. Box 157
Ramsey, NJ 07446
Toll Free: 800-662-2678
Tel: 201-825-7277
Internet: http://
www.severalsourcesfd.org
E-Mail: mail@severalsourcesfd.org

Shepherd Care Ministries

5935 Taft Street
Hollywood, FL 33021
Toll Free: 800-96-ADOPT
Tel: 954-981-2060
Fax: 954-981-2117
E-Mail: shepherd@bellsouth.net

Small World Adoption Program

257 W. Broad St.
Palmyra, NJ 08065
Tel: 856-829-0202
Internet: http://www.swa.net

Small World Adoption Program

401 Bonnaspring Drive
Hermitage, TN 37076
Toll Free: 800-544-5083
Tel: 615-883-4372
Fax: 615-885-7582
Internet: http://www.swa.net

Smithlawn Home and Adoption Agency

P.O. Box 6451
Lubbock, TX 79493
Tel: 806-745-2574
Fax: 806-748-1088
Internet: http://www.door.net/smithlawn

St. Andre Home

283 Elm Street
Biddeford, ME 04005-3983
Tel: 207-282-3351
Fax: 207-282-8733
Internet: http://www.SaintAndreHome.com
E-Mail: adoptioncentral@yahoo.com

St. Elizabeth Foundation

8054 Summa Ave.
Suite A
Baton Rouge, LA 70809-3413
Tel: 225-769-8888
Fax: 225-769-6874

St. Mary's Services

717 West Kirchoff Road
Arlington Heights, IL 60005
Tel: 847-870-8181
Fax: 847-870-8325
Internet: http://homepage.interaccess.com/~stmary/home.htm
E-Mail: stmary@home.interaccess.com

Index

Index

Page numbers that appear in *Italics* refer to illustrations. Page numbers that have a small 'n' after the page number refer to information shown as Notes at the beginning of each chapter. Page numbers that appear in **Bold** refer to information contained in boxes on that page (except Notes information at the beginning of each chapter).

A